ASCENDANCE
OF A
BOOKWORM
I'll do anything to become a librarian!

Part 3 Adopted Daughter of an Archduke Vol. 1

Author: **Miya Kazuki**
Illustrator: **You Shiina**

The Archduke's Family

Rozemyne
The protagonist. She went from being the daughter of a soldier to the adopted daughter of the archduke, changing her name in the process. But her personality hasn't changed at all — she'll do whatever it takes to read books.

Ferdinand
Sylvester's brother from another mother. He is Rozemyne's guardian in the temple.

Sylvester
The archduke of Ehrenfest. He adopted Rozemyne, making her his adoptive father.

Florencia
Sylvester's wife and the mother of his three children. Rozemyne's adoptive mother.

Wilfried
Sylvester's oldest son, and now Rozemyne's older brother.

Karstedt
The commander of Ehrenfest's knights. Rozemyne's noble father.

Elvira
Karstedt's first wife. Rozemyne's noble mother.

Eckhart
Karstedt's oldest son. Works in the Knight's Order.

Lamprecht
Karstedt's second son. A knight who serves as Wilfried's guard.

Cornelius
Karstedt's third son. An apprentice knight who serves as Rozemyne's guard.

The Knight Commander's Family

Summary of Part Two:

After becoming an apprentice blue shrine maiden, Myne built a workshop in the temple, giving food and work to the starving orphans while busily spending her days developing printing through trial and error with her Gutenbergs. However, she was suddenly attacked by a foreign noble brought in by the High Bishop. In order to gain enough status to protect her family and attendants, Myne resolved to become the archnoble Rozemyne, soon to be adopted by the archduke.

Part 3 Adopted Daughter of an Archduke Volume 1

Ascendance of a Bookworm: Part 3 Adopted Daughter of an Archduke Volume 1
by Miya Kazuki

Translated by quof
Edited by Kieran Redgewell
Layout by Leah Waig
English Cover & Lettering by Meiru

Copyright © 2016 Miya Kazuki
Illustrations by You Shiina

First published in Japan in 2016
Publication rights for this English edition arranged through TO Books, Japan.
English translation © 2020 J-Novel Club LLC

Find more books like this one at www.j-novel.club!

Managing Director: Samuel Pinansky
Light Novel Line Manager: Chi Tran
Managing Editor: Jan Mitsuko Cash
Managing Translator: Kristi Fernandez
QA Manager: Hannah N. Carter
Marketing Manager: Stephanie Hii

ISBN: 978-1-7183-5607-8
Printed in Korea
First Printing: April 2021
10 9 8 7 6 5 4 3 2

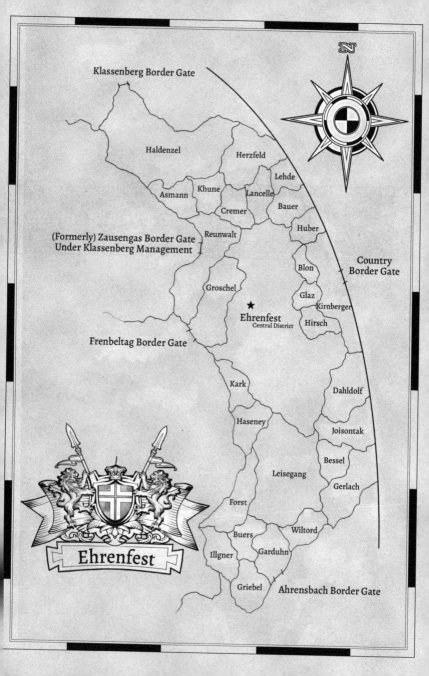

Klassenberg Border Gate

Haldenzel

Herzfeld

Lehde

Khune

Lancelle

Asmann

Cremer

Bauer

Huber

(Formerly) Zausengas Border Gate
Under Klassenberg Management

Reunwalt

Blon

Country
Border Gate

Groschel

Glaz

Kirnberger

★
Ehrenfest
Central District

Hirsch

Frenbeltag Border Gate

Kark

Dahldolf

Haseney

Joisontak

Bessel

Leisegang

Gerlach

Forst

Wiltord

Buers

Illgner

Garduhn

Griebel

Ahrensbach Border Gate

Ehrenfest

Prologue

After seeing Sylvester off to the Archduke Conference, Karstedt headed to the High Bishop's now-vacant room. Together with Ferdinand, he took all of the criminal evidence from inside before sealing off the room.

Then, they proceeded to discuss Rozemyne and the fake backstory they would use for her in greater detail; it would have been a bit of a stretch to use the one Sylvester had improvised on the spot. The idea was to say that Karstedt would let the archduke adopt his beloved daughter for her own protection since, like her mother, she had been born with an enormous amount of mana. But mana alone wasn't enough to earn one the prestige of joining the archduke's family. They needed one more push.

Ferdinand tapped a finger against his temple, deep in thought. "Perhaps we can use the fruits of her workshop. Rozemyne, pitying the horrific state of the orphanage, gave the orphans food and work. Her dedication and novel business ideas drew the attention of the archduke," he proposed.

"Weeping over the orphans and then saving them by providing food and work, hm? That's practically the work of a saint," Karstedt murmured, leading Ferdinand to nod in satisfaction.

"Ah yes, a saint indeed. That should do just fine. And if we add on some embellished tales of Rozemyne's feats, it should be easy to justify giving her the position of High Bishop... What? Karstedt, do not give me that look. There is nothing dishonest about this.

Rozemyne truly did create her workshop to save the orphans. Her ultimate goal may have been to reach a point where she could read books without a care, but that does not change the noble results brought about by her efforts."

Karstedt had heard from Ferdinand that Rozemyne had established a workshop in the orphanage, but after meeting the girl himself, it had been hard to think of her as being anyone capable of something that great.

"As you know, she is skilled in granting large-scale blessings, and as long as she does not speak off-script, she should look just like a saint," Ferdinand continued. "All she needs to do is what she did when healing the earth during the trombe extermination mission."

As he thought back to the healing, Karstedt recalled that Rozemyne had stunned every knight who was present by showing her overwhelming amount of mana—a display that appeared even more impressive because she had immediately followed up Shikza's failed attempt. She was certainly too young to be called a saint, but he couldn't deny that she looked like one—her flowing midnight-blue hair was well kept, silkier than even the hair of most archnoble girls, and her moon-like golden-yellow eyes were like windows into her emotional heart. She had a pretty face as well, and would no doubt grow up to be a true beauty.

Rozemyne had pale white skin largely untouched by sunlight, and soft hands that weren't at all worn down by labor. While this was perhaps simply due to how sickly she was, these were desirable traits rarely seen among commoners. Plus, thanks to Ferdinand educating her, she now moved and spoke so gracefully that it was hard to believe she was a commoner. She wasn't quite refined enough to pass as an archnoble yet, but it would only be a matter of time.

...In any case, the backstory was a little farfetched to say the least. Calling her a saint to convince the nobles that she was worthy wasn't a bad idea, but she would need to cast a powerful blessing or two to seal the deal.

As Karstedt nodded to himself, Ferdinand knitted his brow. "That will be enough to justify her accomplishments, but is it not unreasonable to say that you hid her in the temple for fear of your wives' bullying? Elvira is not foolish, and I find it hard to believe she will cooperate with a cover story like that."

"A fair point, but it's true that Elvira shunned Rozemary."

Both Karstedt's first wife Elvira and second wife Trudeliede had shunned his third wife Rozemary, treating her as a black sheep. The emotional exhaustion this caused was no doubt one of the factors that had led the already-weak Rozemary to collapse.

"You heard that from Rozemary herself, yes? Did you confirm both sides of the story before passing judgment?" Ferdinand asked, eyeing Karstedt closely. He knew that Karstedt had a tendency to side with Rozemary since she was the victim in this situation.

"...I have heard that the root cause was antagonism between Trudeliede's and Rozemary's families. But Elvira, the most influential person in the family at home, deprived Rozemary of any peace by giving her support to Trudeliede, despite the fact that Rozemary was the one she needed to protect."

The dispute had at least been manageable while Elvira was neutral, but everything had fallen apart the moment she picked a side. Karstedt found that frustrating above all else.

"Did you not ask Elvira why she sided with Trudeliede?"

"...I did, and she said it was because I always protected Rozemary. But how could I not have when I saw her being insulted? I have no idea why Elvira gave Trudeliede her support," Karstedt explained, and Ferdinand rubbed his temples with an exasperated expression.

"If Elvira supported your second wife because you were protecting Rozemary so much, perhaps she was just attempting to maintain balance? I was right; it would be best for us to reveal everything to Elvira in order to earn her support. She will determine everything about Rozemyne's future in the female side of noble society."

The largest female faction in ladies' society had been the one led by the archduke's mother, but now that she was gone, the faction that Elvira and Sylvester's wife were in would take its place. Ladies' society was not something that men could easily enter, being off-limits even to Sylvester, so joining this faction would be Rozemyne's best chance at living a peaceful life. But even knowing that, Karstedt couldn't help but feel apprehensive about asking Elvira for help.

"…Ferdinand, would you accompany me when I go to explain this to Elvira? Her attitude will change dramatically depending on whether you're there with me or not."

Ferdinand was the archduke's little brother from another mother, and it was precisely due to his impressive talent that Veronica, the archduke's mother, had treated him coldly since his birth. Karstedt, however, had not only accepted Ferdinand into the Knight's Order, but had also gone out of his way to protect him from malice, treating him with as much respect as he would the proper son of an archduke.

But when the former archduke fell ill and it came time to pick his successor, Veronica's cruelty only intensified. In the end, Ferdinand declared that he had no interest in becoming archduke and joined the temple instead. But even then he continued to help Sylvester with his work, and supported the Knight's Order whenever it was lacking in numbers. Elvira frequently lavished him with praise, saying that if not for Lord Ferdinand, Ehrenfest would have collapsed long ago, so her reaction would no doubt vary depending on whether it was Karstedt or Ferdinand who provided the explanation.

"Very well. Invite me to dinner tomorrow, then. My schedule is packed until tomorrow afternoon."

"Alright. That works well for me too, since we of the Knight's Order still need to conduct our investigation."

Karstedt left the temple and returned to the Knight's Order, where Damuel—who was looking fairly queasy—was being questioned by another knight. He had been carried out of the temple unconscious, but was now sitting up and talking just fine. Apparently, the Order had sent him someone capable of using healing magic.

"Once Damuel's questioning is finished, that will be all for today. We will investigate our prisoners tomorrow," Karstedt declared. As commander of the Knight's Order, he received a round of crisp salutes in response.

In the midst of all that, Damuel timidly asked Karstedt a question. "Lord Karstedt... erm... is the apprentice...?"

"She is fine. You did well protecting her for as long as you did given the disadvantage you were at." A laynoble like Damuel naturally had much less mana than an archnoble like Count Bindewald, so Karstedt was genuinely impressed by how capable he had shown himself to be.

At those words, Damuel slumped over in utter, exhausted relief. "I'm honored," he managed to force out.

The Knight's Order dispersed once Damuel's interrogation was over, and Karstedt headed to the knights' barracks to rest. He thought going home unannounced would cause problems since, as far as they were concerned, he was attending the Archduke Conference in the Sovereignty. *I'm certainly not doing this to avoid talking to Elvira without Ferdinand,* he assured himself, before swinging his hand to retrieve his schtappe and tapping it against a yellow feystone.

"*Ordonnanz,*" he said, and the feystone morphed into the shape of a white bird. "Lord Ferdinand will be visiting for dinner tomorrow. Please prepare for his arrival." Having spoken his message, Karstedt swung his schtappe, mentally ordering the bird to go to Elvira. It returned in no time at all.

"Oh my, Lord Ferdinand? Say no more," it said in a bright, eager voice three times before returning to the shape of a stone. Inviting Ferdinand had been a good idea after all.

The next morning, Karstedt went to interrogate the prisoners. First up was Bezewanst, the High Bishop. Ferdinand had investigated his crimes so thoroughly and down to such a precise detail that Karstedt was honestly exhausted at his persistence. Still, more exasperating than anything was Veronica, who had somehow managed to protect Bezewanst through everything that had happened.

"I'm surprised she protected you for this long," Karstedt said. He had been sure that Bezewanst would kick up a fuss and protest upon having his crimes listed out, but all he did was hang his head. It seemed that he was actually devastated that his older sister was going to be punished by Sylvester.

But in contrast to Bezewanst's surrender, Count Bindewald seemed intent on maintaining his silence; they would have to use the memory-searching magic tool once Sylvester returned from the Archduke Conference. Karstedt didn't know whose mana would be most compatible, but he sure didn't envy whoever had to look through the count's memories. He just prayed that his own mana color didn't end up being the one that most resembled Count Bindewald's.

"My my, Lord Ferdinand. I thank you ever so much for visiting during this busy time," Elvira said. She was wearing a smile three times as pleasant as her usual one, and had bundled up her hair in a particularly exquisite style. Karstedt had just returned home with Ferdinand, and while he was more than used to how differently she treated them, he couldn't help but sigh.

Once they had finished dinner, Karstedt cleared the room of attendants and looked at Elvira. She returned his gaze, quietly awaiting his words.

"Erm… Elvira. My… ah… daughter is being baptized this summer."

"Oh my. And who might her mother be?" Elvira asked, narrowing her dark eyes as if watching Karstedt's every move.

"Ah… Rozemary. It's the baptism for Rozemyne, the daughter I had with Rozemary."

"My my my, now isn't that something. I don't believe Rozemary had any children. Her family would never have kept their silence if she had a child. Do you not remember those fools, and the absurd arrogance they developed after their daughter married an archnoble? How they made unreasonable demand after unreasonable demand of us? You will reignite the dispute between Trudeliede's and Rozemary's families by doing this," Elvira said with a glare, reminding him that Rozemary's relatives had been the initial reason for her being excluded.

Karstedt started to protest, but Elvira continued, interrupting him. "That whole mess has finally calmed down, and you want to start it up again by introducing a child of hers? I shan't allow it… Or, I wouldn't, but given that Lord Ferdinand is here, I can imagine there are some profound circumstances behind all this. I might offer my help depending on what those circumstances are."

"You truly are a wise woman, Elvira. I am in need of your assistance, and I humbly ask for your cooperation," Ferdinand said.

"Oh my, Lord Ferdinand. You always know just what to say."

Ferdinand began to explain the circumstances to Elvira. A talented girl by the name of Rozemyne would be baptized as Karstedt's daughter, and then adopted by the archduke at the very same baptism. Both he and his elder brother the archduke wanted her to be adopted because they had already confirmed that she would be an enormous boon to the future of Ehrenfest.

"Conflict will begin anew if Rozemary's relatives learn of this girl's existence, so I suggest that we hold the baptism without announcing that she is Rozemary's child. I shall raise her as her mother, so that she will not bring shame to Karstedt or our family."

"That would be enormously helpful, Elvira," Ferdinand said. "It seems that entrusting this to you was the right thing to do all along."

Elvira smiled brightly, all traces of sharpness having vanished from her face. As they had all expected, getting Ferdinand to speak to Elvira had proven much more effective than if Karstedt had asked, despite the fact that the latter was her husband.

"I have been educating her to some degree in the temple, so I do not believe she will be an embarrassment, but it will be up to you to finish the job and make her a proper lady who won't stand out within the archduke's villa."

"Oh my. You have educated her yourself, Lord Ferdinand?" Elvira asked, her eyes wide. She was likely wondering whether the infamously harsh Ferdinand, who was brutal even to apprentices in the Knight's Order, was capable of safely raising a child.

Karstedt understood her feelings well; he too had doubted his ears when he first heard it. Ferdinand must have been raising Rozemyne harshly, judging by how gracefully she moved and how skilled she was at playing the harspiel, but she nonetheless trusted and relied on him. It was the first time Karstedt had ever seen a child become emotionally attached to Ferdinand. He still remembered the utter shock he had felt upon seeing Rozemyne hide behind Ferdinand for protection during the trombe extermination.

"I educated her because I believed it was necessary for her to be adopted by a noble," Ferdinand said before beginning to give more details on Rozemyne. "She is a superb assistant when it comes to doing paperwork, and she has an abundance of mana. She has simplistic thinking patterns which makes her easy to deal with, and while she does display a stunning lack of common sense at times, she is not unintelligent. Attempts to educate her will bear fruit. Plus, while she is a fast learner, I am unfortunately incapable of teaching her anything about femininity."

"You may leave that to me. I shall raise her properly."

With that settled, they began discussing their plans. Karstedt asked Elvira to prepare everything for the baptism—a room for Rozemyne would have to be prepared, and the etiquette instructor who had been teaching their boys would need to be asked to teach her as well. Once everything was ready, Rozemyne would be moved from the temple to the Noble's Quarter.

"So I need to prepare rooms and clothes for a girl," Elvira said, her eyes sparkling with excitement. She had only ever raised boys before.

I think we'll be just fine leaving this to her, Karstedt thought, putting a hand to his chest in relief.

Not long after, Ferdinand sent word to Karstedt that he was beginning his examination of Rozemyne. Karstedt left the ongoing criminal investigation to return to the High Priest's chambers in the temple.

"Umm... H-Hello, Father?" Rozemyne awkwardly stammered. Her childish voice made Karstedt break out into a smile; all of his children were boys, some of whom were now even knights, so hearing her calling him "Father" warmed his heart. If Rozemary truly had given him a daughter, perhaps she would have been like this.

"Rozemyne, you'll draw suspicion to yourself if you stutter like that," Karstedt warned.

Rozemyne let out a groan, then quietly murmured "Father" to herself over and over as practice. Seeing her working so hard to survive in noble society so that she could protect her family made Karstedt let out a heavy sigh.

Elsewhere, Ferdinand started spreading out a piece of parchment with a magic circle already drawn on it across the floor. He had preemptively cleared the room of attendants.

Rozemyne peered at the magic circle curiously. "What is this? Does it do something?"

"It will analyze the flow of your mana. You said before that you couldn't move without a certain amount of mana filling your body, correct?"

"...Is such a thing even possible?" Karstedt asked.

Upon entering the Royal Academy, students acquired a schtappe through which their mana could be directed and were taught to compress the mana within their bodies, but before that, they generally poured their mana into magic tools given to them by their parents. Moving mana required stamina and wasn't good for the growth of one's body, so it was widely understood that the less mana kept in your body, the better.

"There is no mistaking that your physical growth is being stunted by the fact that your body is always full of mana. However, I have never heard of one falling ill from having too little or too much mana inside of them."

"What? That's not normal?" Rozemyne asked in surprise, looking down at her own body.

"Indeed, it is not. I will be investigating the flow of your mana in part to determine why this is happening."

"Wow, you can do that? That's really impressive," Rozemyne said, peering at the magic circle and nodding several times, impressed.

Karstedt, in contrast, was glaring at Ferdinand. Not everyone just carried around magic circles that showed the flow of mana within someone's body. "That magic circle is used by doctors, isn't it? Why do you have one?"

"I made it myself, actually, by modifying a common magic circle used for making magic tools. Though I couldn't say whether it is the same magic circle that doctors use, and this is the first time I am using it on somebody other than myself."

Karstedt was at a loss for words. Whenever Ferdinand wanted something, he always ended up making it on his own, and that alone was leagues beyond what most people could do.

Ignoring Karstedt's astonishment, Ferdinand placed four feystones on the circle, one on each of the four cardinal directions, before turning to Rozemyne. "Rozemyne, take off your clothes and shoes, then stand on the circle."

"Huh?!"

"H-Hold on there, Ferdinand!" Karstedt was flabbergasted. Rozemyne was still young, but that wasn't an order you gave a woman so casually.

Regardless, Ferdinand remained unfazed, pointing at the magic circle with a flat expression on his face. "We will not be able to do this once she is baptized and adopted by the archduke. This is our only opportunity. Hurry up and do it."

Rozemyne looked between Karstedt and Ferdinand, then blushed in embarrassment. "No way. That's way too embarrassing!" she said, stepping back cautiously.

While Karstedt pitied her, Ferdinand apparently did not: he just glanced at her and sneered. "I am unsure where this sudden shame is coming from. You were just fine in the bathtub."

"What?! Bathtub?!" Karstedt couldn't believe his ears. *She was "just fine in the bathtub"? Did they bathe together? Ferdinand bathed with Rozemyne?!* Fixing his gaze on Ferdinand, he asked: "Ferdinand, what in the world did you do to this little girl?"

Ferdinand's eyes widened. "D-Do not misunderstand, Karstedt! I am referring to when I observed her memories using the magic tool. I did not bathe with her!" he protested, almost in a panic.

Karstedt calmly determined that Ferdinand must have been telling the truth, given that his usual blank facade had crumbled almost instantly. But still, who wouldn't have misunderstood that? Somebody who didn't know about that magic tool would be convinced that Ferdinand had an interest in young girls. Had Sylvester been here, he would already be gleefully teasing him.

"Rozemyne, you were completely unperturbed back then! Why are you getting embarrassed now, of all times?!"

"I mean, at the time, I was so excited about being able to use (shampoo) and (bath salts) after so long... And I couldn't even see you, so it was like we were just on the (phone) or something, and it was a dream, not reality, so... Anyway! I can't take my clothes off in front of other people!" Rozemyne protested.

Karstedt now knew for sure that the bathing scene had arisen in her memories, and that at the time, she hadn't been bothered by it.

"I am just examining your body. Is this truly more embarrassing than a bath?"

"Yes! If you want to call this a medical examination, then bring a doctor to do it!"

"Can you not just think of me as a doctor? The same thing will happen either way." Ferdinand was so skilled that he truly could work as a doctor, and his personality was such that he wouldn't be satisfied unless he examined her himself.

"Did you not surrender your feminine shame within three days of becoming Myne when you were stripped down by a man who you did not consider to be your father? It has been over three days since you've become Rozemyne. It is time to surrender once again."

"N… N-N… N-No way!" Rozemyne flailed her arms and dashed toward Karstedt, yelling "S-Save me, Lord Karstedt!" She attempted to give Ferdinand a wide berth as he was already standing in between them, but he just effortlessly reached out and grabbed her. "GYAAAH! Let go of me! Gyaaaah!"

"Fool. How many times have I told you to address Karstedt as 'Father'? And from this point on, call me by my name when we are outside of the temple," Ferdinand said dryly, removing the sash and blue shrine maiden robes from the pitifully weeping Rozemyne without an ounce of hesitation. From the side, he looked just like a father punishing a child who was throwing a tantrum. But regardless of how young she was, stripping the clothes off of a woman so forcefully was simply not right.

Rozemyne, now stripped down to the green dress she had worn during Spring Prayer, looked at Karstedt, then reached out her arms with a desperate look on her face. "Fatheeer! Ferdinand is being a creep!"

"Do not invite misunderstandings, you foolish girl." Ferdinand clamped a hand on Rozemyne's head, squeezing it as she squealed for help.

Seeing that, Karstedt considered the possibility that they were much closer than he had thought—though perhaps he was simply trying to avoid facing the reality of their situation. Sylvester, speaking in jest after learning of Rozemyne's immense mana following the trombe extermination mission, had suggested that Ferdinand marry her—and looking at them now, the idea didn't seem so farfetched.

As Karstedt pondered that, Rozemyne's movements began to slow.

"Ferdinand, I believe you are going a little too far. Rozemyne is breathing heavily."

Ferdinand widened his eyes in realization and loosened his grip, creating an opening for Rozemyne to squirm away and leap toward Karstedt. She circled around him, letting out a groan as she hid in the shadow of his cape and angrily glared at Ferdinand. She was like a tiny animal trying hard to appear threatening, and Karstedt couldn't help but chuckle. Sylvester had been right when he said Rozemyne resembled a shumil—all she had to do was say "pooey" and the image would be complete.

Ferdinand crossed his arms in frustration and glared at both Karstedt and Rozemyne. His expression made it clear that he was annoyed things were not proceeding according to plan. "Karstedt, as her father, what do you think of Rozemyne's weakness?" he said, demanding his help in a roundabout way.

Karstedt compared Ferdinand and Rozemyne. Ferdinand's forceful methods may have been a bit uncomfortable to watch, but Rozemyne was weak enough that she was more or less on the verge of death at all times. If Ferdinand was able to help, then it was best to do as he said.

Karstedt hefted Rozemyne up and looked her in the eyes. "Rozemyne, Ferdinand is an expert when it comes to mana. If examining your mana will allow him to discover what potion is necessary to cure you, would it not be wise to let him?"

"Well, I mean... I guess..." Rozemyne stopped glaring and calmed down, seemingly convinced. She did have the rational mind of an adult, after all—unlike other children, she wouldn't throw an actual tantrum or stop listening out of spite. All one had to do was be reasonable and explain things carefully to her.

However, some people did not understand how to be tactful.

"Karstedt, now! Hold her down!" Ferdinand ordered, speaking in the same tone he would use in the Knight's Order. As Karstedt instinctively grabbed Rozemyne, Ferdinand quickly strode over, getting behind her and deftly undoing the tiny buttons lining the back of her dress one by one.

"Hyaaah! Ferdinand, you pervert! Were you a creep this whole time?!"

"I have no idea what you're insinuating, but we have no time for this. Hurry up." Ferdinand finished undoing the buttons and pointed sharply at the curtain around his bed. "Remove your socks behind there. I will be examining your back, so only your torso needs to be bare. ...What is with those defiant eyes? Do you need me to strip your trousers off as well?"

"No! I'll take my socks off, okay?! Happy?!"

"Yes. Do it quickly and waste no more of my time."

Rozemyne scampered behind the curtain, all the while glaring at Ferdinand through tear-filled eyes. He seemed completely unmoved by this, but the sight was enough to send a twinge of pain straight through Karstedt. Why did Ferdinand have to be so cruel to such a young girl?

"You are too cold, Ferdinand. She's a shy and embarrassed little girl. How many times have I told you to be a little kinder to women?"

"That would be a waste of time."

Ferdinand had been abused by Veronica for his entire childhood, and his mother had offered him no protection whatsoever. The experience was enough to leave him somewhat distrustful of women, so unless he saw a particular advantage to being kind, Ferdinand was always extremely harsh to them. Today was no exception.

Karstedt couldn't help but sigh. "As always, you and Sylvester are exactly alike in that you never listen to personal advice, no matter how many times you receive it."

"Do not lump me in with him," Ferdinand said, directing Karstedt an annoyed glare.

That was when Rozemyne, covering her front with her bundled-up clothes out of embarrassment, came trudging out from behind the curtain on bare feet.

"Stand on top of this."

Ferdinand had made the spread-out magic circle by altering one meant to check the flow of mana in magic tools and detect any irregularities. Rozemyne timidly stepped onto it and turned her back to Ferdinand, who whipped his hand to draw his schtappe before getting onto his knees and lightly tapping the magic circle. Mana began flowing into it, and moments later, the mana-filled magic circle shone red and rose into the air. It went through Rozemyne's feet and up to her head, making the flowing mana within her shine red as well. Her trousers hid her lower half, but sharp lines were visible on her back and across her arms.

"Wow! What's going on?"

"I told you that I would be looking at the flow of your mana, did I not? Your hair is in the way." Ferdinand moved her hair aside, looking at Rozemyne's small back with a frown. Karstedt and Rozemyne could have looked at the flow of mana without him, but

Ferdinand was the only one there who could examine the red lines and determine what was wrong with the flow of mana, and where.

After examining her back for a while, Ferdinand let out a heavy sigh and stood up. He looked down at Rozemyne, rubbing his temples and frowning.

"I see you have died before. There are clumps of hardened mana within your chest."

Examination Results and the Noble's Quarter

The examination was embarrassing and horrible—so horrible, in fact, that I declared Ferdinand had crossed a line that now made it impossible for me to marry, which I would use as an excuse to refuse political marriage and stay at home for the rest of my life. But at the end of my examination, Ferdinand told me that I had died before.

...Uh huh. That makes sense. I've been on the verge of death so many times, I'm sure I would have actually died at least once.

I accepted it immediately, but Karstedt looked at me in disbelief. "What does he mean by that? You've died?"

"In the past, my mana has overflowed and nearly killed me more times than I can remember; it wouldn't even surprise me to hear that I've died more than once. What I'm more concerned about is the mana being hardened inside of me. I can still move it around, so I don't really get what you mean when you say it's hardened."

Ferdinand, seeing our shared confusion, continued to rub his temples as he searched for the right words. "Karstedt—when feybeasts die, their mana flows to the organ that usually stores it and hardens. You know this, correct?"

"Hm? Of course. That's where feystones come from." Karstedt nodded like it was the most obvious thing in the world, but I just blinked in surprise.

Um, what? I don't know anything about a mana-storing organ. Are the bodies here built differently from the ones on Earth? They look exactly the same, so I assumed they were made exactly the same too, but...

When cut, we bled. When we cried, tears came out. The whole digestive process was the same, too, so aside from the people here having all sorts of strange hair and eye colors, I had been convinced that our bodies were the same. I hadn't doubted it for a second, and definitely didn't know anything about a mana-storing organ.

"Given that Rozemyne is alive and standing before us today, I believe that rather than completely dying, she revived from a half-dead state. But while she was in that state, her mana returned to her center, where parts of it hardened."

Ferdinand drew a number of charts and explained the situation in detail, and judging from where the mana-storing organ was, I could determine that it was probably my heart. That helped me understand that hardened mana was more or less like a person's arteries getting hardened.

"I believe that Rozemyne has a poor flow of mana due to the hardened clumps of mana scattered inside of her, and that is the cause of her collapsing. The flow of mana accelerates when she gets excited, but cannot flow properly. I imagine that her body knocks her unconscious to contain her emotions and protect itself," Ferdinand said.

"So in other words, she needs to practice containing her emotions. That's something all nobles have to do either way, so perhaps this is for the best."

Apparently me passing out whenever I got too excited was just my body protecting itself, but something as simple as seeing a book room was enough to get me worked up. It was hard for me to imagine ever being able to contain my emotions well enough to stop that from happening.

"Ferdinand, does that mean it'll be okay for me to get a little excited if I drain most of the mana from my body?"

"You should know from experience that you cannot move without mana. I suspect that when you have too little mana, the flow is too weak to push past the hardened clumps, which in turn paralyzes your body. This means you must keep your body filled with a decent amount of mana at all times."

Hmm... I was thinking that mana might just be blood, but it does sound a little different. I don't think that's how blood works in the human bodies I'm familiar with.

"Rozemyne, do you know when it was that you died?"

"What? Umm..."

When I had first become Myne, I was so weak that cleaning the bedroom was enough to make me collapse, and just walking down to the well outside of our house would leave me exhausted. Myne had always been that weak, so it was possible that the mana had hardened before I became her. In all honesty, I had no idea when I might have died.

"Mm... I became self-aware inside of Myne when she was five, so probably then? But if you're telling me that I'm weak because of these mana clumps, then... Well, I've been called weak since I was born, so I don't know when I would have died."

"This is your body we are talking about here. Don't give me that disinterested look." Ferdinand gave an annoyed frown since he clearly wanted more details, but the date of my death didn't seem particularly important to me.

"I mean, does it really matter when I died, or even how many times I died? Right now, I'm alive and well. What's important to me is whether this can be cured. Can you make a potion to fix this, Ferdinand?" I asked while looking up at him, still not quite used to calling him by his name.

He furrowed his brow and let out a sigh. "I can, but it will be extremely difficult."

I had hoped that some kind of magic tool or restoration potion would fix me in a snap, but apparently it wasn't so simple. *Magic tools sure are a lot less useful than I thought.*

My disappointment must have shown on my face, as Ferdinand proceeded to pinch my cheek. "It will be difficult for you, not me."

"For me…?" *What? Is he saying this is something he could make if he wanted to?*

"You need only use a potion meant for bringing one back to life from a half-dead state. It will block the hardening of mana and dissolve any existing clumps. However, obtaining the necessary ingredients is far from easy."

"Are you saying that they're too expensive for even the adopted daughter of an archduke to buy?" *I mean, I can understand that medicine able to bring someone back from the verge of death would be expensive, but I thought for sure that I wouldn't have any money problems once Sylvester adopted me!*

I cradled my head in despair, and Ferdinand shook his head. "It's not the price, but the fact that you have to gather the ingredients yourself. Your mana will be necessary in gathering them."

"This sure is a cruel potion, making people on the verge of death gather the ingredients to make it themselves. How are you supposed to use it in emergencies like that?" I said, pursing my lips.

Ferdinand stared down at me with a thoroughly condescending look. "Are you an idiot? Archnobles gather the ingredients while they are healthy and attending the Royal Academy, so that they can make it ahead of time and carry it with them in case of emergencies. Sylvester, Karstedt, and I each have one on us."

A potion that archnobles carry on them at all times? Wow.

"Well, I'm never healthy. How am I supposed to gather the ingredients?" I asked, hoping for the oh-so-wise High Priest to answer. This time, he didn't give me a condescending look, but rather one of utter exasperation.

"That is why I said it would be extremely difficult for you. Are you just not listening?"

"Rozemyne having to gather those ingredients herself despite her weakness, hm?" Karstedt interjected, wearing a troubled frown as he rubbed his chin. "That should be manageable if we surround her with knights and only have her do the final gathering part. Though even that will be out of the question unless she learns to ride her own highbeast first."

"Indeed. Her training will begin once her baptism and the rituals related to her appointment as High Bishop are finished."

Guuuh, what?! I'm going to have magic training on top of learning the etiquette and common sense of an archnoble? I'll definitely die before we finish making that potion!

"Hopefully we can finish the gathering before Rozemyne goes to the Royal Academy."

"What? Is it going to take that long?"

"At best, it will take one year. At worst, many more. Some laynobles don't finish it during their entire enrollment at the Royal Academy."

We still had three years before I would officially turn ten and be sent to the Royal Academy, but even knowing that, they weren't sure whether I would be able to get all of the ingredients in time. For a moment, I wondered whether taking that long would lead to the ingredients I collected first rotting or going bad over time. But the medicine took a year to make at the very minimum—there had to be some kind of storage method that worked.

"Ferdinand, what will we do for the winter ingredient? There is that one well-known spot by the Royal Academy, but bringing a contingent of knights into the Sovereignty would be an act of war. Where do you intend to gather it?"

"We have no choice but to search for something suitable within Ehrenfest. I have several contenders in mind, and considering the quality we will need, the regular spot by the Royal Academy may not suffice."

"Is that so?"

"The mana hardened so long ago that she does not even remember when it happened. The potion will need to be of an exceedingly high quality to work."

Karstedt and Ferdinand were advancing the discussion themselves. Despite the fact that I was at the center of all this, they were completely leaving me behind. That wasn't exactly uncommon, but I would have rather they explained the things they were talking about instead of just ignoring me.

"Q-Question, please! What determines the quality, or lack thereof? How do you get high-quality ingredients?" I shot a hand up, and they both looked down at me as though they had only just remembered I existed. Given that I was so far below eye level that they couldn't even see me without looking down, they probably really had forgotten I was there.

"The quality is determined by the density of mana where the material is gathered. It also depends on the amount of mana poured into it," Ferdinand began.

"To obtain high-quality ingredients, you will need to carefully select what you gather, and where and when you gather it. Of course, the amount of mana the gatherer has plays a role in all of this, too," Karstedt continued.

"You say 'of course,' but I don't know a thing about any of this. Please explain a little more," I requested, but Ferdinand just shook his head with a look that made his lack of interest in explaining things to me more than clear.

"There is no time for that. We will make the necessary arrangements. All you must do is clear your mind and focus on getting through the baptism ceremony successfully. You will be moved to the Noble's Quarter in three days. Get changed behind the curtains," he said with a dismissive wave of his hand.

The two started discussing which ingredients they would get and where based on quality and efficiency, but as soon as I was done changing, they tossed me out of the room, telling me to go and practice the harspiel or something. I was being left out, as usual. *So mean.*

Once I was outside Ferdinand's chambers, Fran—who had been waiting outside since being sent out with the other attendants—asked me what the High Priest had wanted to talk about. Damuel was standing beside him.

"I've heard that the apprentice—er, I mean, Lady Rozemyne—will be sent to the Noble's Quarter in three days. I imagine it was something to do with that?"

"Yes, it seems they've prepared a room for me. I will be educated in the Noble's Quarter prior to my baptism ceremony, Sir Damuel. ... Or should I just call you 'Damuel' now? Either way, it seems we will be saying our goodbyes for the time being."

Damuel had apparently received healing magic of some kind, which had allowed him to get right back to his duties in the Knight's Order. While I was in the Noble's Quarter, he would apparently be receiving additional training to whip him into shape to become a personal bodyguard to the archduke's adopted daughter. They figured that having someone familiar around would make things easier for me. That said, my status suddenly shooting above his made it hard for us to address each other properly. It would no doubt take a bit of getting used to.

"Also, they examined me to see whether there was a potion that could cure my illness."

"The High Priest had said previously that he would rather not do so without your father's permission," Fran interjected. "I imagine he decided to hold the examination now that Lord Karstedt is your father."

It sure was hard for me to imagine Dad giving Ferdinand permission to strip off my clothes and force me to stand on a magic circle. He'd probably tell him to buzz off, and the thought of Dad being his usual overprotective self made me giggle for a second before a heavy sense of loss gripped my heart.

...Nn. I wanna see my family. I at least wanna see their faces again.

They weren't allowing me to meet anyone from the lower city, the Gilberta Company included, until my baptism ceremony was over. It would take some time for them to get everyone to accept that Myne was dead, and begin laying the groundwork to make people buy their Rozemyne story. I was going to die of loneliness in the meantime. My two new attendants were my only emotional support in these trying times.

"Welcome back, Lady Rozemyne," Monika greeted me when I returned to my chambers, her undecorated emerald-green hair bundled tightly behind her head. Apparently she looked up to Wilma so much that she was even mimicking her appearance. The first thing she had said to me was that she would serve me in Wilma's place, given that Wilma couldn't leave the orphanage.

Monika's dark-brown eyes gave her an air of intelligence, reminding me of a student council member or some such. She and Fran got along just fine as colleagues, and she was a hard worker, dedicating her all to taking over paperwork duties from Rosina. Fran often praised her results, saying that her time spent helping Wilma with paperwork in the orphanage had made her a faster learner than he had expected.

"Monika, Nicola—I have returned."

"Welcome back, Lady Rozemyne. I will prepare tea at once," Nicola said. Her flowing orangish-red hair was tied into two braids, and she headed to the kitchen with a beaming smile. She was an energetic thirteen-year-old girl who just loved tasty food, and I personally called her "Smiley Nicola" since she was always smiling. She was doing basically all of the work Delia had done, and was always excited to help Ella with the cooking.

Both Monika and Nicola had adjusted to my chambers in no time at all, probably partly because they had been visiting all the time during winter to help the chefs. These two provided invaluable emotional comfort for me.

I climbed to the second floor, and there I found Rosina, working through a pile of work Fran had asked her to finish before she left for the Noble's Quarter. It seemed that she had to select furnishings for the High Bishop's chambers, decide on a color scheme, figure out what utensils would be needed, and then write all of that down in a list. A single desk, for example, would need to have its height and overall size recorded in great detail, down to the number of drawers and their dimensions. Karstedt would be using her list to order furnishings of appropriate quality and design.

"Lady Rozemyne, a gift from your father arrived while you were absent. It seems to be clothes for the Noble's Quarter."

Karstedt had sent me clothes to wear when heading to the Noble's Quarter. But it wasn't just clothes for me—there were also outfits for Rosina, my personal musician, and Ella, my personal chef.

"The High Priest told me that we will be moving to the Noble's Quarter in three days."

"In that case, I must hurry." Rosina glanced at the harspiel, her blue eyes gleaming. Her expression made it clear that she was endlessly happy about going from being a gray shrine maiden to a noble's personal musician.

I spent the next three days being fervently trained by Rosina to act even just a little more like a normal noble girl, and in the blink of an eye it was the day of our departure. I finished eating lunch and prepared to head to the Noble's Quarter. I put on the clothes Karstedt had given me and slipped on my leather shoes, then took out the fancy hair stick I used for ceremonies. Ella and Rosina were changing in their own rooms, so I was being changed by Monika, Nicola, and also Wilma, who was visiting from the orphanage to teach the former two.

"I imagine that handling the cooking will be hard for you two since I'm taking Ella with me while Hugo and Todd go to train with Leise, but I trust that you can handle it," I said, and Wilma looked at them while nodding.

"Sister My— Excuse me, Lady Rozemyne's food makes up a significant portion of the divine gifts given to the orphanage, so both of your efforts will be greatly appreciated."

"Don't worry, Wilma."

"We practiced for this all winter. We'll make tons of tasty food."

They had both just moved here from the orphanage, so they knew just how much of an impact a single blue priest or shrine maiden leaving would have on the divine gifts the orphanage received.

"I've told Fran to continue using the same budget as always when buying ingredients, so please do not hesitate to make the usual amount."

"Thank you ever so much, Lady Rozemyne." Monika and Wilma replied at the same time, both giving similar smiles. It was so cute to see how much Monika adored Wilma.

"Lady Rozemyne, I will study hard and learn lots of new recipes to make for you when you return."

"I look forward to that, Nicola."

I finished changing and headed down the stairs with everyone. Upon reaching the first floor, I found Fran, Gil, and the chefs who usually didn't show themselves all kneeling in wait.

"Fran, I entrust you with keeping everyone in order and managing the High Bishop's affairs in preparation for my return. As for the High Bishop's chambers, I do not particularly mind reusing the same furniture, though I imagine that doing so would not please you."

"Indeed. The High Bishop's furniture is not at all suitable for a lady. The High Priest has ordered for it all to be replaced."

The fact that I considered that to be a huge waste of money was probably a sign that I was still looking at things from a commoner's perspective. Nobles cared about appearances, and noblewomen needed to live surrounded by fancy, elegant furniture.

Ferdinand had agreed to leave the furniture in the orphanage director's chambers unchanged since it would be used as a meetup spot for people from the lower city, but the High Bishop's chambers would be visited by blue priests and nobles, which meant appearances were much more important there. It was apparently unthinkable for an archnoble adopted by the archduke to reuse furniture previously owned by a criminal. It wasn't like someone's sins carried over to their furniture, but he was dead set on it nonetheless.

I had no idea what kind of furniture upper-class noble girls tended to use, but as my request to have my chambers filled with bookshelves and books like a library was shot down, I didn't really care how it ended up. Ferdinand, Karstedt, and my attendants could take care of selecting and paying for the furniture.

"Gil, you will be going to investigate some city's orphanage while I'm gone, correct? Take care to stick as close to the Gilberta Company as possible—the High Priest has told the scholars that you're there in my place, but I'm not sure whether you being of a lower status will change things."

"Understood. I shall be careful."

Since I was now an archnoble, Fran had started correcting Gil's speech and behavior even more harshly than usual—after all, we wouldn't be able to interact so casually once I was both the archduke's adopted daughter and the High Bishop. I went ahead and patted Gil on the head while I still could.

And then I stood in front of the two chefs, who on this rare occasion were out of the kitchen. "Thank you both for cooking such delicious meals for me every day. The next time we meet shall surely be in the Italian restaurant. Make good use of what you've learned here."

Karstedt was waiting at the temple's front entrance for me, and once I was there, he escorted me to a carriage. Ferdinand was with him, wearing noble clothing as well. Rosina and Ella would be riding in a separate carriage—one specifically for attendants. Theirs departed first so that they could open the gate to the Noble's Quarter for us.

"I will be off, then. Fran, I entrust everything to you in my absence."

"I await your return, Lady Rozemyne."

Once I had finished saying my goodbyes to all of my attendants, the door to my carriage was shut, and we departed. Unlike Benno's carriage, this one moved incredibly smoothly, not shaking at all. It was actually pretty comfortable. The Noble's Gate was already wide open, and we passed by the attendant's carriage and into the Noble's Quarter.

The carriage passed by the plaza where the knights had been gathered prior to the trombe extermination, rolling down the white paved road that seemed to stretch on endlessly. It looked like a bunch of modest-sized parks were lined up next to each other, but apparently each was a noble's estate. The mansions got fancier the further away we got from the Noble's Gate; it seemed that things getting fancier as you moved away from the gate was true in the Noble's Quarter, too.

Spotlessly clean carriages passed by ours, but I couldn't see anyone walking. Apparently adults just used their highbeasts, and would bring out their carriages when traveling with small children, so there was rarely any reason to walk around outside. That felt pretty weird, since walking was the standard down in the lower city.

"Oh?"

I saw a section where the buildings were large, but packed very close to one another, like a residential area you might find in Japan. We were quite far away from the gate so I had assumed the buildings here would be pretty fancy, but instead they were getting more cramped.

"I see some buildings have big gardens and others don't. What's the difference between them?"

"These are the winter estates for nobles given land by the archduke, called giebes," Ferdinand responded. "As they are only used during the snowy winters, they do not need large gardens."

They were the homes of nobles who lived on their own land from Spring Prayer to the Harvest Festival, only returning to the Noble's Quarter to socialize during the winter. That made sense— you wouldn't really need a big garden if it was going to be buried in snow the whole time you were there. The estates of nobles who served the archduke and lived in Ehrenfest naturally had bigger gardens.

"Is that wall over there where the Noble's Quarter ends?" I asked, pointing at a huge wall that stretched along one end of the Noble's Quarter.

Ferdinand shook his head. "No, the archduke's castle is behind that wall. You will be going there after your baptism."

The mansion that would be my new home was located close to that wall. The carriage advanced through the spacious garden, which did in fact look like a small park, until we eventually came across a pure-white building that seemed to be made of the same material as the city walls and the temple.

"My first wife, Elvira, and my son, Cornelius, live here with me. I have two other sons with her, but they've both come of age and now live in the knights' barracks. My second wife and her son live in a separate building on the estate. You will rarely ever see them, I imagine."

People were lined up in front of the door, which opened just as our carriage arrived. From inside came a single woman, who leisurely strolled our way.

"That's Elvira. She will be your mother from now on. Try to get along with her."

My new mother had dark-green hair gathered up in complex bundles, and wore elaborate clothing covered in embroidery of all colors. Judging by her looks, she seemed to be in her mid-thirties. She gave off a dignified aura even while standing still, and every single movement she made exuded grace and refinement. She was so different from the world of women I was used to that I honestly didn't even know how I should talk to her.

"Um, I appreciate the thought, but how am I supposed to get along with her? I don't know how to interact with a married archnoble woman," I said weakly, but Ferdinand simply mumbled something about ladies' society being outside of his jurisdiction.

"Elvira has only ever been graced with boys before now," he continued. "Why not begin by acting like an obedient daughter? She is not so foolish as to treat the future adopted daughter of an archduke poorly. That said, getting her to like you as much as possible will make your life in ladies' society that much easier."

Karstedt and Ferdinand may have been my guardians, but even they couldn't go to the gatherings and tea parties attended only by women. I would have to find new allies in ladies' society. Right from the start, I had a huge hurdle to overcome.

"Elvira seemed excited about dressing a daughter and preparing a room for her. You would do well to go along with that until she is satisfied."

"Okay. I will do my best to become a living doll." If she was so eager to dress me, maybe I could win her over with some rinsham and hairpins, then seal the deal with sweets that she could bring to tea parties. But either way, I had to start by finding common ground and focusing on that.

"Welcome home, Karstedt. And Lord Ferdinand, I am delighted to see you again so soon."

"Hello, Elvira," Ferdinand replied. "This is Rozemyne, your new daughter."

Ferdinand and Karstedt each placed a hand on my back and gently pushed me in front of them. I slowly lowered my hips in a curtsy, as I had been made to practice over and over again.

"It is nice to meet you. I am Rozemyne. May I pray for a blessing in appreciation of this serendipitous meeting, ordained by the pure rivers flowing from Flutrane the Goddess of Water?"

"You may."

This was the greeting nobles always gave to express that they were happy about their meeting. It was the same one that Ferdinand had given Benno the first time they had met.

"O Flutrane, Goddess of Water. May you grant this meeting your blessing." I put a little bit of mana into my ring as I had been taught, and a bit of green light rose into the air before raining back down.

Elvira, having received the blessing, smiled. "I welcome you into my home, Rozemyne. From this day forth, I am your mother."

...*Well, at least my greeting got a passing grade from her.*

Preparing for the Baptism Ceremony

And so I started my life in the Noble's Quarter, but it was completely different from what I was used to in both the lower city and the temple. The days were filled with one shocking revelation after another, each one making it harder to believe that only a single wall separated these two completely contrasting sides of the city.

The first big difference was the bathrooms. We didn't relieve ourselves in a bucket that we'd empty and reuse—no, there was an actual indoor bathroom with a toilet. However, it wasn't a flush toilet or anything like that. It was a deep hole in the floor, and there was some kind of squishy, slimy thing wriggling around at the bottom. To be honest, I screamed the first time I saw it. Apparently it dissolved our waste, but it would take some getting used to.

Seriously, it's disgusting! And the thought that it might wriggle up terrifies me!

I still refused to go to the bathroom alone at night, asking for someone to walk me there every time I went, but thankfully I still looked young enough for nobody to be weirded out by that. From the bottom of my heart, I was glad I was a noble girl who had at least one attendant following her at all times.

The strange toilet situation aside, the house also had bathtubs—a luxury I had missed so much. The maids would always help me in and wash me, but I wasn't particularly opposed to this since I was already so used to bathing with Tuuli—we had to wash each other's backs since we couldn't reach our own. They used tons of lavish soaps that were noticeably expensive just from the smell, which kind of gave me pause, but that all melted away when they started massaging me. It was wonderful, but they would also use this soap to wash my hair, meaning it always ended up dry and scraggly. It was harder to comb, and all of the glossy silkiness was going away.

"Mother, I have a request."

"Oh my, and what might that be?"

"Please call the Gilberta Company over. Without rinsham, my hair is starting to get damaged."

Elvira had at first looked displeased at the idea of calling over a merchant who did business with laynobles at best, but in the end she consented after I mentioned how silky the rinsham made one's hair.

Benno and Mark arrived on the appointed day with a box packed full of products, both entering the room wearing the sharp expressions they put on during work. I had been hoping Lutz would accompany them, but he was nowhere to be seen. I could guess that he wasn't ready to visit an archnoble's home yet.

Tch. And I really wanted to see him, too.

After their lengthy greetings were finished, Elvira urged Benno to show her what he had brought. "Benno, was it? Show me these products that Rozemyne loves so much."

"At once, my lady." From the box he had brought, Benno took out various jars of rinsham, somewhat fancy hairpins that paled in comparison to the fanciness of the house, and plant paper that could be bought at a cheaper price than parchment. "This jar contains the rinsham that Lady Rozemyne favors, and these are a new set of products with aromas made to match each season. Please smell them at your leisure."

Benno, being the pinnacle of merchants that he was, had made four different kinds of rinsham by swapping up the scrub in the workshop. I had only ever been using the rinsham that I made with Tuuli, so I curiously sniffed the jars as well. One smelled of herbs, one smelled sweet, one smelled crisp, and the last one smelled like nothing much at all. The sweet-smelling summer rinsham was my favorite; its scrub was made from ground-down apfelsige peels and koves that ripened in the summer.

"Mother, I would like to use this rinsham."

"My my, what a lovely smell. Perhaps I shall use it as well."

After buying the rinsham and some plant paper for studying purposes, I recommended the paper with pressed flowers inside to Elvira. "Mother, don't you think this paper would be perfect for letters of invitation? The flowers are very pretty."

"Oh my, so they are. I've never seen paper with flowers inside like this. I wonder what the secret is?" Elvira pondered aloud as she picked up a sheet.

"That is a new kind of paper we have just recently developed," Benno said. "The exquisite spring flowers give an artistic air to the paper that will surely leave a lasting impression on those who receive a letter of invitation made from it."

"But you already have other buyers, no? I would just be following an already existing trend."

The Gilberta Company was primarily used by laynobles and, as an archnoble, Elvira was not fond of mimicking their trends. Archnobles didn't follow trends—they had to make them themselves.

Um, wow. That sure sounds like a pain.

"We do not, actually. In service of Lady Rozemyne, today is the first time we are bringing these out from our store. No other customer has seen them."

"I see. In that case, I shall buy it."

I gave Benno a stealthy thumbs-up from behind Elvira, wearing a smile that said "You're welcome." Benno grinned, and Mark looked away to hide his laugh.

Oh crap, right. I need to act like a proper young lady.

"These are hairpins in the style that Lady Rozemyne has shown a fondness for."

"They are quite pretty, but I would have liked for them to be made using thread at least a little better than this." The hairpins were fancier than the hairpin I had on, but Elvira didn't seem to be entirely happy. I personally thought it was fine, but I glanced at Benno and saw that his eyes were gleaming, like a hunter who had found his prey.

"Of course, we accept custom orders. I believe that we will be able to make hairpins more to your liking if you select the colors and thread yourself. There are many different kinds of flowers and leaves to choose from, too, and the hairpins can give unique impressions based on how these decorations are used."

Elvira began her order by selecting certain flowers from the existing hairpins and describing what colors, sizes, and thread she wanted. Benno wrote it all down and then left with Mark, promising to bring the finished hairpins back later. The Gilberta Company had succeeded in getting an archnoble customer.

"This truly does make one's hair silky. To think that laynobles had been keeping this all to themselves..."

We used the new rinsham not long after, and not only did the luster return to my hair, but Elvira's became silky as well. She was more than satisfied with the result, but couldn't help but be a little displeased that archnobles hadn't known about it before now.

"It's only been a year since rinsham entered the market, and it's more expensive than soap, so it doesn't sell very well," I said. "It may be the ideal product for archnobles, who can afford to spend money on appearances. I'm sure the archduke's wife would love to learn about it as well."

"Oh yes, without a doubt."

Discussions over tea tended to be about beauty and looks. Elvira hadn't seen any archnobles with rinsham or hairpins, and seemed eager to start the trends herself. Up until now, I had always been pulling the Gilberta Company away from their proper business to focus on book-making, so I was more than happy to finally give them some help on the clothing and beauty side too.

You're going to have more work related to beauty products now, Benno. Isn't that just grand? I thought, cheering him on internally.

"Miladies, here are the cookies baked with tea leaves." Ella walked up as quietly as possible and placed a plate in front of Elvira, whose gaze softened as a light, sweet scent wafted into the air.

"I wonder how they shall taste this time?"

As expected, Elvira loved the sweets that Ella made. They were importing sugar from the Sovereignty, but not many recipes for sweets had been developed yet. So far I had introduced pound cake, crepes, and cookies for teatime, and they had all received high praise.

Ella's pound cakes couldn't compare to Leise's, since she hadn't been researching them for a whole year, but they were still good. And since our exclusivity contract had already ended, it would be fine for us to make the pound cake recipe public.

"I would love for you to teach our own chef to make these sweets," Elvira said.

Ella wasn't yet trusted by the chefs on Karstedt's estate; up until now, she had only been making sweets for teatime in a small side kitchen, but it seemed that she had finally earned Elvira's trust. A broad smile spread across her face.

"If you permit her to enter the main kitchen, I can get back to teaching her new recipes for sweets and normal foods that I haven't shown her yet. There are so many more that I would like her to learn."

"In that case, I shall discuss matters with the head chef and make it so."

Elvira summoned the head chef and, as she had said, Ella was given permission to enter the main kitchen in a few days' time, once preparations had been made. It seemed that Elvira wanted to get a bunch of sweets recipes that she could use for tea parties from me before I was adopted by the archduke and my living situation changed. I could imagine that she wanted to start a new trend when it came to sweets as well. Being an archnoble wife in ladies' society seemed pretty rough.

"These smell of tea and taste just delightful."

"Oh yes, Lord Ferdinand quite likes them."

Ferdinand had told me to call him "Lord Ferdinand" when outside of the temple, but honestly, it was so long and tedious to say that I was going to drop the "Lord" part as soon as I could. Incidentally, when I asked whether I should start calling him "Uncle Ferdinand" once Sylvester had adopted me, he immediately started grinding his fist against my head without saying a word. Apparently he wasn't too keen on the idea.

"Lord Ferdinand…? Fascinating."

Elvira loved to discuss Ferdinand, and little tidbits about his daily life were always of great interest to her. The fact that my relationship with Elvira was going so smoothly despite all of my worries was largely thanks to him, really—he came to check up on me once every two days, which put Elvira in a constant good mood.

Though, to be honest, I didn't really know what she was like when she was in a bad mood beyond what I had heard from Cornelius—the third son of the house, and an eleven-year-old apprentice knight. His hair was bright-green, the color of fresh leaves; he had dark eyes; and even though he was growing, he was still a visibly young boy.

Which leads me to something I had never known before moving to the Noble's Quarter—Ferdinand was like a superstar in ladies' society. He was attractive, of good lineage, and a musician on top of being an excellent knight, scholar, and proxy archduke. Not to mention that, as a priest, he had no lover and no plans to take one. I could understand why those watching him from afar would be head over heels for him—on paper, you couldn't really get much better than that.

Whenever Ferdinand came over, Elvira looked at him entirely like a groupie might look at a rock star. She would discuss matters of my education and future with Ferdinand while looking utterly serious, but as soon as he was gone, she would spend all day talking about the precise ways in which he had been wonderful. Not to mention that she even looped the same words of praise over and over again. Cornelius had been forced to listen to it up until now, and was more than glad to be able to push that role onto me.

"The way I see it, a fellow girl would understand Lord Ferdinand's attractiveness far more than I would," he had said.

...Well, not really. I definitely don't understand it.

It was true that Ferdinand appeared to be pretty amazing—he could seemingly do everything, and I would never be able to repay him for how much he had helped me—but his barbed tongue cut deep, and his utter lack of mercy made him kind of scary at times.

To me, Ferdinand wasn't someone to squeal and get all giddy about like Elvira did.

I had tried saying that once, but Elvira brushed the idea right off. "My my, Rozemyne. A kind man incapable of plotting or exterminating his enemies is simply no good at all."

...Noble society is pretty terrifying.

I was studying every day, naturally, but this time I was learning about all of the families who would be gathering at the baptism ceremony. As Karstedt was the cousin of the archduke, all of his family members were archnobles, and memorizing their long names was proving to be quite the ordeal. There were also a lot of landowning counts and viscounts, which meant I had to memorize both their personal and their giebe names, which they shared with the province they kept.

"Learning noble names is really hard. Is there some simple trick I could use to make it easier?" I grumbled to Ferdinand when he next came to visit, but he just shook his head.

"I would not expect it to be easy for you, as you did not grow up among the nobility. But you must learn if you are to continue living here," Ferdinand said, before spreading out a map of the duchy on a table and telling me which provinces my relatives owned, what was famous there, in which order they were visited during Spring Prayer, and so on. I had stayed at a lot of their mansions during spring, which made it easy to put the pieces together and remember them. As Ferdinand continued explaining things to me, I made sure to write everything down.

"It's kind of easy for me to remember my land-owning family members, but the list of scholars and knights working in the castle is just overwhelming. It's like a wall of jumbled letters."

"Hm. In that case, I will offer you a reward to help keep you motivated." Ferdinand grinned and looked at me. "If you memorize all of these names before your baptism ceremony and complete it successfully, on the day you are given the position of High Bishop, I will entrust you with the keys to the temple book room and the shelves inside that hold the most important books."

"Ferdinand, wait... Does that mean...?"

If I had the keys to the book room, did that mean I could go inside whenever I wanted? Did it mean I would be able to read the precious books that I hadn't even been allowed to look at, since they were under the High Bishop's custody?

Seeing my eyes shine with excitement, Ferdinand nodded and gave me a very noble-esque smile. "Indeed. You will be able to enter the book room without my permission, and read the most important books."

"Then I'll do it! I'll learn all of the names, even if it kills me!"

If it meant having unrestricted access to the book room and the new books inside, I didn't mind learning etiquette, doing as much studying as I had to, or listening to Elvira talk her head off about Ferdinand. No matter what it was, I had endless motivation to do it. And so I got right to work memorizing the names, focusing so intently that I didn't even hear Elvira and Ferdinand talking around me.

"Isn't it the High Bishop's duty to manage those books in the first place? Framing her future job as a reward to motivate her is quite clever, Lord Ferdinand. I see you're as good at persuading people as ever."

"This is just her being easy to manipulate."

My studying progressed well—so well, in fact, that I soon ended up collapsing from working too hard. Not long after I recovered, it was time for me to try on my baptism outfits. In her enthusiasm, Elvira had ordered them before I had even arrived on the estate, and for some reason there were four in total. If you asked me, one was more than enough.

"I wanted to be thorough since I didn't know what you looked like at the time. Which one do you prefer, Rozemyne?"

I could guess that saying I didn't care which one I wore would make me a failure of a noble girl, so I obliged and changed into the outfits one by one in front of a large mirror, carefully watching Elvira's reactions all the while. Each one I tried on had a base of white, with blue and yellow embroidery to match the season's divine color and my eyes, respectively, so I had a hard time telling the difference between them. Plus, they all looked good on me; unlike in my Urano days, my appearance was pretty much perfect with no problems to hide. If there was anything wrong with me now, it was my personality, not my looks.

I didn't feel the need to wear anything particularly over the top, but judging by how fancy my normal home clothes and accessories were, Elvira really did like dresses on the more fluffy side. With that in mind, I picked out the two outfits that I thought she would probably like the most.

"I'm not sure which of these I like more."

"Oh, you feel the same way?"

My guesses had apparently been spot-on, and Elvira began to seriously consider which one suited me better. The seamstresses measured me, then started adjusting the clothes to my size. They had initially been made to fit an average child around baptism age, but ended up a little too big on me.

Aww... And I'm a year older, too.

"So? Have you decided yet?" Karstedt came walking in as Elvira continued her deliberation. As the head of the family and the one in charge of the money, his job was to double-check our final decision.

"Oh my, Karstedt. What do you think? These outfits are just adorable, aren't they?"

"Of course. They all look great on her."

"The only problem is, I cannot tell whether this one or this one suits her better." Elvira began comparing extremely minor details like the frills on the skirt and how the chest part was designed, which earned little more than a shrug from Karstedt.

"These kinds of minor details go in one ear and out the other for me. Why not just order both? That way, you can pick whichever one feels right on the day of. Besides, having both would be useful as children tend to dirty their clothes up anyway."

"My my my, what a splendid idea. I'm sold," Elvira said, before excitedly beginning to give instructions to the seamstresses. As I watched out of the corner of my eye, I pulled on Karstedt's cape and whispered to him.

"Father, I'm not going to dirty any clothes, and I really don't need two outfits for my baptism ceremony. I think this is a waste of money."

"The cost of a second outfit is nothing if it means avoiding Elvira's long explanations now, and her regretful griping about how she wished she had bought the other one instead in the future."

It seemed that, by buying them both, Karstedt was in a way investing in the future. If you could buy a peaceful, happy family with money, it was best to do so before it was too late.

...I'm kinda curious about the exhausted look in his eyes. Did something happen, Karstedt?

The day before the baptism, we received word that Eckhart and Lamprecht—Karstedt's eldest and second eldest sons, respectively—would be returning home from the knights' barracks. Cornelius took my hand and pulled me to the door to greet them. As an apprentice knight he commuted to work from home, which meant I saw him every day at both breakfast and supper. But this was my first time seeing my other two elder brothers, since they actually lived in the barracks.

"I'm a little worried since this is my first time meeting them."

"...Haven't you met them already? They've mentioned you before."

In a shocking twist, the two brothers had participated in the trombe extermination mission as knights. I didn't really remember them, since everyone in the Knight's Order wore full-body armor and helmets that covered most of their faces, but apparently they remembered me.

"Ah, looks like they're here." Cornelius, having already learned from experience that I would pass out if he tried rushing me, had an attendant carry me as he raced to the door. "Welcome back!"

"Good to see you, Cornelius," said Eckhart. He was the oldest brother, eighteen years old with dark-green hair and blue eyes. His facial features resembled Karstedt's, and he was a big guy—both tall and muscular.

"Welcome home, Eckhart," I said.

"Good to be back... er, Rozemyne." Eckhart bent over a little to try and make eye contact with me, but Lamprecht just hefted me up to put us at eye level.

"You really are that apprentice shrine maiden I saw. I never would've thought that you were actually my little sister. Hm... You're a lot smaller and lighter than Lord Wilfried."

"Lamprecht, you're scaring her," Cornelius warned in a teasing tone, but Lamprecht just grinned.

"Yeah, looks like I am. Her eyes are like big round saucers."

Lamprecht was sixteen years old and had Karstedt's reddish-brown hair, plus his bright-brown eyes. He was a full head shorter than Eckhart, but still as tall as the average adult—not to mention that he was still growing. And although he didn't seem to be as muscular as either Karstedt or Eckhart, I could feel just how hard his muscles were as he held me.

"I'm home, Rozemyne."

"Welcome home, Lamprecht."

"I work as a bodyguard for Lord Wilfried, Aub Ehrenfest's son. Once he adopts you and you move to the castle, I'm sure we'll see each other all the time. I'm looking forward to it."

Tomorrow was finally the day of my baptism ceremony. Both Wilfried and the archduke's wife had been invited, so I would be meeting even more new family members there.

A Noble's Baptism Ceremony

The day of my baptism ceremony had been busy last year when I was in the lower city, but here in the Noble's Quarter it was even busier. I had been woken up early in the morning and forced to bathe while still half-asleep, and was now being sent to eat breakfast in my normal clothes for the sake of cleanliness. Only once that was done would I be changed into my outfit for the baptism ceremony.

"Good morning, Mother." I went to the dining room once I was done bathing and found Elvira eating breakfast alone.

In the Noble's Quarter, we didn't go to the temple to be baptized; instead, we summoned priests to our homes and held the ceremony there, so the whole house was busy. Food was normally served by chefs in the kitchen, but today our attendants would be serving us. The kitchen was no doubt a war zone right now as everyone busted their butts to make food for all of the guests.

"Rozemyne, please change as soon as you can. Lord Ferdinand is waiting with a gift."

"Yes, Mother."

Elvira finished eating and left, at which point Eckhart entered. He sat down across from me, offering a gentle smile as I scarfed down my food as quickly as I could.

"Morning. And congratulations, Rozemyne."

"Thank you ever so much, dear brother."

Eckhart made some light conversation as he started working through his own plate, which was a relief as I had been worried that we'd eat in silence. "I hear Lord Ferdinand is going to be the priest conducting your baptism ceremony. I'm pretty excited, since this is the first time I've seen Lord Ferdinand agree to conduct a ceremony like this."

"Wait, this is his first time doing one?"

Priests were called to the homes of nobles to conduct baptism ceremonies quite regularly, and since the nobles paid them for this service, it was a valuable source of income. Nobles tried to summon priests of as high of a status as they could, and yet up until now, Ferdinand had never conducted any religious ceremonies in the Noble's Quarter.

It must have been obvious from my expression that I was wondering why, as Eckhart started to explain for me. "The High Bishop used to conduct ceremonies for archnobles."

While archnobles and the archduke knew Ferdinand, they also knew the High Bishop, and so always invited him instead. This wasn't much of a problem for Ferdinand though: he always had a ton of work to do and received income from other places, so he was more than happy to leave these ceremonies to other priests.

"With Lord Ferdinand as the priest, I expect that all of the noblewomen in attendance will kick up quite the fuss," Eckhart added. He explained that since Ferdinand always came to the Noble's Quarter wearing normal noble clothing, the women would probably squeal in delight upon seeing him in his ceremonial priest robes.

...I guess it's like getting excited over a cool uniform? I'm so used to seeing him in his robes that I don't think anything of it, but I kind of get it.

Eckhart and Ferdinand had served as knights together from the start of Eckhart's apprenticeship to the day Ferdinand entered the temple, so Eckhart knew quite a lot about him.

"Lord Ferdinand does everything so perfectly that people are quicker to respect and admire him than curse or envy him. Some even worshiped him back in the day."

I found it a little hard to believe, but Eckhart had apparently earned pocket change while he was attending the Royal Academy by selling information about Ferdinand to Elvira. Perhaps I could do the same and make a good amount of money from it...

"You're the apprentice shrine maiden Ferdinand declared he would be taking custody of, so I'll take good care of you as my little sister. All I ask, Rozemyne, is that you take good care of Lord Ferdinand too. I want him to have as many allies here as possible, and every single one makes a difference."

"Understood."

Eckhart managed to finish breakfast much faster than I could and then left. He finished surprisingly fast considering that we had been talking and he had been eating so gracefully—not to mention that he had started after me. I hurriedly scarfed down the rest of my breakfast so as to not be left behind.

On my way to my room, I bumped into Cornelius, who seemed to be heading to the dining room. "Good morning, Cornelius."

"Morning, Rozemyne. I see they dragged you out of bed too, huh?"

"My attendants woke me up. I've already finished my morning bath and eaten breakfast."

Cornelius had gotten dressed, but still looked very sleepy. I noted that, and he gave a small laugh. "Guess I better eat breakfast then. Ah, right—and congratulations, Rozemyne."

"Thank you ever so much, dear brother."

Once I was back in my room, it was time to change clothes. My attendants laid out two outfits for me to pick from; both matched

Elvira's preferences as far as I could tell, so I just picked the one on the right for no particular reason. I followed my fast-working attendants' instructions on where to put my arms and legs, and was changed in no time at all.

As my hair was being brushed by an attendant in front of a mirror, a small bell rang on the other side of the door. "That would be Mother. Let her in, please."

"Rozemyne, dear, have you finished changing?"

"I have, Mother."

No sooner had Elvira been let in than she walked out of the room again, this time saying something through another door. Moments later she returned with Karstedt, who was wearing a finer set of clothes than usual, and Ferdinand, who was wearing his ceremonial robes and carrying a small box. Elvira stayed back as Karstedt and Ferdinand walked over to me, and honestly, it was pretty funny seeing her gleaming eyes as she stared at Ferdinand from behind.

"Congratulations on your baptism, Rozemyne. Ah, yes, that certainly does look good on you."

"I thank you ever so much, Father."

Karstedt praised how I looked, smiled, and then took my hand. "I'll be borrowing this ring for a bit. I will hand it back during the ceremony," he said as he removed the magic tool from my finger. He had given me the ring so that I could register a hidden room in the temple, and for protection in case the blue priests tried anything, but technically it was something he was supposed to give me during the baptism ceremony.

The children of nobles were given feystone-embedded magic tools at birth to store their overflowing mana. Then, at their baptism ceremony, they were given rings that would help them to use the

59

mana instead. I had never been given the kind of magic tool that children received, but was happy enough offering my mana to the divine instruments. Plus, Ferdinand had said that I had enough mana to quickly fill a feystone if I ever needed to.

Karstedt stepped back once he had the ring and, as if on cue, Ferdinand walked forward with his box. "Congratulations, Rozemyne. May this gift add to your celebration."

"My my, I wonder what he got you," Elvira said, seemingly more excited than I was. "Rozemyne dear, go ahead and open it, if you would."

I thanked Ferdinand, set the box on the table, and then gently opened it, trying to be as graceful as one would expect an archnoble to be.

"Oh my, how splendid!" Elvira exclaimed.

Inside was a gleaming hair stick made using the most luxurious thread. I took it out for a closer look and saw that there were three big white flowers, the edges of which were lined with gold. They were surrounded by small blue flowers decorated in a similar fashion, and hanging from these was a vine of even smaller flowers that resembled wisterias, their colors forming a gradient from blue to white.

...Mom and Tuuli made this.

The flowers in the center used a design that I had taught Mom and Tuuli to make after organizing my deal with Corinna, and I could tell they were involved in part because they resembled the ones on the hairpins from last year. And if they had made the flowers, then I could guess that Dad had shaved down the stick part. The faces of my family flashed through my mind, and the sadness I had bottled up due to being so busy hit me all at once.

"Ah..." Tears started to stream down my face as though a dam had burst inside of me. I had tried not to think about my family over the past weeks, but now they filled my heart. I was frozen, the hair stick in my hands.

"Rozemyne?" Elvira looked at me, her eyes widening in surprise. An attendant, shocked by my sudden tears, rushed over with a small towel and patted my cheeks.

"Calm down, Rozemyne." Ferdinand took the hair stick from my hands and quietly looked down at me, his face expressionless. I wanted to stop, but the tears kept on flowing, like my eyes were broken faucets.

"...I-I can't. They just... keep... Nn... Ngh...!"

Ferdinand glanced around the room, and while he remained expressionless, I could see the faint traces of panic in his light-gold eyes. His brow furrowed deeply and he rapped a finger against his temple. "Karstedt, get everyone out of the room! Do not let anyone inside until I permit it!"

"Sir!" Karstedt, having received a strict order, immediately gathered the worried-looking people in the room together and took them outside. After confirming that he hadn't missed anyone, he left as well, closing the door behind him.

Ferdinand made sure that the door was shut tight, then roughly rubbed the towel against my face. He grimaced hard when he saw that this hadn't stopped my tears from flowing out.

"Ferdinand, hug!"

"Keep the towel on your face. If my robes get soaked, then I am leaving," he said, clearly vexed, before sitting down on a chair, hefting me up, and giving me a hug.

The warmth of another person immediately drained the tension from my body. Karstedt, Elvira, and all of my brothers were kind to me, but I interacted with them a lot less than I was used to. It seemed I had become completely touch-deprived. I clung to Ferdinand, all the while keeping the towel pressed against my face.

"…To think this would happen on the morning of your baptism ceremony," Ferdinand muttered. I had finally stopped crying, and was now pursing my lips instead.

"It almost feels like you did this on purpose. You had to know I would cry if you brought me a hair stick from my parents before my baptism."

"Oh, you think so? I intended for you to rejoice, but I see it had the opposite effect. I will have to remember never to gift you any hair sticks again."

"Wait, please no! I love it! I'm really happy to have it! Please keep gifting me more!"

"You will have to excuse me for not wanting to deal with a situation like this again," he said, deepening his frown. I was so anxious that this just made more tears leak out.

"But I'm telling you, I'm happy… I'm telling you I want more. Ferdinand, you meaniiie! Sniff… Ngh…!"

"How annoying. You truly are a pain to deal with, Rozemyne. What exactly do you want from me?" he asked, and despite how harsh his words were, his tone was sincerely puzzled.

"If you're going to send me a gift like this, please do it several days in advance. I really am happy to get it, but it also makes me miss my family, so I need time to recover emotionally."

"…Very well then. I will keep that in mind for the future. For now, though, you need to stop crying," Ferdinand said, lightly tapping a finger against my head as if to say he had no way of winning against a crying child.

I calmed down after the lengthy hug, and stopped leaning against Ferdinand so that I could climb down from his lap. "I think I'm okay now. Sorry for the trouble."

After I stepped back with the towel, Ferdinand muttered "Trouble indeed" before standing up with a sullen frown and heading to the door. "Come in," he said, and Lamprecht entered with several attendants.

"Excuse me. Mother and Father went to greet the guests, and they..." Lamprecht began as he stepped inside, before coming to an abrupt stop and recoiling at the sight of my red eyes and flushed cheeks. "Rozemyne's eyes are bright red; someone apply something cold to them at once. Mother will kick up a fuss if she sees her like this."

The attendants immediately stepped forward, but Ferdinand, seemingly having only just realized that my eyes were red, reached out a hand to me. "There will be no need for that. Come here, Rozemyne. I will heal you."

The feystone on Ferdinand's ring began to shine, no doubt due to him pouring mana into it. He placed his ringed hand over my eyes and muttered: "May Heilschmerz's healing be granted." A gentle green light shone through my eyelids, which had been shut by Ferdinand's hand, and I could hear the attendants letting out awed noises. The light quickly disappeared, and Ferdinand pulled his hand away.

I slowly opened my eyes to see Ferdinand closely investigating my face. Meanwhile, Lamprecht looked relieved to have escaped Elvira's anger. "To think that you would end up offering healing before performing a ceremony, Lord Ferdinand... We are grateful."

"Healing of this level is no issue at all."

The area around my eyes had apparently been a little swollen. I patted my face and checked in a mirror; everything seemed to be back to normal.

"Lord Ferdinand, what in the world happened to Rozemyne? It would be good to know for the future."

"...We are all busy right now; it can wait until another day. Prepare Rozemyne at once."

Having deftly avoided Lamprecht's question, Ferdinand headed for the door. No way could he reveal that I had started crying after being given a hair stick from my former family, forcing him to calm me down with a hug. I was already sure that he'd think up some excuse before Lamprecht brought this up again later.

As Ferdinand opened the door, the distant clamor of people could be heard, seeming to all be coming from one place. It was almost time for my baptism ceremony.

Attendants set my hair using something like pomade, before tying it tightly behind my head with a cord. They patted on more of what seemed to be hair gel, then weaved the front of my hair into complex braids. The hair stick that Ferdinand had given me was slid in last to finish it off.

With the preparations done, Lamprecht escorted me to a waiting room. It was the closest room to the stairs leading to the assembly hall, where the baptism would be held.

"I'm told the archduke's family has arrived. I'll need to go and greet them, but can I trust you to wait alone? You're not going to run away and hide like Lord Wilfried, are you?"

It seemed that Sylvester's son was like a mini Syl. As his guard, Lamprecht was basically in the same role as Karstedt whenever he had to stop one of Sylvester's rampages. I felt genuine sympathy for how rough his daily life had to be.

"Lamprecht, my dear brother—you say that I would be waiting by myself, but the attendants would remain here with me. I would not truly be alone. And furthermore, I don't have the stamina to escape like a normal child might. You may rest easy and leave."

"That actually just makes me more worried," Lamprecht replied while leaving the room.

Not long after, Karstedt and Elvira came in, having finished welcoming the guests. Elvira immediately walked up to me and peered at my face.

"Lamprecht mentioned what had happened. You cried to the point of your eyes swelling up, and ultimately received healing from Lord Ferdinand, no? Rozemyne, first appearances are very important. You must understand that someone's first impression of you is decided the moment they see your face," Elvira explained, teaching me a fundamental rule of noble womanhood while continuing to check my eyes. "It is a failure of ladyhood to cry and allow your eyes to swell up prior to meeting so many new people at an event such as a baptism ceremony. You must always present your most beautiful self to the world."

Once she was done, we rehearsed the steps for the ceremony. It would begin when Ferdinand, who would be waiting in another room, entered. He would summon me, and then I would walk up to the altar one step behind my parents.

"My my myyy!"

"Kyaaah!"

All of a sudden, I heard the high-pitched squeals of women, so loud that the noise carried through the walls. As I looked at the door, wondering what the heck was happening outside, Karstedt mentioned that it was probably because Ferdinand was here. I thought that was strange. Today was a baptism ceremony, not a harspiel concert starring Ferdinand.

"...I feel like nobody is going to consider me the star of this event."

"Dear, this is the first time everyone is seeing Lord Ferdinand in his ceremonial priest robes," Elvira said. "Our hearts cannot help but flutter with excitement."

One of my few friends back in my Urano days definitely had a huge weak spot for people in particular outfits. Put glasses or a suit on someone and she'd be bleeding from the nose in no time.

...So he's like a boy wearing glasses, except he's a priest? Or maybe this is more similar to a boy in a suit. This is a bit beyond me, but either way, Ferdinand looks a bit too old to be called a boy.

The high-pitched shrieking stopped on a dime as Ferdinand started to speak. I couldn't tell what was being said, but could hear his deep voice reverberating through the walls. It seemed the ceremony was starting.

A small bell rang by the door, which was briskly opened by an attendant. Karstedt and Elvira immediately stood up, and I followed suit, descending the stairs to the first floor one step behind them. When we reached the bottom, I actually gasped at how many people were gathered in the assembly hall.

There were two, or maybe even three hundred people there—a crowd I would have thought too enormous to fit inside a single house—and all of their eyes were locked on me. Their gazes cut kind of deep—or like, they were heavy and bore down on me, making me cognizant that extreme attention was being paid to every single move I made.

...Am I supposed to walk like this?

There was a path running down the center of the hall for us to walk along, and an altar set up by the furthest wall. The divine instruments—which had probably been brought from the temple—

were placed on its steps, and Ferdinand was waiting in front wearing his ceremonial priest robes. It felt entirely like this was my wedding day, except I was alone.

For a second, Karstedt, who was escorting Elvira, shot a worried glance back to me. I returned a small nod to ease his worries. I had already resolved to separate from my family to protect both their lives and my own, and Ferdinand had already promised to give me the keys to the book room if I finished the ceremony successfully.

I had to become the archduke's adopted daughter no matter what. I had to earn the right to freely enter the book room so that I could read the precious books inside. I couldn't let myself fail here.

I shot my head up, put on the smile that Rosina and Elvira had drilled into me, and took my first step. I straightened my back and stared straight ahead, making sure not to look at the ground. My eyes scanned the crowd, but never focused on one point. I walked gracefully, like flowing water; the slowness of my pace meant nothing compared to how elegant it appeared.

In other words, I followed the etiquette that had been drummed into me to a T as I walked to the altar. As I neared the steps, I saw Rosina among the several musicians playing music. She was looking at me as she played, worry clear in her eyes, but I broadened my smile to show that I was doing fine.

As I got closer still, I saw that Sylvester was sitting in the seat closest to Ferdinand, wearing more extravagant clothing than ever before. Beside him was a woman who was presumably his wife, and a boy who looked about my age. That must have been Wilfried.

Seated on the other side of the aisle were my three brothers. Cornelius wore a tense expression as he looked my way, and while my other two brothers weren't showing it, I could guess they were worried as well.

Karstedt stopped in front of the altar with Elvira, then reached out a hand to me. I took it and walked up the steps to stand before Ferdinand. Once I was there, Karstedt and Elvira descended from the altar to join my brothers.

"Rozemyne, today you become seven years old," Ferdinand said as he took out a medal similar to the one I had seen at last year's baptism ceremony. I instantly remembered having to give a blood print.

Not again, I thought with a grimace, earning me a glare from Ferdinand.

"Hold out your hand."

I timidly obeyed, but what he handed me wasn't a knife or a needle—it was a thin stick about twenty centimeters long and covered in gorgeous decoration. Judging by the feystone, I could guess that it was a magic tool. The second I touched it, the stick shone and I could feel my mana being forcibly drained. Meanwhile, the audience started to clap, a sign that this was an intended part of the ceremony.

Ferdinand held out the medal to me, and I pressed the flat end of the stick against it like someone stamping a signature. The mana that had built up inside flowed into the medal, dimming the stick's light as the medal began to glow the seven colors of the rainbow.

"As expected," Ferdinand murmured as he looked at the medal, before immediately putting it away in a small box. "Congratulations, Rozemyne. You are now officially recognized as Karstedt's daughter. A new child has been born in Ehrenfest."

As celebratory applause filled the room, Karstedt climbed up the altar. Once at the top, he held the blue feystone ring high in the air for everyone to see. "I gift this ring to Rozemyne, now recognized as my child by society and the gods," he declared, before taking my left hand just like he had before and sliding the ring onto my middle finger. It changed size, fwooshing down into a ring that fit me perfectly.

"Rozemyne, may you have Leidenschaft the God of Fire's blessings." As Ferdinand spoke, I saw a flash of blue from the corner of my eye. I turned and saw that Ferdinand's ring was shining. Blue light rose into the air, then rained down on my head.

"I am honored, High Priest." I had been told that when Ferdinand gave me his blessing, I would need to bless the audience in return. "I pray that Leidenschaft the God of Fire blesses all those in attendance, and the High Priest for celebrating my baptism," I declared while pouring mana into the ring I had just gotten back. It shone with a similar blue light which swelled before rising into the air, circling around and scattering light across the entire assembly hall. The light was of a different color, but it resembled the blessing I had given my family at our last meeting.

...Whew. And that's the end of the ceremony, I thought, relieved that I had completed everything exactly as instructed. But a stir ran through the crowd. Unlike the calm, coordinated clapping from before, this was the sound of confused people who had just seen something unexpected.

"What in the world? She produced that much light?"

"Just how much mana does she have packed into that small body of hers?"

...Um, what? Did I mess up? I thought, worried by the reaction. But when I anxiously looked up at Karstedt and Ferdinand, they both just grinned ever so slightly. They were clearly planning something.

Karstedt stood behind me and, with a hand placed on my shoulder, whispered in a voice so quiet that only I could hear. "In a standard ceremony, the child only blesses the priest in return. This will give weight and legitimacy to the archduke adopting you."

Sylvester, wearing the grin of a kid who had just successfully pulled off a prank, leisurely climbed the altar, taking one deliberate step after another. The sight was enough to silence the crowd, and a quiet settled across the hall as everyone awaited his next move.

"Congratulations, Rozemyne. You have been recognized as a child of Ehrenfest," he said, facing me at the top of the altar before spinning around to look at the audience. He flourished his cape and continued on, talking in a loud, clear voice that reverberated through the assembly hall. "I shall adopt Rozemyne, here and now."

Most of the audience must not have been informed that this was going to happen, as the hall instantly started to buzz like a wasp nest that had just been hit with a bat.

Adoption

As I looked down at the buzzing audience, I let out an annoyed internal sigh at my three guardians. *Don't just plan things among yourselves! Keep me informed too!* I yelled silently. I understood that they were keeping me in the dark about a lot of things, but a little time to prepare would have been nice given that I was standing on top of an altar in full view of the guests.

"As you have all just seen, Rozemyne has an enormous amount of mana within her," Sylvester said abruptly, not even telling people to quiet down or pay attention first. He was clearly used to addressing crowds as the archduke, and his voice reverberated through the wide assembly hall.

That alone was enough to make the nobles fall silent. Whether it was due to Sylvester's charisma or just another unspoken rule of status-based society, I didn't know, but everyone remained silent and focused their attention on Sylvester as he spoke.

"Her mana is so great that Karstedt determined it necessary to hide his own child and raise her in secret, away from any danger. I am sure you all remember the former High Bishop misunderstanding her presence in the temple and, upon failing to discern her true identity, groaning and complaining of a commoner shrine maiden disturbing the peace."

Well, there it is. Here we go blaming everything on the High Bishop. The ultimate technique: "It's all his fault, not mine."

I knew from talking to Karstedt and my older brothers that the High Bishop had committed so many crimes that Ferdinand had found it tedious just to list them all. So much embezzlement had gone on that just doing the math on it took me forever, and maybe, in the end, adding a single extra crime on top didn't make much of a difference at all. But even knowing that, I found it pretty impressive how Sylvester could stand in front of a huge crowd like this and casually lie without a care in the world.

"Rozemyne was raised humbly, unaware of her parents or status, but even so, her compassionate heart ached at the suffering of those living in worse circumstances than herself. She pitied the children living in the orphanage, and did what no other person would by giving their young selves food and work."

He was speaking so highly of this "Rozemyne" girl that I honestly wanted to ask who he was actually talking about. I mean, he wasn't wrong when he said that I had been shocked by the state of the orphanage, and that I had established a workshop inside to improve the conditions there, but he was making it sound so incredible that I wasn't sure it applied to me at all.

"I heard tales of her inspiring dedication from Ferdinand the High Priest, but I held my doubts. No child could be so compassionate to others nor so successful, I thought, and so I traveled to the orphanage to investigate myself. But there I found Rozemyne, being worshiped and honored by the orphans like a saint. My heart was moved by the sheer extent of her virtue."

...Um, that's way too much exaggeration! Me, a saint?! The only saint I know is Wilma!

I was protesting on the inside, but the archduke saying that he doubted Ferdinand and had confirmed the truth himself clearly made his claims more believable to the people. Those who had previously been murmuring "How ridiculous" or "That can't be true" were now saying "Wait, really?" and "I find it hard to believe, but if he said he saw it himself…"

…Gaaah! I can't stand being on this altar anymore! I wanna shout that I'm not a big deal and that they shouldn't believe him, then run out of the room! Dad, Lutz, save me!

"Furthermore, the work she gave the orphans was quite interesting, and I determined that it could potentially become a new industry for this duchy. Just as I was considering the possibility of spending the next twenty-or-so years spreading it through the duchy, Rozemyne was targeted by a noble from another duchy," he said.

At those words, the crowd immediately started to buzz once more.

"I'm sure you are all already aware of the incident: a villain tried to take advantage of my absence during the Archduke Conference and forged an entry permit to get inside the city. As it turns out, the former High Bishop had leaked information of Rozemyne's heroic exploits and her immense amount of mana. And so, in order to secure her position in our society, and to protect her wealth of mana for the good of Ehrenfest, I shall hereby adopt Rozemyne."

Another stir ran through the crowd, but this time it seemed to be one of acceptance; I could guess that the duchy's mana shortage was felt more harshly by the nobles providing mana than anyone else.

"Due to the execution of the former High Bishop, the lack of priests available to perform prayers and blessings, and her own desire to continue helping the orphans, I will assign Rozemyne to the position of High Bishop from now until she comes of age. Her first duty will be to establish workshops in nearby cities to continue saving the orphans suffering throughout the duchy."

I didn't really care about getting married, so I would have been fine serving as the High Bishop for my entire life, spreading printing and expanding the temple book room, but I guessed that Sylvester wasn't about to let that happen. If he was adopting me to prevent nobles from other duchies coming after me, then I could imagine that he might want me to marry Wilfried in the future. But it sounded like Wilfried was just a mini Syl, which honestly just sounded depressing.

"Ferdinand, if you will." Sylvester took out a piece of parchment from his pocket and held it out to Ferdinand. Something was already written on it, and after glancing over it, Ferdinand gave a nod. It was the official document for the adoption.

Sylvester then took out what looked like a thin, ornately decorated fountain pen from his pocket. He handed it to Karstedt, who signed the parchment before passing it on to me. I had assumed it was something like a ballpoint pen since he hadn't dipped it in any ink, but the moment I took it, I could feel my mana being drained out. Apparently, it was a magic tool that used mana instead of ink. As I used it to sign the sheet, I found that it was indeed just like an ink pen—I could write in exchange for the teensiest bit of my mana getting sucked out.

Wowee, I really want one of these!

I gazed lovingly at the pen for a bit, only to be interrupted by a cough. Ferdinand was glaring at me, and then slowly shifted his eyes to Sylvester. I followed his gaze to see Sylvester holding his hand out and mouthing the words, "Hurry up and give it back."

I felt a sudden burst of anxiety, which I quickly swallowed down before returning the pen as gracefully as I could, forcing a smile as I did so. Sylvester took it and smoothly added his own signature to the sheet, which then shone with golden light just like a magic contract before burning away.

The contract was complete.

As the crowd cheered, Karstedt bent over to pick me up. "Smile and wave," he instructed, speaking quietly enough that only I could hear him among the loud cheers. I did my best to wave while wearing a smile like one I had seen the Japanese emperor give.

As I continued to smile and wave to the crowd, I whispered a question to Karstedt. "Um, is that magic contract limited to the city too? Should an adoption really only be limited to this one city?"

"Only magic contracts for commoner merchants have effects limited to the city. Do not lump them all together," Ferdinand replied in Karstedt's place. Apparently there was more than one kind of magic contract.

Now that the baptism ceremony and adoption were finished, everyone began to talk among themselves while eating meals proudly prepared by Ella and the estate's head chef, who had been working together in the kitchen. Unfortunately for me, I was stuck sitting on the altar in preparation for nobles to come over and greet me. I couldn't exactly be munching away at food while people tried to introduce themselves, so the most I could do was sip drinks while I waited for the greetings to finish.

...Aww, it all looks so tasty. I want to eat too. You're so lucky, Cornelius.

As I watched Cornelius eating happily, I noticed Wilfried break away from the crowd to try and steal some food, only to have his hands blocked by Lamprecht. The archduke's wife walked over, grabbed Wilfried, gave some instructions to Lamprecht, and then came walking this way.

The first people to greet me—and the ones I needed to introduce myself to most—were Sylvester's family. Other nobles couldn't come over to greet me until the archduke's family had. Wilfried was pouting with a slight frown at having been pulled away from the food, but I could tell that both of his parents were ignoring that.

Karstedt introduced me to the three of them. "This is Lord Sylvester, the archduke, and his first wife, Lady Florencia. Beside them is Lord Sylvester's son, Lord Wilfried."

Florencia had light-blonde hair that was close to silver, indigo eyes, and while at a glance she seemed to be a laid-back beauty, the iron grip she had on Wilfried's shirt gave me the impression that she was a strict, no-nonsense mother. Assuming he really was a mini Syl, then I could only imagine how tough it was to keep them both under control at once.

"Lady Florencia is two years older than Lord Sylvester, and has the incredible power of being able to control her husband."

"Karstedt." Sylvester grimaced a bit at that introduction, but Florencia brushed it off with a refined giggle. I could see Ferdinand nodding in agreement. If she really was an older sister-type wife who could keep Sylvester under control, then I would absolutely love to be on great terms with her.

"I am Rozemyne. It is a pleasure to meet you all."

"Elvira has told me much about you," Florencia said. "I assure you that being Sylvester's adopted daughter will not be easy, but we shall get through it together."

Wilfried had the same light-blonde hair as his mother, and deep-green eyes that greatly resembled Sylvester's. To be honest, aside from his hair, he didn't look like his mother at all; his face was literally like a younger version of Sylvester's. He was a mini Syl indeed.

"Lord Wilfried is the same age as you, but as he had his baptism in the spring, that makes him your older brother. Lord Sylvester has two other children, but they stayed behind at the castle today."

Although I was in truth his older sister, the fact that I was repeating my seventh year and only just being baptized made everyone else assume I was younger. Wilfried also apparently had a younger brother and sister at the castle, but they weren't here today since children who hadn't been baptized couldn't be brought anywhere public, even if they were the children of the archduke.

In a shocking twist, Sylvester had somehow managed to have three children despite acting like an elementary schooler. That was legitimately the biggest surprise of the day so far.

...I'm hardly one to talk, but you need to grow up, Sylvester.

"Just consider me your new big bro, Rozemyne. You're as much of a little sister to me as Charlotte is."

"That is oh-so-kind of you to say, Wilfried."

"Yeah, don't worry. I'll look after you," Wilfried said, seemingly satisfied at having established himself as the older brother and, by extension, the more mature sibling. I could already see him dragging me around until I fell unconscious.

Once I had finished meeting the archduke's family, Karstedt raised a hand before any other nobles could approach. Judging by the two people who started coming this way, that had probably been a signal decided upon ahead of time.

"You'll be moved to the castle once your High Bishop inauguration ceremony is over, but now that you're the archduke's adopted daughter, you need knights to guard you at almost all times. These two will be your personal guards starting tomorrow."

As the two made their way through the waves of people, I instantly recognized one of them. The other, however, was a woman who I hadn't seen before, wearing normal noble clothing with low-hanging sleeves.

"It was pretty difficult to find a female knight for you since your workshop's in the temple, and you'll of course be going to the lower city."

I needed a female knight so that she could truly follow me everywhere, but as most only went where noble girls went, they didn't really want to leave the Noble's Quarter.

"These two are going to be the knights who follow you to the temple and beyond. I'm sure you recognize one of them," Karstedt finished, just as the two arrived and knelt before me.

"It's good to see you well, Damuel. I look forward to your continued good service."

"It has been a long time since we last met, Lady Rozemyne. I will serve you to the absolute best of my ability," Damuel said.

Under normal circumstances, it would be unthinkable for a laynoble like Damuel to guard a member of the archduke's family. He had apparently gone from being called an unlucky guy who had almost died alongside Shikza, to someone who had found a metaphorical feystone in the pit of mud known as the temple.

"This fine lady is Brigitte. She's the same age as Damuel. Her skills are unquestionable, and as a mednoble, she has more mana than Damuel. I think you'll find her a reliable ally. For the most part, she'll be your guard when you go to the temple. You'll have other guards when you're in the archduke's castle."

The dark red-haired woman raised her head and looked directly at me with her amethyst eyes. She had broader shoulders and was more muscular than most other noblewomen I had seen, which made it easy to accept that she was a female knight. At a glance, she felt kind of like a reliable older sister, and did seem like someone I could count on.

"Brigitte, I imagine that going all the way to the temple won't be pleasant for you, but I thank you for accompanying me."

"Your wish is my command, Lady Rozemyne."

Having met my knights, it was time for the rest of the nobles to come up group by group to introduce themselves and congratulate me.

"Rozemyne."

I had been greeted by a number of nobles when Wilfried came wandering over, probably bored now that he had filled his stomach. It was a fact of noble society that when the son of the archduke walked over, everyone else had to make way for him, no matter how young he was. The nobles retreated backward.

"Nothing fun's ever gonna happen here. Let's go play," he said, before pulling my arm. "Follow me."

But I was technically the focus of this event, and meeting the nobles was almost certainly an important job for me. My promise to Ferdinand that I would memorize all of their names and jobs to make the ceremony a success spun through my mind.

"Um, but I need to be introduced to everybody..."

"Who cares about that? C'mon."

I turned around in search of help, but Ferdinand just waved a hand and told me to go. "What is wrong with kids playing together? I am sure you would prefer to be with children, Rozemyne, than around all these adults."

...Um, no? I would much rather be with the adults. And should I really be allowed to just leave my own baptism ceremony? I thought, my mouth dropping in disbelief. Meanwhile, Wilfried continued to pull me away. I started following along behind him so that I wouldn't fall over, but he kept speeding up. He pulled me down from the altar and through the throngs of well-dressed ladies, at which point he basically broke out into a run, dragging me right behind him.

"Wilfried, could you go a little slower...?"

"Nah, you need to speed up, Rozemyne. The adults are gonna catch us if we don't hurry."

I'd asked him to slow down and his immediate response was to call me weak. It wasn't hard to guess that he spent pretty much every day running from adults and trying to avoid getting caught, and considering how Sylvester acted, it was easy to imagine Wilfried being an overall problem child.

"You gotta practice every day and get good at finding places to hide if you wanna master shaking off that busybody Lamprecht. A clumsy slowpoke like you is just gonna get caught in no time."

"I don't plan on running or hiding, so if you would please let go of my hand..."

"No way! That'll get us caught, and then we'll be yelled at!"

I wanted to protest and say that he only got yelled at because he ran away from his guards in the first place, but by that point I was breathing so heavily that I could barely even speak.

...Oh no. I'm about to fall unconscious.

"Please... stop... I can't... breathe..."

"Nguh?! Rozemyne?!"

My knees buckled and I hit the ground. The pain as my skin dragged across the ground and Wilfried's shocked cry were the last things I remembered before everything went dark.

That's the second time I've failed to finish a baptism ceremony. Hopefully there won't be a third time...

When I woke up, I was in my room. I sat up in bed and saw Karstedt and Ferdinand playing reversi nearby.

"Finally awake, I see," Ferdinand said.

"...I can still taste it." He must have made me drink that potion again. The awful bitterness stayed in my mouth for so long it was hard to believe.

"As you now know, Wilfried is the spitting image of Sylvester in his youth and listens to nobody but himself. I decided that teaching him how weak you are up front was the only way to ensure he treated you with the proper care going forward, and here we are."

"I think he might end up traumatized from me passing out like a minute into him dragging me away."

Even Mark and Benno had said that their hearts nearly stopped the first time they saw me pass out in front of them, and they had become more than a little overprotective afterward. The same went for Cornelius. Somehow, I got the feeling that the same thing happening to two little kids would be enough to actually traumatize them.

"Undoubtedly. Wilfried has a kind heart despite his clumsy immaturity, so it is easy to imagine this wounding him to some degree. And that is exactly why he will be much more considerate of your health from now on."

Ferdinand didn't hesitate for a second to traumatize a child if doing so was a reliable way of getting the results he wanted as soon as possible. I'd assumed that he was so excessively logical and harsh with me since he knew I was an adult on the inside, but dang, he didn't even show mercy to his own nephew. Ferdinand was kind of mean.

"I see the unhappy look on your face, but this would have happened sooner or later no matter what I did. Wilfried listens to no one, and you cannot keep up with him. Had the same thing happened in the castle, your guards would have been punished for failing to protect you. It is better for everyone if he learns of your weakness and the position you're in now rather than later."

Right. I was entering the castle as the archduke's adopted daughter. If anything happened to me, the knights guarding me would be punished. Wilfried's rampage had ended without any far-reaching consequences since I had only just been baptized and no guards had started guarding me in an official capacity yet, but had it happened at any point beyond today, things would have gone much differently. Other people would have been hurt too.

"Lamprecht was shocked beyond belief as well. As you are the same age as Wilfried, you and he will often spend time together as fellow children of the archduke. His guards will need to understand your circumstances just as much as he now does."

Me collapsing had apparently traumatized Lamprecht as well, since he had been stealthily following behind us as Wilfried's guard.

Sorry, Lamprecht.

"A noble who had coincidentally seen the incident came rushing to inform us, and by the time we arrived at the scene you were in quite the horrible state. Due to how hard Wilfried had been dragging you, there were scrape marks going from your temple all the way down to your cheeks, and blood had started pooling on the white stone floor. There were also scrapes along your thighs and knees, so your white baptism ceremony clothes were stained with blood. You were so still and unresponsive lying on the floor that it was entirely as if you had died."

"Gyaaah! I don't wanna hear that! Ow, ow!" I covered my ears and shook my head hard. Ferdinand looked down at me with exasperation, but Karstedt just let out a laugh.

"Don't let it get to you, Rozemyne. Lord Ferdinand healed your wounds and gave you a potion. He lectured Wilfried and Lamprecht as well. It's all over already."

"...The scrapes are all gone?" It wouldn't have really mattered back in my Urano days, but I didn't want my cute little girl face all covered in scars. I patted my cheeks to check, and Ferdinand grimaced, asking whether I doubted his skill.

...Of course not. No way. I know you're the man himself—the High Priest. I would never doubt your ability.

"In any case, both the ceremony and the adoption concluded without issue. Spend the next two days resting, and if you seem in good health, return to the temple. There we will hold the High Bishop inauguration ceremony." Ferdinand stated our future plans, then left. I assumed that was the end of the conversation, but Karstedt kept looking at me, as if there was something else he wanted to say.

"Yes, Father? Is something wrong?"

"...Rozemyne, did you do something to Damuel?"

"What do you mean by that? Are you asking whether I earned his eternal loyalty through sweets or something?" Maybe he had learned about the parue cakes we would sometimes serve in the orphanage, or maybe... I fell into thought, at which point Karstedt furrowed his brow and shook his head.

"Not that. I'm talking about his mana. The process is slow, but his mana capacity is growing the more he trains. That kind of growth is unthinkable considering his age; he should be just about finished growing by now. Did you give him some kind of blessing without telling us?"

I had never given Damuel a special personal blessing before. At most, he had received part of the blessing I had sent my family.

"...The only thing that comes to mind is the big blessing that I gave my family back at the temple. I wanted it to heal everyone, and both Fran and Dirk received the blessing, so it wouldn't be strange if it also flew over to where Damuel was lying unconscious."

"That blessing, hm...?" Karstedt murmured before cradling his head for a bit.

I hope I didn't mess anything up.

"Rozemyne, tell no one of this. Not Sylvester, of course, but not Ferdinand either."

"Um..."

"Sylvester will never let Damuel hear the end of it."

Apparently the blessing I had given my family was pretty unprecedented in scale, and Sylvester was not only complaining about Ferdinand getting it, but also teasing him for it.

"As his brother and someone who has known him for so long, Ferdinand is skilled and capable when it comes to enduring Sylvester's teasing, but Damuel would never survive."

Considering what had happened back at Spring Prayer, that was definitely something I could agree with. Damuel had nearly buckled under the stress of Sylvester teasing and bullying him. I'd feel bad if my actions caused that to start all over again.

"...I can understand not telling Sylvester, but why shouldn't we tell Ferdinand?"

"You know what a cold-blooded rationalist he is. He wouldn't even hesitate to offer up Damuel if it meant he could escape Sylvester's bullying himself."

"I understand completely. I won't say a word."

Knowing firsthand how harsh Ferdinand's rationalism could be, I silently swore to keep it a secret that Damuel had received my blessing.

Inauguration Ceremony

Ferdinand had told me to use the day after my baptism ceremony to rest. He had most likely told Elvira about this before leaving, given that she also instructed me to stay in bed for the day that morning at the breakfast table. And considering how sometimes my body reacted negatively to being forced back into being healthy with a potion, I was more than glad to comply.

"Rozemyne, do you have a moment?"

"Lamprecht? I do, though I can't leave my bed right now."

"I just came to check up on how you're doing. Lord Wilfried is pretty worried himself, so…"

A glum-looking Lamprecht came to see me before he was due to leave for work, perhaps as a result of the harsh scolding he had been given. He had been so bright and lively yesterday that seeing him so down made me wonder just how hard Ferdinand and Karstedt had scolded him, which made my heart hurt a little. Had I been a normal child, my fall would have ended with a couple of scratches at worst. It wouldn't have traumatized him like this.

"Ferdinand let it happen on purpose as a lesson to Wilfried, so please don't worry about it too much."

"I can imagine Lord Ferdinand wanted it to happen while he was still nearby, since he is capable of using magic and giving potions himself. This ended with no more than a scolding since you were healed almost immediately, but what if it had happened at the castle without any healers around? If you had died there, Lord Wilfried would be far more distraught than he is now."

...Um, why is it that the brutal, cold-hearted rationalist Ferdinand suddenly sounds like a super good person?

"This is something that I should have taught Wilfried myself, without Lord Ferdinand needing to get involved."

Lamprecht was deeply regretting the incident, but if you asked me, Ferdinand was the one who should be regretting traumatizing everyone. He needed to learn to be nicer to other people, myself included.

"Don't worry, Lamprecht. As long as you and Wilfried are more careful from now on, everything will be fine."

"Rozemyne... You were on the verge of death, nearly slain by our hands, and yet you express nothing but concern for us? What enormous compassion..." The light returned to Lamprecht's eyes as his face was overcome by a mix of shock and admiration.

...Oh no. I feel like I've nudged him in the wrong direction.

"Um, Lamprecht, my dear brother, you have the wrong idea. I'm just used to that kind of situation, so a single slip-up doesn't really mean much to me..."

"I see, so your empathy is just that profound."

I feel like nothing I say at this point will change his mind. He's just not listening anymore. Whaaatever.

I dropped the subject, giving up on Lamprecht ever understanding me. That was when he undid a bundle of cloth, from which he retrieved a book. "I asked Lord Ferdinand what he thought I should get you as a gift, and he gave me this, saying it would be perfect for you. I can't say I follow, though."

"That's a book, isn't it?!"

"He said this is a book you've never read before and could finish in a day, but Rozemyne, can you really read a book this thick?" Lamprecht asked dubiously, practically comparing me and the book. But it would be a piece of cake.

"I can read it! I *will* read it! Lamprecht, thank you ever so much!"

"I'm glad to see that you're this happy about it. Well, I have to return to the castle. Rest well, Rozemyne. Okay?"

"Okaaay."

Ferdinand was a brutal rationalist, but he was a good person. He may have correctly predicted that giving me a book I couldn't actually finish in a day would lead to me faking being sick and avoiding going to the temple tomorrow, but that was fine by me.

Thank you, High Priest!

I spent the day rolling around in bed, resting for the first time in ages while reading a book about effectively mobilizing troops during warfare. A lot of the concepts were largely based around magic, which made them pretty hard to understand, but it was really fun trying to figure things out.

When tomorrow came, I felt great, no doubt thanks to the combined powers of Ferdinand's healing and his potion, plus having spent a day reading a book in bed. I sent someone to tell Ella and Rosina that we'd be going back to the temple.

After breakfast, once I was ready to leave, my guards Damuel and Brigitte arrived. They knelt in front of me and crossed their arms over their chests.

"Good morning, Lady Rozemyne."

"Today we are returning to the temple. I ask that you accompany me," I said, and they both responded "Ma'am!" before standing up sharply. I went to stand up too, but Brigitte stopped me.

"Please wait here for a moment, Lady Rozemyne. I will send an ordonnanz to Lord Ferdinand." Brigitte took out her shining wand and tapped a yellow feystone while murmuring *"ordonnanz,"* which turned it into a white bird. She then said "Lady Rozemyne is now heading for the temple" before swiping her wand through the air, sending the bird flying off.

It returned not long after and said "Understood" three times in Ferdinand's voice before morphing back into a feystone. That had really surprised me the first time I saw it, but after living around magic tools for long enough, it just felt kind of normal. I was adjusting to my surroundings shockingly fast, if you asked me.

With our report concluded, Damuel and Brigitte escorted me into a carriage. Ella and Rosina would be following in a separate carriage for attendants.

"Please tell Lord Ferdinand that I said hello. And remember to take your duties seriously, dear."

"Yes, Mother."

Karstedt and Cornelius had already headed to the Knight's Order, so Elvira was the only one to see me off. The carriage started smoothly and we headed to the temple, the pure-white buildings passing by on either side of us.

"Brigitte, have you ever been to the temple or the lower city?"

"Yes, milady, but only while passing through. This is my first time going through the Noble's Gate with the intention of staying."

Brigitte was in fact the little sister of Viscount Illgner—"viscount" being the title given to mednoble giebes—who ruled a province to the south of the city. As such, she had flown over the lower city on her highbeast and passed through in a carriage with her family, but had never actually stayed there or even stepped out of the carriage.

Damuel, having experience in the lower city thanks to me, grimaced a bit and tossed Brigitte some words of encouragement. "The temple's not so bad, but visiting the lower city will be rough for a woman. Good luck."

"Welcome back, Lady Rozemyne," Fran said. He had waited for me at the temple's front entrance. Given that I had been moved to the Noble's Quarter as spring was starting to fade, and that we were now approaching the height of summer, it had been a long time since Fran and I had seen each other.

"I have returned, Fran. Has anything changed since I've been gone?"

"Your room has changed, and Gil has been working like a mad man. With that in mind, I would say that much has changed."

"I'm looking forward to seeing that. Brigitte, this is Fran, my head attendant. Fran, this is Brigitte, a knight and one of my guards."

Once I had finished introducing them to each other, I headed to the High Bishop's chambers. It was at the far end of the temple's noble section, and I remembered passing by it quite regularly during the winter Dedication Ritual.

"Monika and Nicola are preparing to cook in the kitchen now, and Gil is in the workshop. I believe you will all meet after your inauguration," Fran said, before opening the door.

I walked into my new chambers. The decoration and furniture had been changed according to Rosina's list, now looking much more feminine, and with fairy tale-esque flower designs decorating the entire room in shades of red. The chambers barely resembled what they used to look like.

There was one resemblance, though: the altar holding the thirty-ish centimeter tall god statue, bible, and candle, placed thirty centimeters apart from each other with the bible in the middle. I could guess that this was just a necessary part of the High Bishop's chambers, which reminded me—back when I had become an apprentice blue shrine maiden, Ferdinand had said that vowing to serve the gods and being given robes was normally done before the altar in the High Bishop's room. That meant any future blue priests and shrine maidens would say their vows here.

Hm... I wonder whether I'll be able to handle that.

"This certainly is a cute room. It suits you well, Lady Rozemyne. And I never would have thought the High Bishop's chambers would have so much money poured into them," Brigitte said in awe, nodding to herself repeatedly. Karstedt had paid for the entire redecoration, so my wallet hadn't been hurt by it at all.

Maybe I should give a portion of my workshop's earnings to Karstedt to pay for my living expenses.

"The High Priest also instructed that rooms for male and female knights be prepared on either side of the High Bishop's chambers so that Lady Rozemyne's guards can stay the night. Two separate rooms, each with multiple beds. Please do inform me if there are any inconveniences," Fran said, so I went to check out the rooms.

The male room was fitted as a guest room; it was simple, without a single unnecessary thing in it. According to Damuel, it was just like the men's rooms in the knights' barracks. Karstedt had ordered the rooms be made similarly since he figured staying somewhere familiar would be for the best.

I assumed the female room would also be the same as the barracks, but apparently when Karstedt had investigated the female half of the knights' barracks, he discovered that the women had all changed their rooms to suit their personal tastes, leaving the original layout unrecognizable. Karstedt eventually gave up on catering the room to a wide variety of preferences and just ordered for it to be fitted like mine, figuring that a room good enough for the archduke's adopted daughter would be good enough for a female knight of any status.

In other words, the room was feminine. Geduldh the Goddess of Earth was considered the symbol of femininity, and the room was themed around her royal color of red, with bright-pink flower decorations covering everything. It was so cute that I figured a tough woman like Brigitte might be put off by it.

"This certainly is a cute room..." Brigitte repeated the same thing she had about my room, but this time there was a tinge of surprise and worry mixed into her voice. She seemed a bit conflicted about how cute it was.

"Brigitte, um, if you don't like the room..."

"You do not need to concern yourself with that, Lady Rozemyne. It is a guest room; all I will be doing here is sleeping, so there is no need to go out of your way to change the decoration. I will be quite fine," Brigitte said, her amethyst eyes softening as she gave me a gentle smile. I knew better than to doubt the kind words of a cool lady knight.

I returned to my High Bishop's chambers just as Monika left the kitchen. Ella had arrived, and Monika was going to do her normal work while Nicola helped cook.

"Welcome back, Lady Rozemyne."

Once Rosina and Monika finished putting away my things and setting the harspiel in place, they changed me into my ceremonial High Bishop robes. Apparently these were the robes Ferdinand had ordered from the Gilberta Company.

"It seems that, due to a lack of time, they simply altered the previous High Bishop's robes in a haste," Monika said.

I nodded. That made sense. No way did we have the time to wait for cloth of this quality to be prepared from scratch. With the archduke's mother as his older sister, the previous High Bishop had robes made from the highest quality cloth available. It felt wonderful to the touch, and was very light on me. Sadly though, the crest wasn't the one I had spent so long thinking up for the Myne Workshop; instead, it was a lion just like the one on Ferdinand's robes, signifying a child of the archduke.

...Dang. I really liked that crest, too.

I pursed my lips while fiddling with the crest, and Monika gave me a worried frown. "I know that it must be unpleasant to wear clothes worn by the previous High Bishop, but please bear with it for now."

"Oh, that's not it, Monika. I'm just a little disappointed that the crest isn't my own—the one I liked a lot. I don't care who made or wore an outfit as long as it doesn't embarrass me or the people around me. Hate the person, not the clothes."

I had spent years wearing nothing but secondhand clothing. If you were worried about who had worn a particular piece of clothing before you, then you wouldn't be able to wear secondhand clothing at all. Considering that I had once worn an outfit made of literal rags sewn together in order to gather soot, I would probably receive divine punishment if I complained about robes this beautiful.

"You are such a wonderful person, Lady Rozemyne. Everything Wilma said was true," Monika whispered, her eyes glittering, but I had no idea what had inspired her to say that.

I thought for a second, then snapped my fingers in realization. Fran and Gil had seen me walking around the lower city in my raggedy commoner clothes, but Monika only knew me as an apprentice blue shrine maiden, and now the adopted daughter of the archduke. She was convinced I had been suffering in silence as a high-status archnoble used to always wearing new clothes, and since Brigitte was here, I couldn't correct her. I gave up on explaining and decided to just let her misunderstandings be.

"The robes seem to fit you perfectly. With that sorted, I will now discuss today's plans," Fran said once he had looked over my ceremonial robes, heading to a nearby desk. Apparently Ferdinand would be coming here later to discuss a few matters, and then the inauguration ceremony would be held in the afternoon. We also had a meeting planned with the Gilberta Company tomorrow.

...I'm finally going to get to see Lutz again.

By the time Fran had finished his explanation, Ferdinand was just arriving. It turned out that he would generally be coming to my chambers from now on instead of me going to his, since I was of higher status than him as far as the public was concerned. I thanked him for the book he had given Lamprecht, and for preparing the ceremonial robes, rooms for the knights, and so on.

"Still, I'm surprised I'm being inaugurated so quickly," I said.

Ferdinand responded by saying that it was an exclusive ceremony performed within the temple, so there really wasn't much to prepare. I double-checked the ceremony procedures, then asked why we were rushing it so much. Considering that it was a gathering of blue priests, I would have thought that they would be given at least a few days' notice.

"This ritual is necessary for you to use the High Bishop's chambers. Furthermore, if you are not officially inaugurated as High Bishop, I cannot give you the keys to the book room."

"Oh, now *that's* a big deal. We need to get this over with as soon as possible. I'm assuming those aren't the only reasons, though..."

The keys to the book room were definitely important, but it was hard to imagine Ferdinand going through the effort of speeding things up for that alone. There had to be some deeper reasons here.

"The blue priests were informed days ago and pose no issue here; we knew thanks to the potion and healing magic that you would recover soon. But in any case, you should be more concerned with accelerating this small, internal ceremony than anyone else. Otherwise you won't have enough time to finish what Sylvester spoke about, will you?"

"Wait... what did Sylvester say?" I asked, tilting my head in confusion.

Ferdinand drummed a finger against his temple and shot me an annoyed glare. "Were you not listening? I am referring to the eatery and the expansion of printing."

"I remember Sylvester talking about building workshops in neighboring cities to expand the printing industry, but what's this about the eatery?" I asked.

I knew from a hastily written letter Benno had sent me that, in return for letting Hugo and Todd train under Leise, he had let the guildmaster join in funding the Italian restaurant. But that was all; I didn't know any details.

"Benno received a direct decree from Sylvester: he is to meet with a scholar-official, investigate the orphanage of a nearby city, and organize their findings—all before the Starbind Ceremony. Then, he will need to report these findings directly to Sylvester during a meeting at the Italian restaurant."

"Whaaat?!"

"That is naturally too great of a burden for Benno. Help him where you can, especially now that the deadline has been accelerated by your adoption."

Apparently Benno was so overworked that even Ferdinand sympathized enough to try to help out a bit. I nodded hard, feeling the blood drain from my face.

I need to finish this dumb inauguration ceremony as soon as possible so I can get to helping Benno!

The inauguration ceremony was held in the chapel, with the blue priests, their attendants, and all gray priests and shrine maidens who had come of age in attendance. It was being led by Ferdinand, who dryly stated that the previous High Bishop had been dismissed and that the archduke had decided on a new High Bishop. Meanwhile, I was behind a door, waiting for him to call for me.

"...And so, according to the archduke's wishes, the new High Bishop will be his adopted daughter, Rozemyne," Ferdinand said, the door in front of me slowly opening as he spoke. When it was completely open, I could see the rows and rows of gray priests standing silently in the chapel, and Ferdinand standing atop the steps.

"Offer your prayers to the gods and welcome her arrival. Praise be to the gods!"

While feeling nostalgic for the rows of Gl*co poses that I hadn't seen in a long time, I took Fran's hand and gracefully walked to the center of the chapel. I climbed the stairs to the highest point, which allowed me to look over the entire chapel.

There was a row of about ten blue priests closest to us, a few of whom were gaping at the sight of me. Those who knew me as Myne or had mocked me when we crossed paths in the halls all had their eyes wide open in shock, but some were just looking me over with blank, half-interested expressions—most likely the people who had never seen me as Myne and so didn't recognize me. The stark contrast between their reactions made them easy to tell apart.

"Thank you all for coming on this auspicious summer day blessed by Leidenschaft's shining rays. I am Rozemyne, and my father, the archduke, has entrusted me with the position of High Bishop."

"The archduke's adopted daughter? That can't be right! She's a commoner!" one blue priest shouted. Ferdinand repeated the same explanation that Sylvester had given at my baptism, but that wasn't enough to convince the blue priest, who continued his furious protests.

"High Priest, you're the archduke's brother. You would have known if she was an archnoble. You wouldn't have called her a commoner. None of this makes any sense!"

"If even the previous High Bishop—who frequently spoke of being closer to the archduke than anyone else thanks to his high birth—did not know, then it is unreasonable to expect that I would."

There it is! The ultimate technique: "It's all his fault, not mine"! The old High Bishop really is perfect for wrongfully pinning the blame on.

Ferdinand had to resort to the ultimate technique just like Sylvester had, but thanks to that, almost everyone accepted the situation, even if they didn't fully believe it. The gray priests and shrine maidens in particular, who were used to obeying orders from above, accepted it easily without really thinking too hard about it. They would tell the kids in the orphanage about all this later, instructing them to call me "Lady Rozemyne" instead of "Sister Myne" from now on, so that I would be treated one hundred percent like an archnoble even in the temple.

"If you doubt that I am an archnoble adopted by the archduke, you may ask Karstedt, the commander of the Knight's Order, or Aub Ehrenfest, my adoptive father, to see what they say," I declared, indirectly telling them to shut up. And with that done, all that was left was to list my future goals in flowery language and then pray to the gods.

"O mighty King and Queen of the endless skies, O mighty Eternal Five who rule the mortal realm, O Goddess of Water Flutrane, O God of Fire Leidenschaft, O Goddess of Wind Schutzaria, O Goddess of Earth Geduldh, O God of Life Ewigeliebe! We offer you our prayers and gratitude," I said, and the priests all took their positions.

"Praise be to the gods! Glory be to the gods!"

Once everyone had prayed to the gods, I took my leave, Ferdinand taking my hand as I walked down the steps. But about halfway down, I noticed one blue priest deliberately avoiding eye contact, instead looking at the ground. I stopped to take a closer look, and immediately recognized his middle-aged noble features.

"Oh my, are you who I think you are?"

"You know Egmont, Rozemyne?"

"He's the one who made a mess of my book room, I believe. Is that right, Egmont?"

Heheh. Foooound you, I cackled to myself, and despite the fact I wasn't even Crushing him, Egmont paled at once. He desperately flapped his mouth, trying to say words but failing hard as he looked around for help. It was then that he made eye contact with Ferdinand and, a light bulb popping up over his head, hurriedly began to make excuses.

"The previous High Bishop ordered me to do that! I didn't do it by choice!"

There it is again! The ultimate technique: "It's all his fault, not mine!" Goodness, High Bishop, you sure are popular.

However, no ultimate technique would keep working forever. The sin of messing up my precious book room was profound, and my anger for those who spited books was doggedly persistent. Neither would fade by trying to push the blame onto the High Bishop.

"I see. So the High Bishop ordered it, then," I said.

Egmont nodded, his lips curling into a smile—a smile purely expressing the glee of having escaped anger. There wasn't a shred of regret nor any indication of self-reflection. I gave a smile of my own, Crushing him just a little to show I was still angry.

"Your life is mine. Do not think I shall forgive you a second time."

Despite having solved the situation with stunning restraint and perfect logic while avoiding an absolute bloodfest, the second we were back in my chambers, Ferdinand scolded me for going too far. It just didn't make sense.

"That's strange. You're the one who taught me that the most logical and effective course of action is to beat a lesson into someone by emotionally traumatizing them."

"...That is only the case when you are dealing with someone who will not listen no matter what you say," Ferdinand replied with an uncomfortable frown. But as far as I was concerned, it would be a huge problem if Egmont had ignored me and messed up the book room a second time.

"At the moment, I don't care whether or not he's willing to listen. What I want is for all of the blue priests to know that it won't end well for them if they touch my book room. And I accomplished that in quite a rational way, did I not?" I asked with a smile.

Ferdinand gave me a fake smile in return. "Your rationality is spurred by emotion, which makes it all the more terrifying. It is impossible to say what far-reaching impact your actions will have."

"Oh? But your rationality is spurred by complicated plotting, and has quite a far-reaching impact on many things."

As we smiled coldly at each other, I suddenly remembered something important: Egmont being traumatized didn't matter, and now was definitely not the time to be having an evil staring contest with Ferdinand.

"Now then, Ferdinand—the baptism and inauguration ceremonies went perfectly, and we each took care of the dangerous people threatening us. I would like the keys to the book room now. I want to read as much as possible before meeting Lutz and the others tomorrow," I said, breaking into an eager grin as I held out a hand.

Ferdinand shut his eyes tight and cradled his head in his hands. "If you collapse again, expect no potions or any healing from me."

Reunited at Last

I tried running to the book room the instant Ferdinand gave me the key, only to be stopped by Fran.

"Lady Rozemyne, you have been absent for quite some time; there is much I need to report and much we must discuss. The book room is not going anywhere and, while it was only briefly, I am certain that your Crushing of Brother Egmont as the new High Bishop was more than enough to stop him from disturbing it again any time soon. You may read at your leisure once we have finished our urgent business."

I looked between Fran and the door, then scanned the room for anyone who might prove to be an ally. Monika was standing behind Fran; Rosina was polishing the harspiel, showing absolutely no intention of getting involved; Damuel was avoiding eye contact, as to avoid getting wrapped up in the situation; and Brigitte was watching over the proceedings with a frown. It seemed that no one would be willing to support me.

"But Lutz and the others are coming tomorrow, so I want to get as much reading done today as I can," I pleaded. If the Gilberta Company was busy enough to earn sympathy from Ferdinand, then there was no doubt in my mind that I would end up hopelessly busy as well. Today would surely be the last day I could relax and read at my own pace.

But my pleading only earned me a smile from Fran, similar to the one that Ferdinand would always give me. "Rest easy, Lady Rozemyne—there is much for you to read here in this very room. Before you browse the shelves in the book room, please look through and memorize these, all before the Starbind Ceremony." At that, he began piling boards onto my desk. They had apparently been organized by Fran and my other attendants, and detailed a wide range of prayers and ritual proceedings.

But I wasn't the one who recoiled upon seeing the huge stack of boards—Brigitte was. "Wait just a moment—there are simply far too many boards here for her to read. Lady Rozemyne is still young, and this is too much to load onto a child who has only just finished her baptism ceremony."

Fran grimaced slightly. He was no doubt stressed that a noble was contending with him, but nonetheless returned Brigitte a calm look and stood his ground. "Lady Rozemyne must participate in the Starbind Ceremony as the High Bishop. If she were to fail at her first ritualistic ceremony, it would serve as a stain that would tarnish her reputation forevermore. Surely you understand, Dame Brigitte, what happens to those in noble society who have poor reputations."

Fran had learned from Ferdinand how noble society worked while serving as his attendant. He remembered what Ferdinand had needed to be cautious of, and what judgments he had laid down upon others.

"…I understand. It seems I spoke out of turn," Brigitte conceded, before taking a step back. The stress vanished from Fran's face almost instantly, and he held out a board to me.

"Here you are, Lady Rozemyne."

"I wrote that one!" Monika exclaimed, her eyes glittering as she looked down at me. "I worked hard for your sake, Lady Rozemyne."

Not only could I not refuse the innocent smile of someone who had given her all for my sake, but I had approximately zero chance of escaping from Fran, who was standing behind her wearing a smile of his own. Once again, I was reminded that Fran had been trained by the one and only Ferdinand.

Geez, Fran... You're letting him influence you way too much!

"Ngh... Okay, I'll memorize them. To reward both of your efforts, I too will put my all into learning."

"Isn't this great, Fran?" Monika exclaimed. "It looks like putting everything together for Lady Rozemyne really wasn't a waste of time!"

"Lady Rozemyne would never ignore the hard work done by her servants. Now then, Lady Rozemyne, please start by reading the ritual proceedings described here."

Having given up on going to the book room, I tearfully took the wooden board from Fran. *Hmph! These are tears of happiness. I'm just sooo happy to have attendants who care about me so much. Sigh... Soon, my sweet book room... Soon...*

And so, my day was spent learning about the Starbind Ceremony and the duties expected of the High Bishop.

As I ate breakfast the next morning, Gil informed me that Ferdinand and I would be meeting with the Gilberta Company later that day to see how their work on expanding the printing industry was progressing. Ferdinand apparently wanted to receive the report before the scholars had a chance to fudge the data. Once Gil had finished his own breakfast, he burst out of the room to go and let the Gilberta Company know that they would be seeing the High Priest. His trip with the scholars had supposedly been quite the ordeal, but during it he had developed strong bonds of companionship with Benno and Lutz.

Gil had also become a lot better at reading and writing while I was gone, to the point where he could now write reports on his own. His frantic hard work since being thrown in the midst of merchants and scholars had finally paid off. I had patted Gil's head and praised him like I usually did, only for Brigitte to very uncomfortably inform me that it wasn't proper to interact with attendants like that.

Well, it seems that an archnoble girl patting her attendant's head isn't looked upon very favorably. I suppose I could've guessed that much, though...

The Gilberta Company was due to arrive at third bell, and would be staying for lunch once they had given us their report. To that end, Ella and Nicola headed to the orphanage director's chambers once they had finished preparing breakfast in my new chambers. Fran went with them so that he could prepare tea for us, leaving Monika behind to take care of me and accompany me as I walked through the temple. It was standard practice for music to be played during meals attended by the nobility and so, once she had finished breakfast, Rosina also went to the orphanage director's chambers, harspiel in hand. Meanwhile, I stayed behind in the High Bishop's chambers to continue yesterday's memorization.

"Rozemyne, it is time to go." Ferdinand came to my chambers, accompanied by an attendant named Zahm instead of the usual Arno. I was ready to go, and so departed from my chambers with Monika.

"Rozemyne, I understand that you may be excited to be meeting your commoner associates for the first time in such a long while, but remain in control of yourself until I have finished speaking. In return, I will turn a blind eye to whatever occurs in your hidden room afterward, so you may soothe your aching heart as much as you like," Ferdinand muttered as we walked. I could gather that he was allowing me some time to hug Lutz so that he could escape my hugs himself, but honestly, that was more than fine by me.

"Understood!"

We passed through the halls until we arrived at the orphanage director's chambers, at which point Monika opened the door for me. It had been so long since I had visited my old chambers that I was immediately filled with nostalgia. Even seeing the familiar furniture brought peace to my heart.

"I'm glad to see that not much has changed here," I said.

As we waited for third bell, Ferdinand and I discussed the Starbind Ceremony at a table on the second floor. It was going to be a busy day, for sure: the lower city's festival would take place in the morning, followed by the Starbind Ceremony in the afternoon. We also talked about what the orphans would be doing on that day and, following some relentless negotiations, Ferdinand agreed to let us play like we had done last year—so long as Lutz had the time and Wilma stayed behind to keep things in order.

Third bell rang. It wasn't long at all before Gil brought the visitors from the Gilberta Company over, who had been waiting at the gate to the lower city. There was Benno, Mark, and also Lutz.

It looked like Lutz had gotten a bit taller since I had last seen him. His face looked a little more grown up, too. I had been surprised by how much Gil had grown, but it seemed Lutz was maturing fast as well. I pushed down the urge to leap into his arms, instead just offering a little wave. But the second my hand even twitched, Ferdinand glared at me and murmured "Rozemyne" in a low voice.

...I'm sorry. I'll control myself.

"Now then, Benno—I would like for you to tell me what you saw and what your thoughts were during the trip. Hold nothing back; I desire a report that is not from a scholar-official."

"As you wish."

It was only when Benno started talking that I learned that Ehrenfest was the only city that had a temple. Ferdinand noted that it would be ridiculous for provinces to be filled with blue priests as though it were obvious, but I was thinking about things from an Earth perspective, where every city usually had at least one church.

But here, there was only one big temple in the entire duchy; everywhere else had shrines and whatnot dedicated to individual gods. Stores in the lower city worshiped the God of Trade and the Goddess of Water, smithies worshiped the God of Smithing and the God of Fire, and those at the gates worshiped both the Goddess of Wind and the patron deity of travelers. In farming towns, there were small chapels in the winter mansions where all gods were worshiped, but there were no smaller shrines as a result.

As for orphanages, these were generally run by mayors and the leading powers of cities. To preserve peace and order, an archduke several generations ago had commanded that orphanages be constructed near the estate of the mayor. Orphans who were found would be taken in, and in return for giving them food and shelter, the mayors were granted the right to use them like slaves. The orphans were more or less like gray priests and shrine maidens, only with their masters being the mayors and city authorities rather than blue priests.

"The orphanage in Hasse was in a horrifying state," Benno said. It was at this point that Gil stood up to begin his report, wherein he compared the orphanage to how the temple's orphanage had been before the workshop was established. Unlike in Ehrenfest, the orphanages in other towns and cities were not built into a temple. This meant that the orphans living there were not given divine gifts, and, as mayors weren't rich nobles, barely any money was sent to support them. That said, while these orphans lived in unhygienic filth, none of them had been completely abandoned like the children in the cellar had.

"The children aren't locked in the orphanage, so they survive by scavenging for food while gathering in the forest. I think their circumstances should improve at least a little if we can get a workshop running over the summer, before autumn," Gil said, concluding his report.

He had grown so much since his days as a cheeky little brat... Overcome with the same sense of pride that a parent would have looking over their child's straight-A report card, I smiled at Gil and gave him a nod. He nodded back, grinning in satisfaction.

Once Gil had sat back down, it was Lutz's turn to stand and give a report.

"Given that their orphanage does not have divine gifts like in the temple's orphanage, we will need a lot more money to improve their living circumstances. The most problematic aspect here is that the farming towns' orphanages do not consider all orphans equal like the temple's orphanage does. I can't imagine that improving their living conditions will be as peaceful of a process as it was here."

Lutz had grown up in an environment where it was the survival of the fittest, even among family members. For this reason, he had been beyond confused upon seeing how thoroughly equal things were in the temple's orphanage. That equality was the reason everything went so well, but Lutz maintained that it would be wrong of us to assume other orphanages followed a similar system.

"Furthermore, the orphanage director there was much like the blue priests here; should the orphanage start making a profit, there's a good chance that he'll simply steal it for himself."

"In that case," I began, "it might be wise for me to make an entirely new orphanage prior to making the workshop. That way, we can teach them the temple's way of life from the very beginning."

Those who were used to a dog-eat-dog world instinctively knew to obey those stronger than them, so it would probably be easier to use my authority to create an entirely new foundation from which to start. Any city authorities butting in to steal profits would, by extension, be getting in the way of our work on the printing industry—in other words, they were enemies of books, and I would not hesitate to use my authority to eliminate them.

"If we are incorporating the orphanage into the Rozemyne Workshop, I do not mind putting money toward the building costs. But if we make this new orphanage a government-owned business instead, then the duchy will pay for it, right?"

"Is that not obvious?" Ferdinand asked with a raised eyebrow, but Benno shook his head.

"...It may be difficult to make this a government-owned business."

"And why is that?"

"The scholars seem to want to crush the printing industry before it even begins," Benno said, his gaze harsh. Mark quietly nodded beside him. "I do not know what the scholars were told when they were given this job, but they seemed to hate doing it. It was as though they had been forced into doing a job that no one wanted."

Lutz and Gil nodded in firm agreement as Benno spoke. The scholars who had gone with them had apparently given them an extremely hard time.

"Since you asked for my honest opinion, I will say this: it is hard to believe that those scholars were truly put in charge of beginning a new business under the archduke's authority. As a humble merchant, it is impossible for me to determine whether they did not understand the archduke's intention, whether they intentionally want the business to fail, or whether they are simply unintelligent, but with them in charge, the plan will fail without any doubt whatsoever."

Benno had looked annoyed when I wanted to build a branch of the Myne Workshop in the orphanage, but even then, he hadn't told me it was impossible; he had just advised me on the best way to proceed. The situation was seemingly so bad this time that Benno, a merchant with a keen nose for financial success and failure, was convinced that disaster awaited us.

I gasped a little, fearing how likely it was for the printing industry to crumble before it had even been born. But Ferdinand looked nowhere near as concerned; there was a slight grin spread across his face.

Aaah… Yep, there's his evil villain smile. He's probably deviously plotting inside his head right now.

I could already tell that the scholar-officials who had accompanied Benno and Gil were going to be eaten alive. But since I didn't want the printing industry to be sabotaged, I merely looked on, silently giving Ferdinand my full support.

"I see. Your perspectives will no doubt prove useful. Coming here myself was a wise move after all. Now then, moving on—the Starbind Ceremony is fast approaching. How stands the eatery?"

We were approaching a dinner that was not only being attended by the archduke, but his brother, his adopted daughter, and the commander of the Knight's Order as well. My head hurt just thinking about how high Sylvester's hopes probably were.

Benno, however, gave an invincible grin. "Things are proceeding quite well. Construction of the restaurant itself has finished, our chefs are getting more skilled by the day, and we have more trained waiters at the ready. Most of our workers already have a lot of experience with nobles, so I predict that the meal will conclude without any problems."

"Good to hear. Anything else?"

"...That is all I have to report, honorable High Priest. That said, there are some matters regarding the Italian restaurant that I would like to discuss with Lady Rozemyne," Benno said, sharply glancing my way.

Goodness, Benno... What's with that scary look in your eyes? It's not my fault that I couldn't contact you.

"In that case, I shall have Rozemyne help organize your reports and calculate the initial costs of the venture. As the adopted daughter of the archduke, she will need to learn the significance of establishing new industries."

...So you're saying that I need to understand the struggles of those actually doing the work, so that I don't make unreasonable demands like Sylvester? I hear you loud and clear. That said, I won't hold back at all if it brings me closer to getting my books.

"Rozemyne, you may discuss these matters in your hidden room. Damuel will guard you. Brigitte, stand guard here for the time being and finish your lunch."

"Sir!"

At Ferdinand's orders, Monika began preparing Brigitte's lunch, while Fran guided Ferdinand and Zahm out of my chambers. Once I had seen them off, I pressed a hand against the hidden door and poured a small amount of mana into it. The mana flowed from my ring, and the door opened once it had confirmed that the mana was indeed mine. Unlike Ferdinand's workshop, I had no mana restrictions for passing through the door, so anybody would be allowed to enter as long as they had my permission.

"Will those of the Gilberta Company please accompany me? Damuel may guard me as Ferdinand suggested, and Gil can accompany me as my attendant. Monika, in the meantime, please serve Brigitte her food. You may press the feystone on this door if you need me."

Once everyone was inside, I gently shut the door. Inside, my hidden room had a table and chairs like a parlor, and was about three and a half meters per side. It wasn't particularly large as far as hidden rooms went; the more mana you put into one, the bigger the room became, but since mine only existed for me to talk to people about things I didn't even want my attendants to hear, there was no need for me to make it any bigger.

I checked to make sure that the door was tightly shut, then exhaled. I didn't need to hold back any longer. I turned around, ran straight toward Lutz, and leapt into his arms.

"Aaaah! Lutz, I wanted to see you soooo badly!"

"Woah!"

I squeezed him tight, nuzzling my head into his chest as I tried to push out all of the frustration that had built up inside of me.

"I already hate being a noble! I'm stuck spending *all* day studying etiquette and all sorts of other stuff. It sucks. I'm exhausted. When I pass out, they force me back on my feet by making me drink nasty potions that make my head spin. Most of the people I meet are malicious schemers. There's nothing to brighten up my day. My family's not there. You're not there. My new 'mother' and 'father' won't give me any hugs. And, and, and…"

I listed all of my complaints about living in the Noble's Quarter as I clung to Lutz, and he rested his head against mine as if to say he didn't know what else he could do.

"…Uuuh, Myne?"

"No, Lutz, you can't mix that up. You have to call me 'Rozemyne' now." Despite feeling a rush of emotions rise up in my chest at being called "Myne" for the first time in ages, I had to shake my head. "Lutz... Give me a hug since my family can't. I need more. A lot more."

Lutz obliged, wrapping his arms around me like he used to. A big, satisfied smile spread across my face, but everyone watching us was grimacing hard. But that wasn't enough to stop me. I wasn't satisfied yet.

I looked up at Benno, my arms still tightly wrapped around Lutz. "Benno, Benno—I have a request."

"...What?" Benno asked, his exasperated frown turning more cautious as he looked down at me.

"Could you scold me for a bit? Just a little?"

"Wha?!" Benno exclaimed, no longer looking at me with the guarded expression he always gave nobles. That alone was enough to make me feel happy.

"It might be because of my high status, but nobody is willing to scold me in Karstedt's estate. Everyone praises me no matter what I do, and it's honestly kind of gross. I'm not even doing anything praiseworthy!"

Both my etiquette instructor and my personal tutor put me on such a high pedestal that it was actually uncomfortable. Not even Karstedt or Elvira would scold me, either; whenever I messed something up, they just smiled as though they were going to cut me off entirely, which was genuinely terrifying.

Benno listened to me with his head down, trembling all the while, then suddenly shot back up. "You're letting your guard down too much, you idiot! You're already a thoughtless airhead who walks into trouble like a dumb baby; don't make things worse! They're gonna exploit the hell outta you!" he yelled, unleashing his thunder on me.

"Yes, that's it! That's what I wanted! Aah, that's much better!"

The fact that even Benno's rage was enough to make me giddy with nostalgia showed just how much I had been suffering lately. I let out a sigh of satisfaction, which Lutz met with a heavy contrasting sigh of exhaustion. He slumped his shoulders, then leaned against me a little.

"Man... You haven't changed at all, huh? You're a noble now, but it's still the same old you on the inside."

"I mean, people don't change that easily, do they? What're you even saying, Lutz?"

Surely it would be more surprising if I *wasn't* the same old me. I had certainly gotten better at hiding my true self, and I was holding myself much more like a noble, but I was the same as ever on the inside.

"See? I told you," Benno said to Lutz in a somewhat defeated tone. "Going from being a commoner to an archnoble isn't enough to change her at all."

Lutz ground his teeth in frustration and glared at me. "Dang it... Give me back all the tears I cried over never being able to see Myne again!"

"Okay. I'll give them all back and more through hugs."

I thought that was a pretty good idea, but Lutz immediately turned me down. Weird. But either way, I had treated my Lutz deficiency, and I felt great.

"If you're done there, can we get back on track? I want to talk about the fluffy bread we're gonna sell in the Italian restaurant," Benno said, his eyes gleaming with the enthusiasm of a merchant.

How to Make Fluffy Bread

"When you say that you want to make fluffy bread, do you mean you want to know how to make natural yeast?"

"Yup, that's right."

I pursed my lips and fell into thought. Fluffy bread was my trump card to stay on top of other restaurants. Even if the chefs who knew all of my recipes were stolen away from us, the secret of yeast would remain with me. I had expected the guildmaster and Leise to be our rivals, but they had joined the restaurant as partners—Leise was even teaching Hugo and Todd recipes. In all honesty, I didn't see any need for me to give fluffy bread to the store.

"I imagine that Sylvester will be looking forward to all sorts of unique foods, so I'll prepare yeast ahead of time for the meal I'm attending. Hugo and Todd will be able to make the fluffy bread just fine since they've done it before, but I'm not going to tell anyone how to make the yeast just yet. Please continue to run the store without fluffy bread for the time being."

"Huh?!"

The bread Leise made in the guildmaster's house was hard, as was the bread I ate at Karstedt's estate. The Italian restaurant would already be attracting customers by serving the kinds of food that nobles ate, which meant it didn't need fluffy bread.

"And why's that? Weren't we gonna start selling it?" Benno asked, his eyes wide. Mark and Lutz looked just as surprised. Benno seemed to quite like the fluffy bread, so he probably wanted to know the recipe for personal reasons, too.

"I had intended to introduce the bread to show that nobody else could make the food that the Italian restaurant was serving, but now that the guildmaster is on our side, who in the world would try to copy us? Who would face you and the guildmaster head-on at once? Nobody. We're going to stand unopposed."

"...Ngh, well, I guess you're right about that."

There were other stores big enough to do business with nobles, but nobody stood a chance at beating Benno and the guildmaster when they were working together. And since the Italian restaurant targeted such a wealthy demographic, introducing several similar stores would lead to so much overlap that they'd all fail. One also had to consider how hard Benno had worked to prepare the food, chefs, waiters, and so on. Setting up the restaurant required an amount of work and financial investment that most merchants would balk at. Benno had only started this venture due to feeling competitive toward Leise and the guildmaster, but most people weren't ridiculous enough to step foot into an entirely new industry out of spite.

"Not to mention, I need the fluffy bread a lot more than the Italian restaurant does."

"You need it? Why? Aren't you already eating it every day?"

"...I've been told that, since I'm the archduke's adopted daughter now, I need to start new trends."

In the world of nobles, it wasn't dignified to follow after those who were beneath you. That wasn't just Elvira's personal philosophy, either—it was a fact of life for all archnoble women. The invention and spread of new things created demand, which in turn stimulated the duchy's economy, and it was the nobility's duty to keep the economy thriving.

In other words, as the archduke's adopted daughter, I needed to start coming up with trends that would make nobles want to spend loads of money.

"So basically, that's the situation. I'm tied up in annoying noble stuff and I need to spread the fluffy bread through the archduke's castle and the archnobles to secure my position in society. I think it'll be fine to share the recipe with the Italian restaurant once it has spread through my mother's faction. If you already have the guildmaster on your side, then you don't need a trump card like yeast to boost you up, do you?"

"C'mon, the more trump cards I have, the better," Benno said with a dissatisfied look, before conceding that he understood nobles had their own noble problems to deal with.

"I still intend to make and sell the things I want through the Gilberta Company, so don't worry about that. You'll just have to give up on selling fluffy bread in the store from day one."

"Alright. Nothing wrong with adding to the menu over time."

Trends flowed most easily from the top to the bottom, especially when it came to high-class stuff. It was easy for me to forget since I made them myself and had them available all the time, but rinsham, plant paper, hairpins, and picture books were all expensive enough that not everyone could afford them. The purchasing demographic was limited to those with money, and since those on top weren't allowed to follow those beneath them, I would have to spread my new ideas starting from the top.

"In any case, I fully intend to personally guarantee that the restaurant's slogan that 'even nobles eat here' will hold weight. Hopefully that's enough for you."

"Wait, 'personally guarantee'? What're you planning here?" Benno asked with a wince.

Wow. It looks like he doesn't trust me at all. Well... not that I didn't know that already.

"During the first trial run, when we have the owners of other large stores eating there, I'll participate as one of the restaurant's founders. The new High Bishop giving the restaurant her seal of approval will give you all of the prestige you need, right?"

"Well, regardless of what you're like on the inside, you're still the High Bishop and the archduke's adopted daughter. The customers are gonna freak the heck out."

"I'll just be saying hello and then leaving, not participating in the meal myself. I wouldn't want them to be so scared that they can't even taste the food," I said. Just popping my head in and saying some generic line about looking forward to their continued patronage would be enough to do the trick. Plus, if those big store owners started flocking to Benno in the hope of getting connections with nobles and the archduke, it would be easier to get their help when it came to expanding the print industry.

"Either way, I think you should leave as much of the restaurant to the guildmaster as possible. You don't need to put that much of a burden on yourself, do you?"

"Just to be clear here, the guildmaster isn't the one joining us; it's his granddaughter." Benno was the only adult among those funding the restaurant, so he had said that he needed to give it his full attention, but personally, I got the feeling that it would be totally fine to leave the whole thing to Freida.

"Having Freida on board is pretty comforting—she'll make sure we're earning a profit, and her whole family will almost certainly toss in their support as well. I think you'll be fine taking a step back."

Despite everything Freida said, her family did take good care of her. And much like Benno, her whole family had a keen nose for profit, and would no doubt throw their full weight behind the Italian restaurant to ensure that they reaped as much financial gain as possible.

"But the moment I take too big of a step back, they're gonna steal the whole operation, y'know?"

"Um, well... I think you're going to be so busy with the printing industry that you won't have any choice but to leave the Italian restaurant to them by the year's end. You should just be satisfied that you'll still be an investor and will get some of the money it makes," I said, looking from Benno, to Mark, to Lutz. They were all wearing expressions that showed they weren't following me at all. "Benno, you just said that you didn't think the scholars were motivated enough to make the printing industry a success, right? Well, whether or not they're motivated doesn't matter at all."

"Even though it risks bringing the whole plan down?" Benno asked with a dubious expression.

I nodded. "Just so you know, Sylvester gave an announcement to a bunch of nobles at my baptism ceremony. He said that he expects the printing industry to have spread throughout the duchy within the next twenty years or so, and judging by the evil look on Ferdinand's face earlier, I'm sure those rude scholars are going to be gone in no time. If anything, you should be worrying about our plans being accelerated even more."

I had known just by looking at Ferdinand's face that he was plotting some kind of trap. Hopefully it was one for the unmotivated scholars, but there was a chance that this was all a test to see how useful the Gilberta Company really was—in which case, Benno would be in serious trouble if he let his guard down.

"...Don't make such a baseless prediction."

"It's not baseless," I declared, firmly puffing out my chest. "It's a confident assertion based on my past experiences."

While Benno continued looking at me doubtingly, Mark crossed his arms over his chest. "Thank you very much for your valuable advice. We will hold it very close to our hearts."

"Mark…"

"Master Benno, no matter how busy we may be, we must not avert our eyes from the truth: it is in our best interest to do as she advises, and prepare ourselves for whatever unreasonable demands we may be given." At those words, Benno, Lutz, and for some reason even Gil and Damuel, all hardened their expressions.

…It sure is rough to serve under someone who has such unreasonable expectations.

"So, Benno, is that everything you wanted to talk about?"

"Yeah, but—"

"No buts. I want to speak to Gil and Lutz," I said, leaning forward to get a closer look at them.

Even though I had gone to other cities and the winter mansions of farming villages myself, I had spent most of our journey on a highbeast, and everyone was always really tense because of all the nobles around us when we were riding in our carriages. Plus, it wasn't as though we had been on a normal trip—all we had done was offer our prayers and then move on to the next place. I wanted to hear what a normal trip had been like, especially since Lutz had finally visited another city, just like he always wanted.

"So, you two… How was your first time visiting another city? How different was it from Ehrenfest? Did the carriage bouncing make you feel sick?"

"Man, it bounced so much! It only took us half a day each way, but on both journeys, Gil was so sick that he could barely sit straight."

"Hey! You weren't doing so great yourself, Lutz!"

Their eyes gleaming, Gil and Lutz started telling me all about their first trip. They spoke about how the carriage had bounced way harder than it did when in the city, how the noble scholars had been so smug that they both wanted to punch them in the face, how the other cities were so tiny and had so few people compared to Ehrenfest, how the orphanage was so bad that it reminded them of a year ago, and how they both resolved to give the dead-eyed orphans in rags a new lease on life.

"I see you both worked hard and didn't give up, even though it was your first time in a long carriage ride. You've got my thanks. Gil, I'm not allowed to pat your head outside anymore, but I'll give you all of the praise you deserve in here."

Gil ran over and knelt down so that I could pat his head, accepting my praise with a broad, happy grin. "I thought you weren't ever gonna praise me again, no matter how hard I worked."

"Well, I can only pat your head in here from now on. Being of a high status is a lot more annoying than I thought it would be."

Once I was done patting Gil's head, I went to do the same to Lutz, but he dodged my hand and said that he wasn't interested. That was a bit vexing, so I gave him another hug instead. Now that I had heard their honest thoughts, it seemed like establishing printing workshops in the orphanages would be a tough ordeal.

"Benno, Mark—what do you think it'll take to bring printing into the orphanages?"

"They barely have any people, and those who are there are mostly just weak kids. You'll probably be better off having them make paper instead of doing any printing. It's pretty hard to use the printing presses that Ingo's making," Benno said as he stroked his chin.

Mark gave a troubled smile. "Ehrenfest, where the archduke resides, may be large, but the nearby cities are nowhere near as populated."

"In that case, it might be smart to divide the paper-making and printing industries. We can have them make paper in this region, while the workshop in the temple focuses exclusively on printing. Or alternatively, we could focus on finishing mimeograph printing as soon as possible. That way, even weak kids would be able to print," I said, counting my ideas on my fingers as I listed them off.

Benno scratched his head and looked down at me exasperatedly. "Rozemyne, do you have the time to be making inventions like that?"

"Right now? Not at all. That's why I thought it would be fastest and easiest to just drop the pretext of negotiating with city authorities to find compromises, and instead just use my authority to establish new orphanages with workshops in them, whether they like it or not." Plus, if I went ahead and added a chapel under the guise of spreading the good word of the gods, I could even make excuses for visiting the orphanages myself.

"Woah there! You're already going crazy with power?! Weren't you always talking about how you didn't like confrontations and stuff?"

"I don't like confrontations, but this won't even be one. Considering my status, they'll literally have no choice but to do exactly what I say. I have a way to eliminate anyone who gets in the way of my book-making, so I might as well use it to make things easier."

To be honest, there was so much being thrown around that I had to learn—so many orders, jobs, and duties, among other things—that I was sure my brain was about to explode. I didn't have the leeway to casually discuss matters with the authorities of small cities in order to find compromises or whatever.

If I can use my authority to make my problems go away, then I might as well do just that.

"Who the hell gave a girl like this so much power?!"

"My adoptive father, the archduke."

"…Gah! There's no way I can pick a fight with him!"

Benno was cradling his head in his hands, but when it came to matters like this, one needed to have their priorities in order. And my first priority was making as many books as possible. It was a goal that mattered to me more than anything else, so I was willing to use all of the money and power at my disposal to achieve it. Fulfilling my duties as the High Bishop and the archduke's adopted daughter was nothing but a means to an end, and I didn't want to waste my time on those standing in my way who were no match against my new authority.

"You might say I'm going crazy with power, but under normal circumstances, a little girl who just finished her baptism ceremony like me would never have this much control. This is only possible since Sylvester is even more impatient than I am."

That seemed to ring a bell for Benno, and he let out a despairing groan. Mark placed a hand on his forehead as well. As expected, Sylvester's rampage was giving everyone in the Gilberta Company a hard time.

As I watched them start to seriously discuss with stiff expressions what unreasonable demands Sylvester would give them at the meal, Lutz took out a folded sheet of plant paper. He glanced around, before handing it to me with a whisper. "I figured that I should give this to you before I leave. It's a letter."

It was written on the paper that I had bought as Myne, then asked Lutz to give to my family so that they could write letters without needing to worry about the costs. Between Myne's death and Rozemyne going to the Noble's Quarter, I had consulted Ferdinand and written a letter to Benno requesting that he organize the arrangement.

According to Ferdinand, the story in the lower city was that a noble had killed Myne, and my family had been given a portion of the money confiscated from him as an apology. But my family had apparently refused to take it, since they would feel like they had sold me for money. I could see them reacting like that.

So, that money and Myne's wealth instead went to me, and I could use it however I liked. If I sent my family some ink and paper and a letter asking them to write back to me, then they wouldn't have much choice. And if they sent me letters, then I'd be a little less lonely.

Eheh. I'm so smart.

"This letter was written to the Myne who died, so don't expect it to be addressed to 'Lady Rozemyne' or anything."

I anxiously opened the first letter from my family, and immediately saw Tuuli's clumsy lettering scrawled across the page. She wasn't used to writing yet, and it was her first time using ink, so there were smudges all over the paper. Some letters trailed in the wrong direction, and others were fused together, so the only line I could actually read was, "I'm doing great, Myne!"

"Um, I hate to ask, but... what does this say?"

"Oh," Lutz began, "that line says that she started studying sewing at Corinna's workshop. This line here's from your dad; he says that Kamil's starting to move his head around. And this bit is from your mom; she's been real worried about whether you've been getting sick or not."

Dad needed to know how to write for work, and I had seen his handwriting during my time at the gate, so even though it definitely had some quirks, I could read it without issue. But Mom had only just started learning, so her handwriting was even harder to read than Tuuli's. The worst part, however, was that they had all written on the same small sheet of paper; they had gone through the effort of sending me a letter, and yet I couldn't even read it.

"...Lutz, could you ask them to use one sheet of paper each? I can't read it when all of the letters are overlapping."

"I did tell 'm that. But they just said that it'd be a waste of expensive paper."

That was something I could definitely see them saying. I had used Myne's savings to buy the paper and ink, since I knew both would be too expensive for my family to afford. I wanted them to use the paper freely so that I could at least read the letters.

"I'll tell 'm that you won't be able to read it unless they use a sheet of paper each."

"Thanks, Lutz. I'll quickly write a response. Could you give it to them for me?"

"Sure."

As I looked around the mostly empty room, thinking that I would need to go and fetch some writing utensils and paper, Mark suddenly pulled out a writing set from his belongings and placed it on the table. "I shall lend you these. It would be best for you to write the letter here."

"I can always count on you, Mark. It's amazing how you always know exactly what to do," I said, before borrowing Mark's stuff and instantly starting my reply. I wrote that I was busy, but doing great too.

With that done, we had finished discussing everything we needed to keep private, and so exited the hidden room to begin lunch. As Brigitte had already finished, she swapped places with Damuel, and came over to join us.

"How was lunch, Brigitte? Did it suit your tastes?" I asked as my own food was being prepared. Brigitte was a regular noble, and as the Italian restaurant's opening was drawing ever closer, I wanted as many noble opinions as I could get.

"Absolutely. It was beyond delicious. You have excellent chefs, Lady Rozemyne. I must admit, I'm quite looking forward to being your guard now," Brigitte replied. Her sharp, refined expression didn't falter, but I noticed that her amethyst eyes were wrinkled in the beginnings of a smile. If she was going that far to compliment the food, then it was safe to say that she really did like it.

Just as I let out a sigh of relief, I noticed a reddish-orange braid come into my peripheral vision.

"Lady Rozemyne! I made half of this!" Nicola exclaimed, beaming a proud smile as she brought over our plates. Back before I had left for the Noble's Quarter, she had told me that she wasn't confident enough in her cooking skills to serve me, but her brimming excitement was enough for me to be able to tell that she had become a lot more skilled since then. I was looking forward to digging in.

"Lady Rozemyne, do you have any new recipes? I want to try making more things. I love tasty food, and the best part about serving you is the food I get to cook. I'll work as hard as it takes to make even more tasty food!" she declared without an ounce of hesitation.

I couldn't help but chuckle. "I'll have some more new recipes written for you by tonight. I trust you and Ella to learn them well."

But I would first be teaching them how to make natural yeast, under the understanding that they were not to share that information with anyone else. Once that was done, I wanted them to master sweet recipes that would most likely be popular with archnoble women. There were rooms that were apparently kept ice-cold through the use of magic tools, so maybe it would be best to focus on making cold sweets, especially in a hot season like this.

Maybe I could try putting a book together called "Rozemyne's Recommended Recipes" once the printing industry has taken off...

Starbind Ceremony in the Lower City

As the Starbind Ceremony approached, I spent all of my time in the temple. I memorized the words for the prayers, kept up to date on Nicola's progress making natural yeast, and discussed the restaurant's menu and our report to the archduke with Benno and Lutz in the hidden room in my orphanage director's chambers.

Today was a day when Benno and Lutz were visiting from the Gilberta Company, so we were talking in my hidden room.

"I'll be returning to the Noble's Quarter for the Starbind Ceremony. I'll ask Sylvester about the date and time while I'm there."

"Yeah, please do," Benno replied.

We had finished everything that we needed to do before the big meal. Benno's eyes seemed kind of lifeless, but he would have a chance to get some rest beforehand.

"Well, that should be it," Benno said, before letting out a huge sigh of relief and rubbing his eyebrows. "Seems like I made it."

"...So, Lutz—what're you doing for the Star Festival?"

"Same thing as last year, I guess? I'm gonna be eating lunch in the orphanage."

It wouldn't be hard for me to arrange for extra food to be made for Lutz, and then join him for lunch, but given how close Benno looked to dying from overwork, I wasn't sure whether Lutz would have the time to look after the orphanage.

"Are you sure that'll be okay? You're not too busy?"

"Well, we've finished everything we've absolutely gotta get done, and it's not like I can just spend the festival resting at home, y'know? Besides, I'll be able to relax more at the orphanage. The food's better there, too."

The Star Festival involved the whole city.

Everyone who wasn't related to someone getting married or getting married themselves would go to pick up taue fruit as soon as the gates opened, and spend the day tossing them around. Once that was done, they would eat in the plaza and then prepare for the nighttime part of the festival. As such, it wasn't a time when you could just stay at home and relax; you would be chased out and made to help others.

"Make sure you don't throw all of your taues. Save a few, okay?"

"I know," Lutz replied with a grin. He really was the same as ever.

But despite everything that would be going on during the festival, I still couldn't see my family, no matter how much I wanted to. I had thought that I would be able to see them by having them volunteer to look over the temple's orphans during the festival, but they had to turn me down since they had prior engagements. And Tuuli hadn't even shown up once, despite saying that she'd drop by the orphanage every now and again.

"...Tuuli just isn't coming, is she?" I asked under my breath.

Benno snorted, then broke into a huge grin. "Tuuli's real busy at the workshop she has a lehange contract with. Not only has she been studying sewing on her days off, but she's been teaching those in Corinna's workshop how to make hairpins."

"Wha?"

"According to Corinna, she's sucking in tons of technical knowledge at a crazy fast rate. Her last promise to you was that she'd become a first-rate seamstress, remember?"

I could feel tears well up in my eyes as Benno told me how hard Tuuli was working—something I hadn't been able to pick up from her letter. She was dedicating everything she had to keep her promise to me.

"Your dad's been super busy too," Lutz added. "The Knight's Order looked into why a noble from another duchy was able to get inside despite the archduke's orders, and the commander of the east gate ended up getting punished for not keeping his men informed of critical information."

The commanders of the other gates had all confirmed that Dad had told them the archduke was absent and would not be providing any new entry permits, and that they had immediately informed their men on duty. And yet, despite him guarding the gate that saw the most traffic and being the first one to have been informed, the commander of the east gate had delayed telling his men.

The Knight's Order had determined that this was an unforgivable error. And since Dad had lost his daughter and worked so hard to capture the noble who had illegally entered the city, he was promoted to fill in the new vacancy. He was now the commander of the east gate.

"He's gotta work a lot more these days. He actually cried about how he barely even has the time to eat with his family anymore."

"Oof, I can imagine that…"

Everyone was just too busy to come, then. I slumped my shoulders in disappointment, only to have Lutz flick me on the forehead.

"Don't feel so down. Tuuli already has plans during the festival because she's coming to see you," Lutz said, earning him a wide-eyed stare from me. He grinned and continued. "She's gonna wait outside the temple's doors and try to blend in with the married couples' families. When the couples leave, you're gonna be up at the altar in the chapel, right?"

Tuuli had apparently told Lutz that she wouldn't be able to see the new High Bishop if she stuck with the orphanage kids, and that the whole family was going to be waiting at the doors to see me, even if it was only going to be for a brief moment.

"Go ahead and show her what you can do, okay?"

"Ngh... I'll go over all of the prayers I need to give once more."

Now I could feel the nervousness of someone performing in a class play while their parents were watching. I wanted to do the best I could since my family were going out of their way to come, but at the same time, I was scared of what might happen if I messed up.

I said goodbye to Benno and Lutz, the former looking like an exhausted ghost, and then headed for my room in the High Bishop's chambers. Lutz had said that he'd be spending the festival with the orphans, so I needed to talk to Wilma about what the orphans would be doing on the day of the Starbind Ceremony.

"I will now be heading to the orphanage. Who shall accompany me?"

"Please entrust this duty to me, Lady Rozemyne." Monika beamed a smile and rushed over to me, endlessly happy about getting to see Wilma.

I looked up at Fran. "Please continue your work here, Fran. I shall discuss the orphanage's plans for the Starbind Ceremony with Wilma."

Fran paused his discussion with Zahm and nodded. "Monika, take good care of Lady Rozemyne. Fare thee well."

"Fare thee well, Lady Rozemyne."

Fran and Zahm both crossed their arms and knelt as Monika and I exited the room together. Naturally, my two knight bodyguards followed from behind.

Ferdinand had been sending his attendant Zahm to help Fran with High Bishop-related work as of late, supposedly because Zahm had the most experience dealing with the previous High Bishop. Ferdinand always brought Arno around with him, so I hadn't seen Zahm enough to have a particularly strong opinion about him. But what I did know was that he, not Arno, would be the main liaison between Ferdinand and me now that I was the High Bishop.

I had been under the impression that Ferdinand always had Arno accompanying him, even when dealing with the previous High Bishop, but I wasn't too familiar with what sort of jobs he gave his attendants. This was probably a good change for Fran, though; he had always used to treat Arno like his superior, but here he was talking to Zahm as a coworker.

"Wilma, Lady Rozemyne is here," Monika said once she had opened the doors to the orphanage.

"I thank you ever so much for coming all this way. Did the High Priest say anything about the High Bishop traveling here personally?" Wilma asked, looking worried. It seemed that she hadn't expected that I would continue visiting the orphanage, given that the previous High Bishop had never done so.

"I am the High Bishop, and I shall do as I please. The High Priest won't forbid me from doing anything as long as I remain safe and am not embarrassing myself as a lady."

In fact, when I had gotten Ferdinand involved in the plan to make orphanage workshops in other cities, he had told me to do a bunch of saint-esque things. No way would he protest me visiting the orphanage.

"So, about the day of the Starbind Ceremony..."

The blue priests would be taking all of their attendants to the Noble's Quarter, the reason being that there wouldn't be anybody to look after them when they returned home otherwise. Ferdinand didn't need to do this as he had his own estate in the Noble's Quarter with its own set of attendants, but he did it anyway since the others did.

"Since I'm the archduke's adopted daughter, I can't bring people into the castle unless I have received explicit permission ahead of time. For that reason, my attendants will all be staying in the temple. Rosina is the only one I can bring."

Personal musicians were essential for feasts, which was why I was able to take mine with me to the castle. I could also bring Ella as my personal chef, but throwing her into the chaos of an unfamiliar kitchen preparing for a huge wedding ceremony would be outright cruel. I had asked her what she wanted to do, and we decided that she would stay behind until it was time for me to live in the archduke's castle.

"I will have Ella and Nicola prepare the orphanage's food. I've also sent word to the other blue priests that, despite their absence, their chefs will still need to prepare food as usual."

Every year, the orphanage went without dinner on the day of the Starbind Ceremony since all of the blue priests were absent, but it wasn't as though they were taking their chefs with them. They had chefs at their family homes, and so didn't need to bring their own. That was why I had ordered the blue priests to continue having food prepared, even while they were gone.

In return, I would change how the donations offered up to the temple during the Starbind Ceremony were distributed. The previous High Bishop had taken half all for himself, and then given the rest to those who sucked up to him the most.

I was planning on distributing it equally, but Ferdinand had stopped me. Noble society was finicky about status and appearances, and considering what might happen after I was no longer the High Bishop, equal distribution was a no-go. In the end, we settled on me getting a quarter as the High Bishop, Ferdinand getting another quarter as the High Priest, and then the blue priests getting the remaining half. Those who hadn't sucked up to the High Bishop had all fervently agreed, while those who had stayed silent, looking blatantly annoyed.

"That means we won't need to worry about food," Wilma said. "I truly am thankful for this, Lady Rozemyne."

"Also, Lutz will be coming to bring everybody to the forest, just like last year. Please allow him to eat lunch in the dining hall with everyone else. There shouldn't be too much confusion, since it's all the same as what we did last year. Just please watch over them carefully so that they don't disturb those in the lower city."

"As you wish," Wilma replied, giving me a smile and a nod. Then, as I scanned the dining room, her smile clouded just a bit. "If you're looking for Delia, she is napping with Dirk."

"How are they doing?"

I had been told by Monika and Nicola when I had first summoned them to make them my attendants that the blessing light had flown to Dirk as well. And while I knew that Delia's life wasn't in danger, I was still worried about her since Wilma had told me that she was struggling a lot, and was unable to fit in with the others.

"They're both doing well. Delia no longer tries to care for Dirk entirely on her own to the point of collapsing, and has learned to ask those around her for help. That said, Dirk has recently started to crawl, and Delia has her hands quite full chasing him around and cleaning up after him. It is now a daily occurrence to see Delia running after Dirk while yelling 'Geez.'"

"Really? I'm glad to hear it." I sighed with relief, and Wilma gave me the smile of a saint.

"Lady Rozemyne, I truly do feel blessed to serve you."

"Huh? Wilma...? Have I done something special?"

"I know that it must be difficult to serve as the High Bishop at your age, but I am absolutely, *absolutely* certain that you will succeed." Wilma gave me a gentle look as she spoke, and I could have sworn that I saw a halo shining above her head. Or maybe, in this world, it would be the lights of a blessing. It felt as though she had given me a blessing even though she didn't have any mana.

...Wilma seriously is a saint. I have seen a goddess, and her name is Wilma.

And so, the day of the Starbind Ceremony arrived. Monika woke me up early in the morning, and I quickly finished a simple breakfast.

"Lady Rozemyne, I will be going to the orphanage."

"Say hello to the children for me, Gil."

Second bell rang not long after Gil left. As I bathed, I thought about him, Lutz, and the kids who were about to head to the forest. You were really supposed to be given a holy cleansing in a water bath before a ritual, but I knew that would make me sick in no time. Regular hot water would suffice as long as I properly cleaned my body.

"No, Monika. That will lead to wrinkles here, see?" Rosina said. As my personal musician, she wasn't allowed to do the work of an attendant, but since Monika and Nicola were struggling to put my ceremonial clothing onto me in the proper, aesthetic way, she was taking on the role of a tutor.

"Do I put this here… and then pull this here?"

"That's right, Nicola. Now it looks just fine."

I knew that I couldn't wear just anything on the first day I was appearing before the public as the High Bishop, but it was taking Rosina a lot of time to teach Monika and Nicola how to make the clothes look their best on me.

I know it's because she used to serve the High Bishop, but now I know how truly impressive it was for Delia to know how to put on ceremonial clothing from the very start.

Once my High Bishop robes were on, a broad sash woven from black and gold thread was slung over my right shoulder and clasped in place with a brooch. The second, much thinner sash that was tied around my waist was also decorated in black and gold, which made it obvious at a glance that this was a ritual for obtaining the blessing of the King and Queen gods.

Elvira had given me some hair product, instructing me to do my hair properly like a noble even when I was in the temple. To that end, Rosina was using her experience having done Christine's hair to instruct Nicola and Monika on the complex ways in which noble girls were supposed to set their hair. They bound my hair in black and gold cords, then experimented putting my hair stick in at various angles as they tried to determine what would look the best. The hair stick in question was the one Ferdinand had given me for my baptism ceremony.

"High Bishop, please move to the chapel," said Zahm.

I hesitated for a second, not yet used to being called the High Bishop, and Fran immediately stepped in for me. "Lady Rozemyne, let us depart," he said, taking my hand and leading me along.

I began walking after him, taking care not to step on the hem of my robes. In my normal High Bishop robes, the part by the middle sash was folded so that the hem only reached my knees, but my ceremonial robes were long enough to hide my entire legs, just like the dress of an adult woman would. I was in great danger of stepping on it and falling over.

Behind me was Monika. She was walking carefully, the large, ornately decorated bible meant for the High Bishop clutched to her chest. Meanwhile, Nicola was in the kitchen helping Ella to prepare lunch.

"The High Bishop is entering the room." Ferdinand's voice rang out and the gray priests opened the doors to the chapel for me. The blue priests lined up before the altar waved the sticks in their hands, and the sound of a thousand bells echoed throughout the chapel.

I took the huge, heavy bible from Monika and slowly walked down the middle carpet. To my right were the blue priests, and to my left were just about a hundred pairs of newlyweds.

The lucky husbands and wives each wore clothing themed after the divine color of the season they were born in. Those happily leaning against each other were most likely those who were marrying for love after having grown up together in the same neighborhood or some such, while those standing expressionlessly were those who had marriages arranged by their families. In the worst-case scenario, some of the couples here were only just meeting for the very first time.

But everyone's expressions changed when they saw me, no matter their personal circumstances. Some dropped their jaws, some looked at each other in disbelief, and others whispered among themselves. There probably would have been a huge fuss if sound-dampening magic tools weren't being used like they had been during my first baptism ceremony.

When I reached the altar, I handed the bible to Ferdinand, who proceeded to set it on the top step. The lack of weight in my arms eased my tension a bit. But as I climbed the first step up to the altar, I immediately trod on my robes. I could feel the fabric stretching out; I would absolutely fall over if I tried to keep going.

As I froze in panic, having no idea what to do, Ferdinand picked me up and set me down atop the altar. It was clear through his cold smile that he was calling me a fool.

...I know, I know. I'm sorry.

"This is Lady Rozemyne, the archduke's daughter and the newly appointed High Bishop," Ferdinand said to introduce me. At those words, several of the newlyweds stiffened. That was a reasonable response; anyone would be surprised upon learning that they had just been whispering about the archduke's daughter.

In the midst of all that, Ferdinand began to preach words of celebration and recite a tale from the bible in a clear, resounding voice. It was a story about how the King and Queen gods—the God of Darkness and the Goddess of Light—were first married, the problems they faced, and how they had combined their powers to overcome them. It then turned into a story about them having kids, and, when it came time to celebrate the marriage of their children, it turned into a lesson about the Starbind Ceremony. Incidentally, unlike the previous High Bishop, Ferdinand had this all memorized and didn't have to read from the bible at all.

It was the High Bishop's job to recite tales from the bible, but my voice was still childish and lacking in power, plus I ended up running out of breath whenever I tried reading aloud for too long, so Ferdinand was telling them in my place. All I would be doing was watching the people offer up their prayers and gratitude to the gods, then giving them a blessing in return.

"Now then, let us offer our prayers to the gods. Praise be to the gods!"

The blue priests assumed the praying position, then so too did the newlywed couples. I absentmindedly flipped through a few bible pages as I watched over them.

…What the heck?! The words to the prayers are written right here! High Bishop, you cheater! I worked so hard to memorize them!

I recoiled upon seeing that in the margins of some pages, the words to the prayers had been written out in handwriting that I didn't recognize. I had been so busy memorizing the boards that Fran and Monika had written for me that I never had the chance to reread the bible in my new chambers. But the words to the prayers were right there; I hadn't even needed to memorize them.

As I pouted angrily, Ferdinand spoke again. "Now, we shall proceed to grant you the blessings of the gods." Then, he instructed the couples to kneel. It was my time to shine.

…Well, I went out of my way to memorize this stuff. I might as well go all out.

I closed the bible, inhaled deeply, and poured mana into my ring.

"O mighty King and Queen of the endless skies, O God of Darkness and Goddess of Light, hear my prayers. May you grant your blessings to the birth of new unions. May they who offer their prayers and gratitude to thee be blessed with thy divine protection."

Once I had prayed to the married King and Queen gods for their blessing, black and gold light swirled in my ring before flying up to the ceiling of the chapel and exploding. It scattered in all directions, raining down on the newlyweds.

They all looked up at the ceiling, their jaws dropped in disbelief. Even the blue priests were wearing the same shocked expressions. Ferdinand was the only one who remained unfazed.

"She gave a true blessing, despite not wielding a divine instrument?" a nearby blue priest murmured.

I looked at my ring, remembering that becoming a blue priest was the fate of nobles who didn't have much mana, or those from impoverished families who couldn't afford magic tools. Naturally, none of them had magic tools with feystones in them. Blue priests only had access to divine instruments to pour their mana into, which worked in a similar fashion to magic tools, so it was impossible for them to give a blessing without one.

...Wait, did I mess up here? I thought, timidly looking up at Ferdinand, only to see that he was wearing the grin of someone whose evil plot had just succeeded. *Oh. This is just part of his "make me a saint" plan or whatever.*

"Your future will no doubt be bright now that you have obtained the blessings of the King and Queen gods," Ferdinand declared, just before the gray priests pushed open the creaking doors to the chapel. The dazzling summer sun reflected off of the white stone walls, brightening the room at once. At the same time, the quieting magic tools lost their effect, and the married couples immediately erupted in excited chatter.

"Wow, so that's a blessing! He said that's the archduke's daughter, right?"

"Apparently that's a blessing from the King and Queen gods. The new High Bishop's pretty amazing for someone so tiny, huh?"

"This year is the first time that this blessing's happened, right? My brother didn't mention anything like this."

The newlyweds exited through the wide-open doors, all thrilled by how different the Starbind Ceremony had been from what they had heard and expected.

"We got a crazy good blessing. I'm totally gonna dodge all the taue fruit thrown at us!" one man confidently declared, as the grooms prepared to guard their brides while running to their new homes.

"The High Bishop shall now depart," Ferdinand intoned.

"No, I think I will watch until they have all gone," I replied, staring fixedly through the door. I could see a single family not throwing any cheers to the newlyweds, nor searching for a particular pair. They were merely peering into the chapel.

Just as Lutz had said, my whole family had come to see me as the High Bishop. The fact that they were looking all around the chapel made them look completely suspicious compared to the rejoicing couples. It was painfully obvious that they had come here for a different reason than everyone else.

You're standing out! You're all standing out so much!

They looked so funny that I couldn't help but smile. Holding back the urge to call out to them, I thumped my chest twice with my right hand. They noticed that, and made the same motion in return.

"...I see," Ferdinand said with a nod of understanding, before beginning to instruct the surrounding blue and gray priests on what to do next. It seemed that he was going to let me do what I wanted here.

While Ferdinand pretended not to notice, I made contact with my family that was for all intents and purposes as direct as indirect contact could be. I touched my hairpin and shook the flowers a bit, making Tuuli jump with joy. Mom held up Kamil in his sling so I could see him; he was moving his head around. And Dad was looking at me with a massive grin on his face. I stayed on the altar until all of the newlyweds had gone, and the doors had been closed.

By that time, the gray priests had finished cleaning up the chapel, and there wasn't even a single blue priest still around. It felt as though I had just woken up from a happy dream.

Ferdinand quickly walked over, his brow furrowed, and lifted me up off of the altar. He then strode out of the chapel, where he handed me to an already waiting Fran. "Hurry up and finish your lunch, Rozemyne. We do not have much time."

I gave a big nod and said, "Okay." It had only been a brief encounter, but my heart was filled with warmth at having finally made contact with my family.

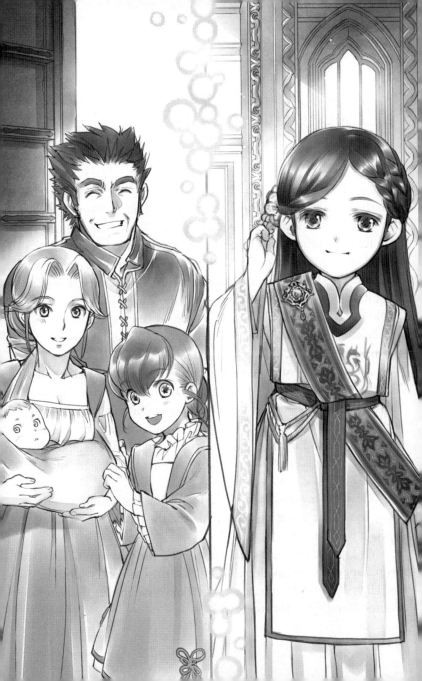

The Archduke's Castle

"So, Fran—what is the Starbind Ceremony like in the Noble's Quarter?" I asked as I ate lunch in the High Bishop's chambers.

Fran's eyes wandered uncomfortably. "The same cannot be said for most other blue priests, but, as the High Priest already has attendants at his estate in the Noble's Quarter, there was never much for me to do. His other temple attendants and I would simply wait in the estate for his return. We were given the same food as usual, and while the High Priest allowed us to use our time there to rest, we struggled to relax without any work to do. As a result, we would all usually gather to discuss work-related matters."

Apparently, Ferdinand's attendants were all serious workaholics. The fact that he thought he was giving them time to rest, unaware that they were in actuality listless and uncomfortable without work, brought tears of sympathy to my eyes—metaphorical tears, at least.

"I would feel more at ease staying behind in the temple. The Noble's Quarter is… not a particularly pleasant place for gray priests to be," Fran added quietly.

I lowered my eyes. It was easy to imagine how much prejudice there was in the Noble's Quarter, and the thought made me a little hesitant to go there.

As I sipped my post-meal tea, I heard the footsteps of several people approaching my door. Given that the only other room past the High Bishop's chambers was the ritual chamber, it was safe to assume that they had business with me.

"Rozemyne, did I not tell you to hurry?! You are the last one to appear. Everyone else is waiting!" Ferdinand stated angrily as he strode into my room.

"Okay, okay!"

I hurriedly gulped down the rest of my tea, slid off of my chair, and exited the room with Rosina. My guard knights, both of whom had been keeping their backs rigidly straight since Ferdinand's loud entrance, were following behind us.

The plan was for me to stay at the archduke's castle for the night. Karstedt and Elvira had already prepared a room for me, having sent over clothes and other such things, so I was told that I wouldn't have to bring much myself. All I needed was my ceremonial High Bishop robes.

Rosina climbed into the same carriage as the attendants, while I stepped into one with Ferdinand and my knights. I wasn't sure whether it was because they were of a lower status or because they had been trained as apprentice knights by Ferdinand, but Damuel and Brigitte both seemed smaller and more restrained than usual once we were inside.

We passed through the wide-open Noble's Gate to enter the Noble's Quarter, and then headed over to the massive wall stretching out along its far end. Here we passed through another huge gate, bringing us to the archduke's castle—or at least, bringing us to where we could see it. It was a radiant, elegant shade of white, seemingly made out of the same material as the temple and the Noble's Quarter. It looked to be either three or four stories high from the outside, but as I had previously lived in the lower city where six- to seven-story buildings were commonly packed together, the castle itself didn't seem particularly large. That was probably why it seemed to lack some oomph for me.

But boy, was it big. In fact, there was so much land between the gate and the castle that walking between the two would be a bit unreasonable. I honestly wanted to ask them to lend some land to the people living in the cramped lower city. The sheer amount of space was probably a signifier of wealth, and I could see buildings I didn't know the purpose of dotting the lengthy expanse leading to the castle grounds.

"Those buildings are where the tutors and forest rangers live. There are also farms and orchards, training grounds for the Knight's Order, barracks for the knights, and a smattering of gardens for tea parties. You will be living in the northern building. The western building is where the archduke's second and third wives will live when he marries again."

I watched as the training grounds and beautifully kept gardens passed by the carriage window, until we eventually reached the castle's northern entrance. The entrance on the southern side was for workers such as scholars, knights, and nobles who had administrative business with the archduke, while the northern entrance was used by private visitors and the archduke's family.

...Yeah, anyone would struggle to feel at home if you had to walk through a crowd of busily working scholars to reach your house.

I watched Rosina descend from the attendants' carriage and have the servants take several pieces of luggage from inside. She was the only one who got out, and once our belongings had been taken care of, the carriage departed. Ferdinand's attendants were probably heading to his own estate.

Once Rosina had prepared everything, the door to our carriage was opened. Damuel and Brigitte alighted first, then Ferdinand, who held out a hand to help me climb down. Memories of Damuel's failed attempt immediately flashed through my mind. I looked down to make sure that I could reach the steps, only to earn an immediate scolding from Ferdinand. "Don't look down," he murmured quietly so that no one else could hear.

"I have to. I'll fall if I don't watch where I step," I protested in an equally low voice. Ferdinand briefly closed his eyes, then hefted me into the air and set me down on the ground. I gave him a bright smile and said, "I thank you ever so much," but all he did was sigh.

Why?!

The northern entrance had opened in the meantime, and I saw several people coming out to greet us. There would normally be a lot more, but everyone was busy due to the Starbind Ceremony.

The butler-esque older man at the front knelt down, and all those behind him followed suit. "Welcome home, Lord Ferdinand. And I presume this is Lady Rozemyne. May I pray for a blessing in appreciation of this serendipitous meeting, ordained by the vibrant summer rays of Leidenschaft the God of Fire?"

"You may," I replied.

"O Leidenschaft, may my young mistress be blessed. It is a pleasure to meet you, Lady Rozemyne. I am Norbert, and I am in charge of the attendants in this castle. I look forward to serving you." A fluffy-looking blue light flew toward me as he spoke, which I accepted into me. I hadn't been wrong to think that he looked like a butler; he pretty much was one.

"I am Rozemyne. I trust you to serve me well."

Norbert stood once he had finished his self-introduction and turned. "Now, would the reassigned knights please step forward." I froze in place, having no idea why my knights were suddenly being reassigned until Ferdinand took it upon himself to explain.

"As Damuel and Brigitte are both unmarried adults, they must attend the nighttime feast that follows the Starbind Ceremony. It is about time for them to be getting changed in the knights' barracks."

"Oh, I see."

It wasn't hard to guess that the feast would be a place for unmarried people to search for partners, just as the lower city's nighttime feast was. For today, I would be assigned apprentice knights who had not yet reached adulthood.

"Cornelius. Angelica," Norbert called.

Two apprentice knights sharply stood up and stepped forward. One was Cornelius, my older brother, and the other was Angelica, a young-looking girl who seemed to be about Cornelius's age. She had light-blue hair and dark-blue eyes. It was clear that Brigitte was a female knight from the striking aura around her, but Angelica hardly seemed like a knight at all—she was an adorable little girl with lithe, slender features. I would have more easily accepted that she was an attendant.

"These are Cornelius and Angelica, who will serve as your guards," Ferdinand said. "You already know Cornelius, so I shall spare you his details. As for Angelica, you can consider her to be your guard for the Noble's Quarter. Her appearance makes her quite fitting for standing guard during feasts and tea parties." His words were enough for me to trust that Angelica was skilled enough to be a knight, but the fact that she was such a pretty little girl still made the thought a little jarring.

The knights switched places, and I began walking through the castle. All around me were pure white staircases, and equally white hallways that stretched into the distance. The only injections of color were the carpets spread across the floor, which were blue to represent the divine color of summer, and the tapestries hanging on the wall. Nobody explained what was behind any of the doors we were passing.

We climbed to the second floor and, while walking down yet another hallway, I saw a separated mansion through the window. I pointed at it, and Ferdinand explained that it was the northern building. This was where the archduke's children lived once they had finished their baptism, and it was connected to the main castle through a hallway that joined onto the second floor. I assumed that was where we would be heading, but Norbert stopped at a nearby door instead.

"Please follow me. I shall introduce you to your attendants, Lady Rozemyne."

My two guards stood beside the door while Ferdinand and I entered with Norbert. It was a parlor-esque room that had a bench, several chairs, and a table, near which a truly old-looking woman who seemed like a physical manifestation of the word "granny" was standing. Ferdinand's mouth twitched slightly the second he saw her—an unusual reaction for him.

"Rihyarda, are you to be Rozemyne's...?"

"That's right. Lord Sylvester personally asked me to look after her."

As I looked between Ferdinand and Rihyarda, Norbert took a step forward to introduce her. "Lady Rozemyne, this is Rihyarda. She will be your head attendant here."

"I appreciate your service," I said, giving the curtsy that Elvira had drilled into me. Rihyarda broke into a grin.

"I see that Lord Karstedt has raised you right. I always like to see someone who has such good manners. Lady Rozemyne, I am Rihyarda. It will no doubt be a pleasure to serve you," Rihyarda said, before beginning to shout out instructions. "You're Lady Rozemyne's personal musician, yes? I've heard from Lord Sylvester that you're very skilled. Norbert, take her to where she needs to be. I know that you need as many musicians as you can get today."

Norbert crossed his arms over his chest. "At once, Rihyarda. I entrust the rest to you." At that, he exited the room with Rosina. He would apparently be taking her to a meeting of musicians preparing to play at the feast.

"Now then, milady—it's time for business," Rihyarda said, and I reflexively stood up straight. "First, bathing. We will need to adjust your hairdo to match current trends. Once you are bathed, you will change clothes and eat with the family. Then, you will change into your ceremonial robes and attend the Starbind Ceremony. Once the ceremony is over, you will return to your room, bathe, and sleep. Any questions?"

For a second, I had assumed that I would only be changing my clothes, but hearing Rihyarda mention bathing made me realize something—I needed to ask whether they had rinsham here. I hadn't forgotten how dry and gross my hair got when washed with soap.

"Excuse me, Rihyarda. I need something called rinsham to wash my hair properly. Could you ask my mother to prepare some? Without it, my hair gets dry and brittle. I would rather have an outdated hairstyle than damage my hair by using soap."

Rihyarda's eyes widened as she listened, and then she let out a cackle. "A precocious one, aren't you! My my my... Well then, consider it done. Could you ask Lady Elvira to handle this, Ferdinand, my boy?"

...You're going to make the High Priest run an errand, Rihyarda?! And you're calling him "my boy"?! Holy cow! That doesn't suit Ferdinand at all!

I looked away from Ferdinand, holding back the urge to laugh. Seeing the look on his face now would absolutely make me burst into laughter.

"...Rihyarda, could you stop calling me 'boy' already?"

"I will when you get married, my boy."

Ferdinand is losing! Wow! Rihyarda is incredible! I so wish I could laugh right now. I'd be rolling around, pounding my fists against the floor!

Ferdinand, no doubt having figured out what I was thinking, shot me a cold glare before walking to the balcony and morphing his feystone into a highbeast. He jumped onto it, and off into the sky he went.

"I figure he'll be back in no time. Let's have some tea while we wait," Rihyarda said, having already started to prepare some.

"Erm, Rihyarda... May I ask what your history is with Ferdinand, Sylvester, and my father?"

"I'd tutored Lord Karstedt since he was a little boy, and then I was Lord Sylvester's wet nurse. It was more than a little tough for me since they both just loved to move around; neither one would ever sit still. I've known Lord Ferdinand since he was a young boy too, going all the way back to when he was first brought to the castle."

...Wow! To think there existed a powerhouse who's known the whole trio since they were kids!

Rihyarda was the widow of an archnoble, and already had grandchildren. Once Sylvester was too old for a wet nurse, she continued serving him as an attendant, and had now become my attendant at Sylvester's request.

Mm... I just hope I haven't taken away one of the few things keeping our berserk archduke under control.

We waited for a short while and, soon enough, Ferdinand returned with a small jar. He landed on the balcony and turned his highbeast back into a feystone before coming inside.

"Thank you kindly, my boy."

"How many times must I ask you to stop...? No matter. I will be going to Sylvester's office. Rihyarda, look after Rozemyne."

After observing the very rare sight that was Ferdinand running away, wearing an uncomfortable grimace as he did so, I was taken to my room in the northern building where the archduke's children lived.

"Here we are, milady."

Boys stayed on the second floor, and girls on the third. It was set in stone that boys would leave the building when they came of age, with the next generation's archduke moving to the main building while the others moved to residences outside the castle. Girls, on the other hand, were technically allowed to stay until they got married. At the moment, Wilfried and I were the only ones living here.

We entered through the second-floor hallway connecting the building to the main castle, which led us to a staircase. When I looked around, I noticed that there were knights standing in front of a door a little further in; that was probably Wilfried's room. I instinctively glanced around for Lamprecht, but then remembered that he was an unmarried adult noble. No way would he be here. He was definitely busy preparing for the feast.

I went up to my room on the third floor, which was located right beside the stairs. The second I opened the door, I could tell that the inside had been prepared by Elvira. It was just like my room in Karstedt's estate and in the High Bishop's chambers—in other words, it was very cutely decorated with red and pink flowers.

"You must feel right at home here, hm?" Rihyarda commented as she led me to the bathing room. She speedily stripped off my clothes and started roughly washing my hair with the rinsham, quickly getting out the gel, or whatever it was. I could feel it run down my face as Rihyarda dumped hot water on my head; opening my mouth now would be a disaster, for sure. I sat perfectly still, feeling like a vegetable being washed before getting chopped up.

"You make this so easy, Lady Rozemyne. Couldn't be more different from those little rascals."

She had apparently bathed Karstedt and Sylvester the same way, as her eyes were wrinkling with nostalgia. It was kind of heartwarming to see her love showing so clearly on her face.

"Goodness, your hair is so silky. Is this because of the rinsham?"

"Indeed. After you've used it once, you can never go back," I said, recommending the rinsham to Rihyarda.

"Please wear this at dinner," she said, looking through the wardrobe and taking out a fancy dress that Elvira had prepared for me.

Given that today was the Starbind Ceremony, I would need to wear clothing that was even more proper than usual. She secured my hair again using the gel stuff, then pushed in a hair stick. It was the one that Elvira had ordered from the Gilberta Company.

"Never seen a hair ornament like that before," Rihyarda said, peering curiously at the hair stick. That reaction all but confirmed that me wearing this as the archduke's daughter would start a massive hair stick trend.

Sorry, Benno. I know you're getting some much-needed rest, but I think you might have more work coming your way soon.

Once I was changed, Rihyarda guided me to the dining hall, where Sylvester and Ferdinand were already seated and discussing something. She took me to the seat beside Ferdinand.

"So you've come, Rozemyne," Sylvester said.

"Hello... Father? Lord Sylvester? It's been a while. May I ask you a question?"

"Just stick with 'Sylvester.' Drop the 'Lord' part, though—gotta maintain some distance for political reasons, but not too much. And sure, go ahead. What's your question?"

I went ahead and asked him what time and on what day the Italian restaurant gathering would take place. Sylvester may have had a date settled in his head, but he hadn't told us anything.

"...Everyone's gonna be busy tomorrow recovering from the festival, yeah? And on the day after tomorrow, I'll be busy seeing off the nobles who got married. So that leaves us the day after that. We'll go to the temple at third bell, then move to the eatery at fourth bell."

"Understood. Is there anything in particular that you would like to see on the menu? Or anything that you don't want to see?"

"Just give me stuff I've never eaten before."

"...How am I supposed to know what you've eaten before, Sylvester?"

"Something like what I ate at Spring Prayer will do just fine."

I knew that Sylvester liked new, unique things; the planned menu seemed like it would go down just fine.

As I asked about the things that Benno had wanted me to double-check, Florencia entered the room. And then, when our conversation was about done, Wilfried entered. His expression softened with relief when he saw me. As expected, he really had been torn up over what had happened during the baptism ceremony.

Once Wilfried sat down, Sylvester stood up. "Looks like everyone's here. Let's get started, then."

Wearing a sharp expression befitting an archduke, Sylvester gave divine greetings before proceeding to discuss the Starbind Ceremony, among other things. In the meantime, waiters were busily yet gracefully buzzing around the room, serving us food from large platters.

Sylvester had said that everyone was here, but Wilfried's younger brother and sister were nowhere to be seen. It was just

Sylvester, Florencia, Wilfried, and myself, with Ferdinand as our only guest.

"Ferdinand, where are the other kids?" I asked.

"Those who have not had their baptism are not allowed to attend," he replied.

As unbelievable as it sounded, noble children weren't even allowed to eat with their families before they were baptized. It was apparently forbidden for them to sit with adults until they had been taught proper manners. I probably only considered that such a bad thing because I had loved eating with my family so much. A childhood spent eating alone felt sad, somehow.

But I was apparently the only one who thought so. Everyone else here was a noble who had been raised that way—even Wilfried was sitting upright at the table. Nobles were taught that they must not stand up until the meal was over; back during my baptism ceremony, disaster thankfully hadn't struck until the meal was already done.

For today only, dinner began before sixth bell. It was fairly early as far as dinners went, but this was a formal dinner that lasted longer than normal, and for good reason—it was the last meal that people who were getting married had with their families.

Once the meal was over, Charlotte and the newly two-year-old Melchior were brought to the dining room by a wet nurse. They were both tiny, and I couldn't see them while seated.

"Goodnight, Father. Goodnight, Mother."

"Sleep well, Charlotte and Melchior."

They embraced and said their goodnights before immediately leaving. According to Ferdinand, that was the only time they ever saw or interacted with their parents. It was such a dry and barren exchange that I could barely believe my eyes.

"Goodnight, Father. Goodnight, Mother," Wilfried said while standing up, before immediately leaving as well.

I did the same, and together we started to make our way back to the northern building. Wilfried was going to be stuck in his room again, but I needed to change straight into my High Bishop robes and head to the large assembly hall where the Starbind Ceremony would take place.

When we reached the stairs and it came time for us to go our separate ways, Wilfried let out a murmur. "Er... It's good to see that you're doing alright, Rozemyne. Sorry about all that."

"Everything turned out just fine thanks to Ferdinand's healing and potions. I'm sorry for worrying you."

Looking relieved at having gotten the chance to apologize, Wilfried headed to his room. I climbed the stairs to return to my own, only to find Rihyarda standing in wait with a bundle of clothes in her arms the second I stepped through the door.

"Now then, milady, let's hurry and get you changed. More newlyweds are arriving as we speak."

Starbind Ceremony in the Noble's Quarter

"Ottilie, undo her sash for me."

There was another attendant standing in wait with Rihyarda—a woman who looked about the same age as Elvira, and seemed to be called "Ottilie." They both worked together to take off my dress, and all I could do was stand there and let them do their job. My shoes were changed, and my ceremonial High Bishop robes were put on me. They both worked super, super fast, no doubt being very used to changing the clothes of children.

Nicola and Monika had struggled to get me into my ceremonial clothing that morning, but Rihyarda and Ottilie had dressed me in no time at all. I watched in the mirror as the smaller sash was tied around the beautifully pleated robes, and the larger one was placed diagonally across my chest alongside a ton of other decorative ornaments.

When the box of ornaments was empty, Rihyarda took a step back and looked over me before giving a firm, satisfied nod. As I looked in the mirror, I noticed that there was only one part of me that remained unchanged. I reached up a slow hand to touch my hair stick. I wanted to switch it out for the one that my family had made me.

"Rihyarda, may I ask you to swap this hairpin for... that one over there, with the summer colors?" No sooner had I asked than Rihyarda switched them, thus completing my outfit.

"And off we go." Rihyarda guided me to the big assembly hall, Cornelius and Angelica naturally following as my guards.

"Eeek?!"

"Careful now!"

On my way down the stairs, I stepped on my dress and would have fallen had Cornelius not instantly reached out and caught me.

"I thank you ever so much. My normal robes only reach down to my knees, and I still haven't gotten used to walking in these longer ones..."

"You need to hitch it up a little as you walk, milady." Rihyarda hitched up her own skirt a bit and then took a few steps to demonstrate.

I had assumed that it was forbidden as I hadn't seen anybody else doing it, but apparently it was fine to raise the hem a little. But just as I thought that this would make things a lot easier for me, Rihyarda launched out another warning.

"Be careful not to hitch it up too much. You don't want your legs showing."

I didn't care about people seeing my ankles since my normal robes only went down to my knees anyway, but I kept my protests to myself. Rihyarda stood on top of even Ferdinand; I had absolutely no chance of winning against her.

I hitched up my skirt a little as I walked, taking great care not to step on the hem, only to have Rihyarda step in front of me, wearing a frown. "Excuse me, milady," she said, before bending down and picking me up. I blinked in surprise as she walked off at a speed much faster than I would have ever expected from an old granny. "If we keep going at your pace, seventh bell will ring before we reach the hall."

Seventh bell was apparently when the Starbind Ceremony started, and Rihyarda had determined that we'd be late if she let me keep walking. But honestly, it wasn't really my fault; the castle was just so ridiculously big. The distance between the northern building—that is, the living quarters—and the public assembly hall was way too far for a child to walk. And then there was the fact that we had to take a bunch of turns instead of going directly toward the hall, which made the journey even longer than it needed to be. I had half a mind to demand that carriages be allowed in the halls.

Rihyarda carried me almost the entire way to the assembly hall, setting me down a short distance from the hallway leading inside. She looked me all over to make sure my clothes hadn't been creased or anything.

"This is as far as I can take you, milady. Walk straight down the carpet and up the altar at the end. Lord Sylvester will be there."

"Okay."

I turned the corner to see a big hall, illuminated by shining things that looked like lamps. Candles were used as sparingly as possible in the lower city to save on wax, so it was standard for everything to go pitch-black once the sun had set, but here in the Noble's Quarter, these tools that worked like lamps were used plentifully. Though they weren't as bright as, say, the ones powered by electricity on Earth, the pure-white walls made everything feel much, much brighter.

"...It certainly is bright in here."

"You don't have these in the temple? They're magic tools that amplify the small light from candles," Cornelius explained as we walked. I nodded. The doors leading to the assembly hall were wide open, and I could already see a ton of people gathered inside.

"The High Bishop has arrived," announced a voice.

The assembly hall had a massive ceiling like a gymnasium, and was divided into two by a black carpet with gold edges. Newlyweds and adult unwedded nobles were waiting on either side, talking among themselves.

I faced forward and walked down the carpet as quickly as I could, feeling a whole room of curious eyes watching me. But despite my best efforts, I was still walking far slower than most people would appreciate—something that was made especially clear when I heard Cornelius whisper a supportive *"You can do it."*

I began to climb up the altar when I reached the end, and, thanks to being able to hitch up my skirt, managed it without stumbling. That alone made me feel as though I had completed a huge, arduous task.

"Over here, Rozemyne," Sylvester said. He was calmly sitting in a chair atop the altar as Rihyarda had said he would be.

Karstedt was standing behind him, and motioned with his eyes for me to take the seat beside the archduke that had been prepared for me. I did just that.

"Rozemyne, where is your bible? How are you going to perform the ceremony without it?" Sylvester asked, his tone incredibly worried. Ferdinand hadn't written the bible on the list of things that I had to bring to the Noble's Quarter, so I hadn't even considered it as something I would need.

"I know the words to the prayer, and Ferdinand will be reciting the tales from the bible himself. There won't be any problems at all," I explained, and Sylvester appeared to visibly relax.

"As long as you can give the blessing. Oh, by the way—I'm gonna be the one reciting the tales."

"I see."

Now that I was atop the altar, I was free to gaze around the assembly hall like a teacher looking over their class from the podium. *Oh, there's Ferdinand.*

"I see there aren't any women around Ferdinand. Why is that?"

I could see women watching him from a distance and squealing in excitement, but none were actually trying to approach him. Maybe everyone had found out what a nasty personality he had. At this rate, it seemed unlikely that he would ever escape from Rihyarda calling him a boy.

"Only a fool would take this opportunity to find a romantic partner and waste it talking to a celibate priest," Sylvester said. Honestly, it made perfect sense. The only question I had was why in the world Ferdinand had bothered to join the crowd at all. "Rozemyne, do you want Ferdinand to get married soon? I'd bet he's working you to the bone in the temple and piling tons of work on you. Must be rough."

"Actually, it's quite the opposite—I would be in more trouble than anyone if Ferdinand quit being the High Priest. I know that this would be very unfair on him, but I would like him to remain single until I come of age, at the very least."

I scanned the crowd looking for any other familiar faces and noticed Brigitte standing alone by a wall. She seemed uninterested in joining the crowd, but I didn't know whether that was a good thing for her.

"What happens if you don't find a marriage partner here?"

"Depends on your family and why you couldn't find a partner. You're talking about your knight, huh? Finding a partner's gonna be real tough for her," Sylvester said with a frown as he looked over at Brigitte as well.

"Why is that?"

"Family stuff."

According to Sylvester, Brigitte's father had died three years ago, at which point her older brother—who had only just come of age—inherited the position of Giebe Illgner. Brigitte was engaged at the time, but the man she was due to marry and his family saw weakness in her older brother's young age, and planned to take control of the entire Illgner house.

Finding that despicable, Brigitte expressed her displeasure and put an end to the engagement. While their families were of about the same status, the man's family had more experience in a variety of fields, and there were more than a few cunning schemers among them. To this day, they were giving Brigitte's inexperienced older brother as much trouble as they could. Although she had saved her family from being taken over by canceling the marriage, her choice had also ended up putting her brother through enormous hardships, which made her incredibly depressed.

Brigitte had requested to be my guard knight before anyone else, wanting to gather as much influence as she could to help her older brother, even if she had to go to the temple and the lower city in the process. Her unyielding determination gave her the strength to go somewhere that all nobles hated, all to protect her family and the lives of her province's citizens.

Tears welled up in my eyes as I listened to the story, which caused Sylvester to look at me with shock. "Why're you crying?! What about that was worth crying over?! This kinda thing happens on a daily basis, doesn't it?!"

"I-I mean…" *I'm just weak to stories about strong family bonds. Especially right now…*

The father was also recognized as the central pillar of the family in the lower city, so most fell upon hard times when he died—especially when his successor hadn't been fully raised yet. Benno had only just come of age when his father died and had mentioned that not only had most of his employees quit, but he had been regularly tormented by the guildmaster. If a commoner merchant had that hard of a time, then I could only imagine what a giebe who had to lead an entire province would go through.

"I had no idea that Brigitte was in such a bad situation... Father, Sylvester—what can I do to help her?" I asked Karstedt and Sylvester, respectively.

"Her situation might improve a little if you can introduce her to some good houses, but given her personality, that's not gonna be easy," Sylvester said. "She's pretty self-conscious about how people see her, but at the same time, she doesn't really fit in with everyone else. Just look at what she's wearing. That should tell you everything you need to know."

I took a closer look at Brigitte. It was pretty easy to guess that she was wearing something trendy as her clothes looked similar to what tons of other women were wearing, but the style didn't suit her very much at all.

"It seems like she's chasing after trends to avoid looking out of place," I observed, "but the clothes don't look good on her, so she ends up looking half as pretty as a result." In all honesty, Brigitte looked way cooler and more attractive in her usual knight gear.

"Yeah. She's tall and muscular, so girly outfits don't compliment her at all."

"Now, that's not true. Plenty of girly outfits would look just fine on Brigitte, assuming they were the right style and color. Though everything that comes to mind would go against current trends..."

"Alright. In that case, how about you make the trends? Women don't have long to get married; it's said that a girl who's still single when she's twenty will be single for the rest of her life."

...Um, that's asking a bit much. I can't just up and make trends in a snap.

I puffed out my cheeks in a pout and tried to think of more clothes that would look good on Brigitte, all the while continuing to scan the crowd. I had a feeling that Damuel would be having just as hard of a time as she was.

Lamprecht wasn't too hard to spot, considering that he was tall enough that his head poked above the crowd of women surrounding him. It seemed he was so popular that he would have his pick out of just about anyone he wanted. There was no need for me to worry about him.

"I see that my dear brother Lamprecht is surrounded by women. Do you think he'll be married by next year?"

"I imagine he'll be single for a while longer yet," Karstedt explained while staying on guard. "He fell in love with a girl from another duchy back in the Royal Academy, and she's not of age yet. There's a chance that her family won't actually let her marry him when she does come of age, so it might not happen at all."

...Wait, is this a long-distance relationship? And what was that about an opposed family? Is this Romeo and Juliet? I needed more details; there was no romance in my own life, so I lived vicariously through the love lives of others.

"Is it just me, or is Eckhart not here?" I asked.

"I've been wanting him to move on and look for a new wife, but it seems like it's going to take him more time to heal," Karstedt replied.

"Um, what?! Nobody told me about this."

Eckhart had apparently married once before, but his wife had passed away. I was getting a little concerned about how little I actually knew about my new family.

"It's still a sensitive issue for him, so it doesn't come up much. Rozemyne, please take care not to talk about Eckhart's marriage or his late wife."

"Of course."

I continued looking for Damuel as I mulled over all of the shocking revelations that were being dropped, but the crowd was so thick that I couldn't see him. I had no idea where he could be. But just as I got increasingly serious in my search, seventh bell rang out.

Sylvester smoothly stood up and took a step forward, flourishing his cape behind him. "Now begins the Starbind Ceremony. All newlyweds, step forward!"

Eight couples entered the assembly hall. Their outfits had much fancier designs and used more gorgeous cloth than the outfits I had seen in the lower city this morning, but their colors still matched the season the wearer was born in. The couples started to walk forward, keeping a set amount of space between each pair. Cheers, claps, and pleasant words of celebration filled the room, contributing to the joyous atmosphere.

Once the couples were lined up in front of the altar, Sylvester began to recite a biblical tale in a resounding voice. It was fairly abridged compared to what was written in the bible, but he definitely had it memorized. The old High Bishop really had been a complete and utter failure.

Once he was done retelling the story of the God of Darkness and the Goddess of Light, Sylvester began calling out the names of those getting married.

"Bernadet, son of Baron Glaz, step forward with Lagrete, daughter of Baron Blon."

The named couple climbed the steps of the altar. Sylvester confirmed that they wished to get married, then handed them the pen-like magic tool that he had used when signing my adoption papers. Once they had both signed the contract spread in front of them, it disappeared in a small burst of golden flame. Once all eight contracts had vanished, loud cheers echoed through the hall.

"The High Bishop shall now bless the newly joined couples."

It was finally time for me to do my job. I stood up and walked forward to stand beside Sylvester.

"Go a little nuts," he whispered, though I could hardly hear him since he was so much taller than me. It seemed that he also intended to push the legend of Rozemyne the Saint.

I poured a bit more mana into my ring than I had back in the temple and took a deep breath, before raising my hands and beginning to pray.

"O mighty King and Queen of the endless skies, O God of Darkness and Goddess of Light, hear my prayers. May you grant your blessings to the birth of new unions. May they who offer their prayers and gratitude to thee be blessed with thy divine protection."

Black and gold light swirled in my ring before shooting up to the ceiling, just as it had in the temple. The two beams of light twisted around each other before eventually bursting into tiny specks of light, which scattered and rained down onto the newlyweds.

"Oooh…"

Awed voices filled the assembly hall, followed by a brief moment of silence before the hall erupted in cheers once more. Judging by the mix of surprise and joy on the newlyweds' faces, it was safe to say that my prayer had been a success.

"The High Bishop shall now depart. May she be blessed for granting such a large blessing despite her youth!" Sylvester declared. All those present took out their shining wands and held them up, making them shine even brighter with mana. They looked exactly like concert glow sticks, and while it was a pretty sight, I felt deathly embarrassed knowing that they were all for me. Walking calmly in the midst of all that was too great of a task for me; I sped across the carpet as quickly as I could manage, wanting to flee from the source of my shame as soon as possible.

The large doors to the assembly hall closed once I had passed through them—what followed would be a feast that only adults were allowed to attend. The knowledge that my job was now done coupled with the fact that I would normally be asleep by now made my body feel suddenly heavy out of nowhere.

"Are you alright, Rozemyne?"

"Cornelius, I think I have reached my limit."

Cornelius hurriedly picked me up, knowing full well that I could pass out at any moment. But despite being a lot bigger than me, he still didn't have the arm strength to carry me very far. "Sorry, Angelica, but could you hurry and call Rihyarda for me?"

Angelica gave a firm nod, and was gone in the blink of an eye. A second later, she came running back. "Rihyarda will be here at once."

"Thanks. I owe you one, Angelica."

"My my my!" Rihyarda exclaimed as she rushed over a brief moment later. She hefted me up and began carrying me back to my room. "Now, if you aren't just the easiest person to carry. Light and docile. How about that!"

Rihyarda was apparently more than a little strong thanks to always having to catch Sylvester and lug him back to his teachers when he was a kid, or drag him out of bed and into his office whenever he tried to avoid work. She told me various stories as we made our way back, then set me down when we eventually reached my room. I could feel myself teetering the moment my feet touched the ground.

"Milady, you have to bathe before bed."

I just wanted to jump into bed and go to sleep, but Rihyarda refused to let me sleep while the gel was still in my hair. She and Ottilie stripped off my clothes before putting me in the bath, and I rested my head against the tub as they washed my hair with rinsham. The hot water was making me more and more sleepy.

"Careful now, milady."

"Mm…"

By the time I was out of the water and having some kind of scented oil put on me, I was already falling asleep.

"Wake up, milady. You have to wake up, Lady Rozemyne."

"Okaaay…"

I continued to sway sleepily as they washed away the scented oil, rubbed me dry, dressed me in my sleeping clothes, and then supported me from either side as they guided me into bed. The next morning, I ended up bedridden with a fever.

"Ngggh… Ferdinand… My head hurts…"

"Bedridden as expected, I see."

Ferdinand had come to see me right after breakfast. Although the plan had been for us to return to the temple that morning, he had predicted that the tight schedule would be enough to make me collapse. He was completely right.

"Why are you so calm about this, Ferdinand?!" Rihyarda demanded. She only had experience raising abnormally healthy kids like Karstedt and Sylvester, so seeing me collapse with a fever out of nowhere and for no real reason was throwing her off big time. Her voice had come out sharp as a result, whether she intended it to or not.

Completely ignoring Rihyarda's scalding remarks, Ferdinand held out one of the potions that had been hanging from his waist.

"She performed two religious rituals, each of which required a significant amount of mana, on top of spending an entire day moving around. It was more than obvious that she would end up bedridden. She needs only to drink this and get some rest."

"What do you mean she only needs to get some rest?! If you knew that she was going to get sick, why didn't you stop it from happening?! This is the kind of situation where you should be putting that big brain of yours to use!" Rihyarda barked quite unreasonably. Maybe being raised by her was the reason why Sylvester had such unreasonable expectations of other people.

"Rihyarda, it is an unfortunate fact that Rozemyne's poor health cannot be planned around. It is inevitable that she will fall ill, no matter what you do. If there was something that could be done about it, then I would have done it already." He was wearing a troubled expression and had his hand placed on his forehead, but Ferdinand gave an explanation to Rihyarda rather than simply silencing her like he would anyone else. He really couldn't win against her.

I reached out from my bed and gently tugged on Rihyarda's skirt. "Rihyarda, please don't get mad at Ferdinand. He made sure to brew a potion that would help get me better. He is a bit of a meanie, though, and refuses to improve the nasty flavor…"

"My my my… In that case, drink up and get some rest, milady."

With a small grin, Rihyarda took the potion from Ferdinand. The green liquid inside swished about as she handed it over to me, and the condensed smell of a potion pierced my nose the moment I opened the small bottle. The bitter taste that I had been forced to consume so many times before immediately arose in my mind like some kind of nightmarish phantom. It terrified me, but I steeled my resolve and gulped the potion down in one go. The quicker the pain was over, the better.

"…Wha? It… doesn't taste that bad." It was bitter, to be sure, but not so much that I wanted to roll around on my bed, flailing my limbs in misery as I had before.

Hearing my whisper, Ferdinand shot me a glance. "I improved the recipe, though it seems that was out of character for a *meanie* such as myself."

"U-Um… G-Gosh, Ferdinand, how *do* you do it? Intelligent *and* kind. My goodness… What a shining example of a good person. Ohoho…"

Ngh… That glare stings… I hurriedly dived under my covers to avoid Ferdinand's sharp, piercing glare.

The Archduke and the Italian Restaurant

I had expected to return to the temple after lunch, but, as my fever was still going strong come noon, Ferdinand decided to stay behind. He sent his attendants back to the temple without him, and it wasn't until later that afternoon that my fever finally went down.

"I suppose that should suffice," Ferdinand said. He put me onto his highbeast and we returned to the temple accompanied by Damuel and Brigitte, who followed on either side of us.

"Damuel, did you find a wife?" I asked, having ultimately failed to spot him during the feast last night. He furrowed his brow sadly and shook his head.

"...Unfortunately not. Though I have been blessed with the opportunity to guard you, Lady Rozemyne, I have still been demoted to the rank of an apprentice knight."

It would be hard for someone to consider marrying Damuel while he was serving his punishment as a mere apprentice, to be sure, but he was still a knight of the archduke's adopted daughter. In my opinion, it would be fine for him to set up an engagement before his punishment was up. Damuel also seemed to be getting more and more precious mana thanks to my blessing so, as far as I was concerned, anyone who decided to marry him would be getting a great deal.

"Well, there's always next year to look forward to," I said.

"It's hard to be too optimistic, but I'll try my best. How did things go for you, Brigitte?" Damuel asked casually.

I watched Brigitte timidly, already knowing about her circumstances. She lowered her gaze the moment our eyes met.

"...I canceled a previous engagement following the passing of my father. I cannot imagine that there will ever be a second chance for me," Brigitte said, wearing such a stiff expression that my urge to help her somehow grew even stronger.

We descended to the Noble's Gate and returned to my quarters, where Fran opened the door with perfect timing and welcomed us inside.

"Fran, but how? We didn't send word of our return."

"I noticed the highbeasts descending toward the Noble's Gate," Fran said coolly, as though it were the most natural thing in the world. In reality, he had probably been looking out the window the whole time that he was waiting for us. He really was a model attendant. I looked up at him, and he knelt down so that we could make eye contact. "Lady Rozemyne, it appears that you are not feeling well."

"You think so? Ferdinand gave me a potion, and my fever's gone down, so..."

As I touched my face and hands to check my temperature, Ferdinand shook his head. "I trust Fran's word more than yours. Fran, put Rozemyne to bed. Do not let her do anything else today."

"As you wish."

The two settled the matter without even giving me a chance to speak. At this rate, I would be forced into bed against my will.

As Fran picked me up and headed to my room, I asked him a question. "Fran, could you send a messenger to the Gilberta Company?"

Fran shook his head. "Please postpone it until tomorrow," he said, using Ferdinand's order as a shield. It was true that I wasn't feeling particularly well, but there was stuff that I had to do. The last thing I needed was being stuck in bed, unable to do anything.

"It's very important. Sylvester has decided on the day he'll be visiting the eatery. I need to let them know."

"You can do that tomorrow," Fran replied, refusing to budge an inch.

I pursed my lips. "Very well, then. Sylvester and Father will be visiting the temple beforehand, but I'll tell you the date tomorrow as well."

Fran's shoulders twitched. The moment he heard that he was personally involved, a look of worry washed over his face.

"Tell me, Fran—can you predict the exact day that my adoptive father, the archduke, will be coming? Making preparations will be quite difficult if you're not warned far enough in advance, no?"

"I understand. I will send a messenger to the Gilberta Company, but please make do with just a letter. A meeting would be too much. With that said, erm... when is he coming?"

"The day after tomorrow."

At those words, Fran rushed to the High Bishop's chambers, his eyes blinking rapidly. Not only would he need to organize the room to avoid any possible embarrassment, but he also needed to prepare tea and food appropriate to the archduke's tastes, and there was a chance that what we had on hand wasn't of a high enough quality.

"Please rest as soon as you've written the letter, Lady Rozemyne."

"Yes, I know."

Having secured Fran's permission, I hurriedly wrote a letter to Benno. I mentioned the date and time that the lunch would be taking place, how many people would be attending, and added some general warnings concerning the menu, then closed by asking them to send someone tomorrow afternoon to pick up the natural yeast.

"Gil, sorry to ask when you've only just gotten back from the workshop, but could I ask you to deliver this to the Gilberta Company?"

"As you wish."

Once I had finished my letter, Monika changed my clothes for me. As I crawled into bed, she made sure to give me a firm reminder that I was not to leave my bed until dinnertime.

"Monika, how was the festival at the orphanage? Did the children have fun?" I asked.

"Yes. This year, Wilma joined them in the taue throwing. The divine gifts were plentiful thanks to your request that the blue priests continue to have food prepared, and making the soup was not as tough as it was last year."

I lazed about in bed as Monika told me what had happened while I was gone, and before I knew it, Gil had returned from delivering the message. "They've already finished preparing. Benno said they'll be ready no matter when you come. Also, Leon will be coming by tomorrow to get the natural yeast," he said, holding out a response that Benno had written to me.

I opened the letter, feeling relieved that he was on top of things, as always. Inside, he described that Freida and the guildmaster would be participating in the lunch as fellow contributors to the establishment. They both knew that Myne and Rozemyne were the same person, and he wanted me to tell the archduke that ahead of time.

I didn't feel much better when the next day came around, so Fran forbade me from entering the director's chambers or the book room. After some negotiation, I was able to convince him that I wouldn't be able to rest without books to read. He brought me some from the book room, which meant that I could spend the whole day reading in bed. It was a very fulfilling, blissful day.

In the afternoon, Nicola came to inform me that Leon had come for the natural yeast. Meanwhile, Fran was busily moving in and out of my room, preparing for Sylvester and Karstedt's arrival.

The plan had been for Sylvester, Karstedt, and their guards to arrive at third bell on the day of the lunch, but Sylvester was apparently so enthusiastic that he arrived well before third bell. I had been practicing my harspiel with Rosina when Ferdinand guided the excited-looking man in, and Ferdinand and I exchanged exactly the same grimace.

"Sylvester, please don't come sooner than promised," I said.

"Rozemyne is correct. How many times do I need to tell you that other people have their own lives, too?!"

"Alright, alright. But what's the issue? We're still gonna be heading to the eatery at the time we agreed on," Sylvester said, casually blowing us off.

Karstedt placed a weary hand on his forehead and explained that, despite how it may seem, he had held Sylvester back for as long as he could.

Eckhart and Cornelius were standing behind them. It had been agreed that Eckhart would be coming from the very start since Karstedt needed a guard while he was eating, but Cornelius was underage, and I was pretty sure that no plans had been made for him to come.

"Cornelius, will you be joining us?" I asked.

"Yeah. I'm your bodyguard too, after all." He thumped his chest twice and gave me a confident grin, but I had a feeling that he was only here because he didn't want to be left out of something that seemed like fun.

I looked to Eckhart for confirmation, who explained with a teasing look that, since guards ate on alternating shifts, Cornelius had offered to serve as his partner. It seemed that he had basically forced his way into joining.

"No point sending him back now that he's here. Give him a visitor's welcome too, Rozemyne; he's your family."

"Sylvester, aren't you and the High Priest family as well?" I asked, looking at Ferdinand in hope that he would handle Sylvester himself. He looked down at me, and, with a grimace, noted that he would handle him once the meal was over.

While Fran was preparing tea, I allowed Sylvester and my brothers to investigate my chambers while I began writing another letter to Benno. I needed to tell him that I was bringing more guards than we had anticipated. He had seemed so confident about his food stores that a single extra person probably wouldn't pose much of a problem, but knowing something like this ahead of time would likely make things a lot easier on him emotionally.

I also recorded how people were dressed, and asked that he feed this information back to Freida and the guildmaster. It would be best if everyone dressed fairly similarly. I could imagine that a single person wearing different clothes and sticking out would make them extremely uncomfortable.

"Rosina, please give this letter to those who come to get you."

"Understood."

Rosina would be playing harspiel for us during the meal. A carriage from the Gilberta Company would be sent for her ahead of time at third bell so that she would arrive at the eatery before us. Today, she was wearing a light-blue dress that I had purchased through Benno for this specific occasion, and it looked incredible on her.

"Lady Rozemyne, I must be going. I shall see you soon," Rosina said with an elegant smile, before fleeing the room of archnobles prior to third bell. Nicola, who was basically descending into a small panic over our visit from the archduke and the commander of the Knight's Order, watched her go with envy.

"Nicola, please serve cookies to everyone. You may taste-test them and choose the tastiest ones."

"Yes, milady! You can count on me."

Amused by how eagerly Nicola rushed to the kitchen to begin taste-testing, I headed over to Sylvester, who was enjoying the tea that Fran had served him. Despite the fact that it was just before lunch, he was stuffing his face full of the cookies that Nicola was serving him while raving about how good they were. Cornelius watched on with frustrated envy, unable to eat as he was standing behind him as a guard.

When fourth bell rang, more carriages arrived from the Gilberta Company. One was for me, Ferdinand, Sylvester, and Karstedt; another was for my brothers, Damuel, and Brigitte; and the last was for Fran and Ferdinand's three attendants. Our sizable train of three carriages headed toward the restaurant.

"What the heck's wrong with this carriage?!" Sylvester exclaimed, his eyes flared open in anger. He was clearly annoyed that commoner carriages shook, unlike the ones in the Noble's Quarter.

"This is just how carriages in the lower city are. The ones in the Noble's Quarter use magic tools, remember? And the roads there are flat and straight."

"Rozemyne, can't you use that knowledge of yours to fix this? Forget about books; these carriages are a travesty."

"...I'd never even ridden in a carriage before coming here. I don't know a single thing about what could be done to fix them."

I never had any interest in the structure of carriages since I had never had any plans to ride one. I might have read a paragraph or two about how suspension was used to lessen the impact of the shaking, but I didn't remember enough details to give Johann a concrete order.

"And it smells just as bad as it did last time," Sylvester commented, scrunching up his face in a grimace and no doubt recalling when he had passed through the lower city to go hunting. Given that Karstedt and Ferdinand were also wearing stiff frowns, I could tell that they were thinking the same thing.

"If you hate it that much, why don't you dedicate some of your budget to improving sanitation in the lower city?"

"Is that truly something you could fix with money?" Karstedt asked, looking at me with great interest. There was so much anticipation in his voice that it was actually kind of painful.

"...The smell would, for the most part, disappear if we could build a proper sewage system. I don't know everything that would entail, though."

"Are books seriously the only thing you know about?! Sheesh, your knowledge sure is useless half the time!" Sylvester bellowed at me. But his yelling wouldn't change that my interests had always been focused on a single point that I prioritized above all else: books. I could think about other things once they were taken care of.

"Why would I bother to remember precise details about things I don't need or care about? Do you remember everything you've ever learned, Sylvester?" I asked.

"I leave that job to Ferdinand."

...Why are you proudly puffing out your chest?! That's not something to be proud of!

I looked at Sylvester, feeling exhausted before we had even arrived at our destination. "Sylvester, I would like to preemptively inform you of who will be joining us at the meal," I said, before going on to explain everything that Benno had asked me to in the letter. I mentioned Freida and the guildmaster first, adding that they knew me from before my baptism.

"Hm. A merchant who has a sharp nose for profit, huh? Got it. I'll decide on how to deal with him once I see him."

We arrived at the Italian restaurant midway through Sylvester's sentence. He closed his mouth and put on the archduke face that he wore in public. This was a pretty big eatery since it was in the north of town, but it was the same size as the other six-story buildings around it. From the outside, it was almost impossible to tell that it had been modeled after the mansion of a noble.

The attendants alighted from their carriage first carrying our things, then the guards disembarked from theirs. Once the outside of the restaurant had been cleaned and cleared of any obstacles to make the walk to the front door easier, Karstedt descended from the carriage with Ferdinand, then helped me down, leaving Sylvester the archduke to climb out last.

The three carriages lined up next to each other were drawing the attention of passersby. Even those who didn't know who we were could tell at a glance that we were obscenely rich, and an increasingly growing peanut gallery started to form a reasonable distance away.

"Let's hurry inside, Sylvester," I suggested.

The door was shut behind us as we entered, blocking off most of the outside's smell and freeing us from the intrigued eyes of the public. I let out a sigh of relief and turned around to see Benno, Mark, the guildmaster, Freida, and the waiters, all kneeling with their arms crossed in front of their chests.

It had been a long time since I had last seen Freida, but I couldn't casually bring that up since I wasn't Myne anymore. Feeling a bit lonely, I listened to Benno give a lengthy greeting as their representative.

"We are the owners and employees of the Italian restaurant. May this serendipitous meeting, ordained by the vibrant summer rays of Leidenschaft the God of Fire, be blessed by the gods."

"May this meeting be blessed."

When I had last visited the Italian restaurant, its interior decoration hadn't even been finished yet. It looked entirely different now: there were ornate window frames and doors, the walls were adorned with tapestries, carpet had been laid, and various paintings and flower-filled vases served to punctuate the already opulent atmosphere. The entrance hall was furnished with benches and chairs so that it doubled as a waiting room, and I could see the decorations that Rosina and Fran had picked out some time ago.

"This is the room where your honorable guards will be eating. As it was not built with serving nobles in mind, it is of a slightly lower quality than the main dining hall, but I beg your forgiveness for this."

Benno was referring to a simple room which had a sizable table and several chairs. It was apparently an eating area for staff members, but could also be used as an extra waiting space while the main room was being cleared. Since it hadn't been designed for actual customers, the fact that it was too simple for noble guards could hardly be helped.

"This is the dining hall."

"Impressive. Feels like one that a mednoble or laynoble might have. It's hard to believe this is in the lower city," Sylvester said.

"I appreciate your kind words," Benno replied, visible relief on his face. The restaurant that he had spent so much time and money on had gotten direct approval from the archduke himself, so I could understand his reaction.

Elaborately carved, waist-high wainscoting ran along the wall, alongside a number of shelves that were decorated with expensive-looking plates and vases, plus a picture book that I had made and the origami wishing crane that I had given Benno a very long time ago. The tables were polished to a glossy sheen, and had as many napkins and menus as there were people seated. There was also a vase of seasonal flowers in the middle of each table, kept short enough that it wouldn't obscure the vision of customers seated across from each other. They had even added a cute little bell used to summon the waiter. I gave a big nod of satisfaction.

"Now then, please follow me."

Once we had looked around the restaurant to our hearts' content, we were guided to our table. Eckhart stood at the door facing the table, while Brigitte stood on the other side of the door, outside the room. Meanwhile, Damuel and Cornelius headed to the side room.

"I shall now introduce those who funded the establishment of this restaurant. First is Lady Rozemyne, the archduke's adopted daughter. The menu being served today consists largely of recipes provided by her. Next is Gustav, the guildmaster of the Merchant's Guild, and his granddaughter, Freida. They contributed greatly to the training of our waiters and chefs."

Benno introduced the archduke to those who would be eating with us, and that was when I learned the guildmaster's name for the first time—Gustav.

"You two, huh?"

Sylvester shot Freida and the guildmaster a piercing glare, knowing that they knew my past as Myne. The guildmaster was always so domineering and arrogant in my memories, but here he was practically cowering as he kept his arms crossed over his chest.

"Gustav and Freida, I hear that you are both wise individuals—that you have sharp noses for profit and the skill to seize opportunities that others would miss. In that case, I imagine you both already know what to do. Am I right to think that?"

"Of course. We will do everything in our power to assist you, my lord."

"Good. Soon, my daughter will be starting a significant new industry. I ask that you aid her efforts."

Sylvester indirectly ordered them to assist Benno without dragging their feet, and it seemed that the guildmaster fully intended to do just that. He was kind of a greedy person, but he had saved my life before; it was a relief to know that he'd be staying on our side.

Freida, feeling more at ease now that the archduke was no longer staring daggers at her, made eye contact with me. We both smiled and nodded at each other. She would be living in the Noble's Quarter when she grew up, so I wanted to make sure we stayed on good terms.

While Benno was giving his introductions, Fran was with Ferdinand's attendants preparing the cutlery and dishes we had brought ourselves. The waiters were taking care of everyone else's dishes, and I spotted Leon among them.

The food itself was brought on a serving cart covered in pots and big plates. The attendants and waiters started taking the plates off, each preparing to serve their respective bosses. Fran would be serving the archduke today, while Zahm would be serving me. Status-wise, the archduke needed to be served first, but this was the first time that anyone was working here, and nobody wanted to be the one to improperly serve the archduke these unique dishes. After a brief discussion, it was decided that Fran was the most used to my cooking and should thus serve the archduke, while everyone else observed what he did.

"So this is today's menu, huh?" Sylvester picked up the board that had been set on the table in front of him and looked it over with great interest. I could see a grin forming on his face as he saw the list of various dishes that he had never eaten before.

Leon began by serving fluffy bread, so freshly baked that it was still steaming. Its enticing aroma stirred my hunger, making me want to eat as soon as possible. Karstedt and Ferdinand looked at the bread in surprise, since it didn't look like the bread they were used to, while Freida and the guildmaster shot glances in my direction.

Fran smoothly set a plate down in front of Sylvester. On it was a mound of potato salad made with handmade mayonnaise, partly surrounded by steamed bird and vegetable salad, which had been shaped into a crescent and topped with faux Italian dressing.

"O mighty King and Queen of the endless skies who doth grace us with thousands upon thousands of lives to consume, O mighty Eternal Five who rule the mortal realm, I offer thanks and prayers to thee, and do partake in the meal so graciously provided."

Once everyone's food had been served, we all offered prayers. Once that was done, I picked up my fork; those who invited others to a meal ate first, partially to demonstrate that the food hadn't been poisoned.

...Yup. Tasty.

I chowed down on my food, and saw that Sylvester was immediately digging in. His love for new things was evident by how he ignored the vegetable salad and instead went straight for the potato salad, which he had never seen before. That was the complete opposite to Ferdinand, who went for the familiar-looking salad before anything else.

I watched Sylvester carefully to see how he would react. He chewed for a moment, then widened his eyes in shock and looked at me. "...Rozemyne, what is this stuff? I've never tasted anything like it before," he said, his deep-green eyes shining with excitement. He was apparently fond of potato salad.

"It's called potato salad. You boil potatoffels, crush them, put in other vegetables, and mix it all together with (mayonnaise). Does it suit your tastes?"

"Like I said, I've never tasted anything like it before, but it's not bad. Yeah, not bad at all."

He really did seem to like it, which reminded me that Lutz's brothers had all been super pumped too back when I had first taught them how to make mayonnaise. They said that it made bitter, previously nasty vegetables actually taste good. Incidentally, I had never made mayonnaise by myself since becoming Myne; mixing the ingredients required a lot of strength, and as there were no electric mixers or anything, I had no choice but to ask for help.

Karstedt, seeing Sylvester ignore the vegetable salad entirely to focus on the potato salad, tried some potato salad himself. He chewed for a bit, then nodded. "Its flavor is certainly unique, but not in a bad way."

It was only once he had seen both of their reactions that Ferdinand took a fairly small bite himself. His expression barely changed, but given that he then put even more in his mouth, I could tell that he was satisfied with how it tasted.

Benno had been observing the three archnobles to see how they reacted as closely as I had, and, upon seeing their approval, he relaxed his shoulders a bit and started eating from his own plate. He, Freida, and the guildmaster had all eaten the practice dishes made by the chefs, so while they did enjoy the food, none of them looked surprised in the least while eating.

"Sylvester," I said as I saw him reaching to get more potato salad, "please try the other salad." He hadn't even touched the steamed bird yet.

With a small grimace born from a hatred of vegetables, Sylvester stabbed a fork into his salad. He chewed loudly for a bit, then blinked in surprise and took another bite. "Rozemyne, this salad's unnaturally good. What kind of sauce did you put on it?"

"I put (herb dressing) on it. It's made of plant oil, salt, citrus fruit, and some edible herbs, but the flavor changes depending on what you make it with."

In this world, it was standard practice to cook sauces, and most of them were made using meat juice. They even put a sauce that was similar to gravy on vegetables. That tasted good in its own way, but it often led to the vegetables getting all greasy, which I wasn't too fond of.

"What're the white chunks on top of the vegetables? Looks like bird meat, but they're soft and taste kinda different."

"Bird meat is right. It took extra time to prepare, but the flavor was worth it, don't you agree?"

Even Sylvester with his distaste for vegetables readily finished the whole salad, then tried asking Fran for seconds.

"Sylvester, if you fill up on salad now, then you won't be able to eat any of the other food we've prepared," I said.

"Ngh. Good point."

I picked up a portion of fluffy bread and tore off a bite-sized piece, indicating that others could do the same if they wanted. It was still steaming hot, and the sweet scent of freshly baked bread rose into the air the moment I pulled it apart. I tossed the piece into my mouth, enjoying the warm sweetness and soft mouthfeel.

Mmm... Tastes like Hugo's baking. Even though they were using the same recipe, Hugo's bread always came out slightly differently from Ella's thanks to his higher level of precision and skill. A smile spread across my face as I enjoyed the familiar taste, at which point I noticed Freida eagerly grabbing a piece herself. It seemed that she had been carefully waiting for me to try some first.

The moment that Freida touched the still-warm bread, she looked up at me in surprise. She hadn't expected that it would be so soft, and squeezed it in her hand a few times as if confirming that she wasn't mistaken. She then tore off a piece and ate it. Her eyes shot open wide, and she placed a hand over her mouth as she chewed. The sparkles in her brown eyes grew steadily brighter, and I could easily tell that she was calculating the potential for profit in her head.

"Lady Rozemyne, I have never before eaten bread this soft, or that tastes so naturally sweet on its own. I would very much like to serve it here."

As expected, she jumped on the opportunity. I had expected as much since I hadn't even taught Hugo how to make the natural yeast, instead just giving him the yeast I had made myself.

Now then, how should I turn her down? I thought, only to have Sylvester grin and interject before I could say anything.

"Freida, right? Sorry, but that's not gonna happen. This bread is a secret recipe that I'm gonna use to surprise nobles in the winter," he said, before looking at me with gleaming green eyes. I fully intended to use the fluffy bread to strengthen my position in noble society, so I had no disagreements there.

"Sylvester is correct. I allowed the chefs to make this bread since Sylvester and Father were visiting, but it will only be revealed to the world come winter."

"I see. That is a shame," Freida said with a smile before taking another bite. From what I understood, Leise was her only chef, and I could imagine that she wanted her to try some too.

"It certainly tastes good, but... Hm..." Karstedt, who was halfway through his third bread roll, furrowed his brow in thought. "The bread being this soft actually makes it a bit unsatisfying. I reckon that I could keep eating these forever and still never feel full."

Chewing was an important factor when it came to feeling full and satisfied. I made a mental note that Karstedt liked harder bread; making sure that he had as much fluffy bread as was needed to satisfy him would probably be a huge blow to my wallet.

"And this is (consommé) soup."

A large pot of soup was wheeled into the room on another cart, and an aroma that caught everybody's attention immediately filled the room. The clear amber-colored soup inside had no vegetables or anything mixed into it, and had been cooked just enough that the umami had concentrated. Nothing in this entire region would taste anything like it, since here it was completely normal for people to boil vegetables and then toss away the broth.

"It smells nice, but there's nothing in it," Sylvester said with a confused look after watching Fran pour some soup for him. In the culinary world here, everyone understood soup to be a pile of vegetables that were boiled to the point of being overcooked. Soup that lacked visible ingredients simply did not exist.

"The flavor becomes more apparent when there isn't anything in it. I think you'll be surprised by how tasty it is," I said, bringing my face close to my bowl so that I could enjoy the smell. It had a thick aroma that made my mouth water.

I dipped my spoon into the amber soup that had been delicately strained over and over again, and the appetizing smell grew even stronger as tiny ripples spread along its surface. Then, I put the spoon into my mouth, rolling the consommé over my tongue to enjoy the concentrated umami taste. The thick, deep flavor had a surprisingly refreshing aftertaste, and I couldn't help but sigh in awe. Hugo had obviously worked hard on it. Maybe it was because Hugo had so much more experience, but honestly, this was several times better than the consommé that Ella had made.

"I'll be the judge of that," Sylvester said, putting a spoonful of soup in his mouth. His eyes shot open, then started to gleam with delight as he immediately ate some more. On his third spoonful, he moved the soup around in his mouth while blinking in confusion. "What flavor is this?"

"It has hints of meat, vegetables, and all sorts of other things in it. It's a soup that has a concentrated umami taste. It can be used to add flavor to other meals, too."

Ferdinand tightly knit his brow, a look of pure bewilderment on his face as he ate the consommé. You would think that an expression like that would be a sign that he hated it, but the speed at which he was eating suggested otherwise.

"Ferdinand, you seem confused about something. Does it not suit your palate?"

"Hm? Ah. No, I find this soup to be quite beautiful," he said. While I sat there confused as to why Ferdinand would praise the food for its appearance rather than its taste, he wiped his mouth with a napkin and explained. "Indeed, it truly is beautiful. You can tell from a single sip how deep the flavor is, and how many ingredients were used to form it, no? Each has its own delicious taste, but here they have been fused and condensed into one. And yet, there is nothing in the soup itself. It is so clear that one can see through to the bottom. The soup has a beauty that has been refined to perfection."

It was still a bit hard for me to understand what he meant, and I definitely hadn't expected him to talk about it at such length. It seemed safe to assume that he really liked the consommé soup.

"The next course has been prepared," a waiter announced, pushing over another cart. On it was another main dish: the (macaroni gratin). It had been baked in small ceramic bowls, which were now set on wooden plates with handles to make them easier to hold.

"These brown bowls are extremely hot, so take care not to touch them under any circumstances. Please hold the wooden parts when eating."

Everyone could tell from a single glance that the gratin had only just been taken out of the oven. Steam was coming off of the still-bubbling white sauce, and the cheese atop it was moving. The aroma coming from the white steam carrying the crisp smell of cooked cheese was irresistible.

Since this world lacked macaroni, I settled on making handmade farfalle pasta. It complemented the white sauce well, and nobody would have to worry about any boiling sauce getting caught inside and scalding their tongue. It was perfect.

"Rozemyne, is this baked cheese?"

"It's something similar. Take care not to burn your tongue while eating."

There were several commonplace noble recipes that involved putting cheese on birds or vegetables before baking them, and I had eaten meat sauce before, but nothing here tasted like white sauce. Maybe it didn't yet exist, or maybe I had just coincidentally never tried it.

I wrapped some of the hot cheese around a piece of farfalle, blew on it, and then put it in my mouth. Strong feelings of joy washed over me the moment it touched my palate. Since the ingredients here were somewhat different, the resulting dish had a flavor unlike what I was used to, but this was a recipe that my Earth mom had used to make back in my Urano days.

"Rozemyne." Sylvester took a single bite before looking at me with narrowed eyes. "How is this anything like baked cheese? It tastes nothing like what I'm used to."

"Well, it's cheese, and it was baked in an oven, so I think it's fair to say that they're similar."

"Everything else is completely new to me. What's this droopy white stuff, for example? I like it."

I had elected to make a menu of recipes that resembled what you might expect to find on a kids' menu at a family restaurant specifically for Sylvester's visit, and it seemed that this decision had been a resounding success. I couldn't help but let out a small giggle at the sight of Sylvester's glimmering green eyes as he scooped up the white sauce.

"This is white sauce. It's made using butter, milk, and flour, with salt to taste."

As I thought, white sauce didn't exist here. Karstedt took one bite of gratin before setting his fork down. I looked over to see him staring at me, a serious expression on his face. He must have not liked it.

"When you were living with me, I tried a lot of those strange sweets that you had your chef make, but she never made anything like this outside of the baptism ceremony. Did your chefs make this food too, Rozemyne?"

Sylvester raised his head with a "Come again?" the moment that he heard Karstedt say "strange sweets," but I ignored that and replied to Karstedt.

"My mother is not so careless as to trust the kitchen to a chef who has only just arrived. My chef earned her trust by making sweets, and only recently have we begun exchanging recipes. It will still be some time before she allows my chef to make actual meals."

"I see. 'Some time,' hm…?"

Elvira prioritized getting sweets recipes for her tea parties. From what I could remember, I hadn't exchanged more than a few normal recipes with her, and Ella had told me that she had mainly been tasked with making sweets during the baptism ceremony. It was a shame that I'd ended up passing out before actually getting to eat anything.

At that moment, Cornelius walked into the room with a satisfied smile, having finished eating first. "I am here to relieve you of your duties," he said to Eckhart.

Guards were ordered to eat quickly since they ate in shifts, but, as I understood it, they were being served the same things that we were. And judging by how Cornelius was happily patting his stomach, he had eaten his fill.

Eckhart, who had only been able to watch everyone else eat, power-walked out of the room, his flat expression not faltering for a second. Damuel and Brigitte were probably changing places outside the door.

A cart was pushed into the room right as Eckhart left. It was the second dish of the meal and the first with meat.

"I prepared this thinking that you would like some meat dishes, Sylvester. It's called (Hamburg steak) stew," I said. I was sure that he would like it, and as expected, his eyes were gleaming.

In truth, making Hamburg steak here wasn't easy since mincing meat was so much work, and buying ground beef flat-out like I would back in my Urano days just wasn't an option. But Hugo and Todd had worked hard for my sake. They used knives to chop the meat like crazy until it was adequately minced, then wrapped cheese inside so that it would flow out when cut. Next, they peeled the skin off of a yellow tomato-like vegetable called a pome, which was diced and cooked in consommé soup before dipping the grilled hamburger into the soup to stew it further.

Freida and I were already getting full, so our Hamburg steaks were only half as big as everybody else's. As my fork pierced the small, round piece of meat on my plate, clear juices flowed out, followed by thick yellow cheese a moment later.

"Something's coming out!" Sylvester yelled.

"That's cheese," I replied, pulling my knife away to show the sticky cheese stretching along with it. I cut off a bite-sized piece of steak, making sure to cover it in cheese sauce, and then placed it in my mouth. "Mmm... Too good." Nothing could beat pome sauce made with high quality consommé.

Sylvester must have been really impatient, because he lunged at his own Hamburg steak the second I took a bite of mine, hastily slicing off a piece and forking it into his mouth. His eyes widened, and he nodded hard. "Ooooh! This tastes great! I like this the most out of everything I've tried so far."

"I knew that I could count on you to like it, Sylvester. I'm glad it suits your tastes so well."

Karstedt and Ferdinand ate silently, the former cutting his steak into big chunks which he eagerly chewed through, while the latter smoothly sliced his into small pieces which he gracefully consumed. But despite their differing approaches, the meat was disappearing from both plates just as quickly.

"How is it, Ferdinand?"

"You used the soup from before to make this sauce, correct? The taste is excellent. Profound, even. To think that it could be used in this manner as well..." Ferdinand seemed to really like the consommé, and once again began to eloquently extol its virtues at great length.

...Mhm, right. It's very beautiful. Om nom nom... Mmm! Hamburg steak is just sooo good!

Having made his way through the main dishes, Sylvester was leaning back with a blissful expression on his face. But things weren't over yet—there was still one more course. I was already full, but I had a second stomach when it came to dessert.

I can make it. I can keep going!

As the attendants set down plates and busily moved around to prepare tea, Leon came in pushing a cart and announced the dessert for the day. Atop the cart were shortcakes, which had been cut into five centimeter-wide squares and were decorated with seasonal fruit. Pure white cream was piled on top of each one, with a gleaming red rutrebs crowning the center—it was the very image of a strawberry shortcake.

It had been extremely tough to make. Managing the oven's heat wasn't easy, so it had taken a long time to reach a point where our attempts could be described as a success. That said, when it did eventually happen, it definitely was tasty. Judging by how the pieces that Leon had brought out were cut, I could guess that the sides had gotten too hard to eat. They had probably only brought out the edible parts.

Another cart came in carrying the cake that we had prepared ahead of time, just in case the shortcake didn't come out right. It was a cake that I particularly liked called a mille crepe, which was made by piling crepes on top of one another and slathering a thin layer of cream between them. To make it look even more beautiful, it was covered with a layer of orange sauce made from cooking the juice from an apfelsige with sugar. Its refreshing summer smell and taste complemented the cake well.

Atop the last wagon pushed inside were two pound cakes: one made using tea, and the other made using plenty of distilled liquor for the men who weren't too fond of sweet things. Leise had baked these ahead of time meaning that they had been able to sit overnight, so the flavors should have definitely settled.

Sylvester looked at the various wagons that Leon had pushed in and immediately asked me which dessert was best. I told him to pick whichever one he liked, at which point he started to glare from cake to cake, fiercely deliberating which one he wanted. I was absolutely certain that he was yelling "Everything! Gimme everything!" on the inside.

Leon would of course obey if Sylvester actually ordered everything, but waiters weren't allowed to speak unless spoken to. He had finished preparing the tea and could do nothing but watch him waver in his decision. He looked increasingly distressed, then ultimately turned to me for help.

"Sylvester, there is no need to think so hard about this. They were cut into small pieces ahead of time so that they could all fit onto your plate at once."

"Smart thinking! In that case, I'll take them all," Sylvester declared, flaring his nostrils in satisfaction.

…Well, the fact that Sylvester picked them all should make it easier for anyone else who wants to taste-test each one. Sometimes him having the heart of an elementary-schooler comes in handy.

It hadn't been too long ago that I had eaten one of the shortcakes prepared by Ella, so I selected the mille crepe instead, as planned. Meanwhile, Ferdinand and Karstedt requested one of everything, Benno asked for one of each of the pound cakes, and Freida and the guildmaster opted for the shortcake.

I leisurely enjoyed my cake while sipping my tea; the apfelsige's sharp flavor tasted great alongside its restrained sweetness.

Those of us who had eaten these cakes before to taste-test them in the early stages all appeared very satisfied as we enjoyed our favorites, while Sylvester, Ferdinand, and Karstedt each seemed to eat in their own unique way. Sylvester had his eyes closed and seemed to be comparing the taste of each dessert; Ferdinand was eating them one at a time, wearing a contemplative frown the entire time; and Karstedt cleared his plate in the blink of an eye before requesting seconds.

Pretty good, huh? I'm glad to see that our first customers are so pleased, I thought to myself, feeling the satisfaction of a job well done.

Making a Monastery

Sylvester wore a satisfied grin as he sipped his tea, having completely devoured the desserts. "Not a bad lunch, if I do say so myself. I honestly wasn't expecting much from a lower city eatery, but the food tasted good enough to prove me wrong."

"Your praise is greatly appreciated," Benno said, his voice containing the emotional sincerity of someone who had pushed themselves to their absolute limit to make sure the meal was a success. Freida and the guildmaster seemed just as pleased, beaming at the knowledge that they had successfully hosted the archduke, of all people, at their eatery.

"I'm very interested to see what the future holds for this restaurant," Sylvester said. Then, his expression hardened; everyone straightened their backs, sensing that things were about to get serious. "Alright, Benno—it's about time you tell me what you learned on your trip. Clear the room."

On Sylvester's order, Benno directed the waiters and attendants to leave. Rosina stopped playing music and exited as well, her harspiel in hand. Only now could they go and eat lunch.

Benno hesitated for a moment, then turned to look at Freida and the guildmaster. While they were unrelated to the orphanage investigation, we would need as much help from the guildmaster as we could get when branching out the Rozemyne Workshop.

"Freida, you may leave, but I would like to ask the guildmaster to stay and listen."

"...Benno, why are you keeping him here?" Sylvester asked.

"Gustav is the guildmaster of the Merchant's Guild. He has better connections with Ehrenfest's major stores than I do, and we will be able to progress a lot quicker if word spreads about the business we are setting up here."

In other words, the guildmaster would no doubt be wrapped up in whatever Sylvester's next unreasonable demand for Benno was, so it was more convenient for him to stay and be involved from the start. I could guess that Gustav would soon have to whip his old body into shape to keep up with us.

My sympathies. But, well... maybe he'll be fine, since he still seems to be full of energy?

"Hm. Very well, then. Eckhart, guard the door. Everyone else, ensure that nobody attempts to come in."

Once the guards that were lined up in front of the door had received Sylvester's orders, they did exactly as they were told: Eckhart stayed behind, while the other three left with Freida. As they passed through the door, Mark entered and stood behind Benno.

The door closed, and silence fell over the room. We had planned ahead to weather whatever storm was going to hit us today, but we were dealing with Sylvester here—there was no telling what he might demand.

As tensions rose, Ferdinand looked at Benno. "Your report, then."

Benno faced the archduke and repeated what he had already told Ferdinand. He very carefully explained the orphanage situation, the financial state of the city, and then how the plan's success depended on the scholars put in charge. I could guess that Sylvester had already heard everything from Ferdinand, as his expression didn't change in the slightest as he listened to Benno. The report was only being repeated for the sake of appearances, and so that Gustav could hear.

"Hm. With all that in mind, Rozemyne, what do you think we should do?" Sylvester asked, shifting his gaze to me once Benno had finished.

I exchanged looks with Benno, then turned to face Sylvester. "I believe that, despite the cost and effort that it will involve, we need to set up an entirely new orphanage and workshop. I would like the workshop to operate under my rules, and do not wish to have any unnecessary disputes with the city's authorities."

I went ahead and explained the differences between the orphanage in the temple and the one in the city. Sylvester nodded, encouraging me to continue.

"Right now the temple has very few blue priests, but an excess of gray priests. I think it would be wise to send several gray priests and shrine maidens over to a new orphanage and workshop, where they can teach the orphans how to live and work according to the principles developed here. To that end, I would appreciate it if we could build a small chapel of sorts for these gray priests to live in, which would also give me an excuse to visit."

Having an entire new building constructed for the orphans would be beneficial in both protecting them from harassment from the city's authorities and smoothly adjusting them to our way of life. It would also help us to prepare for the printing business expanding over time.

Once I had listed out everything that I discussed with Benno, Sylvester shot a glance his way. "If we make this workshop, would you have the tools ready soon?"

We had already ordered the tools ahead of time, just in case Sylvester told us to borrow space in the city and run a workshop from there while we waited for the orphanage to be built.

Benno gave a firm nod. "We have already begun our preparations. But, depending on the number of orphans and how old they are, they may not be strong enough to print."

"Are you suggesting that the workshop focus on making paper, then?"

"Yes, Sylvester. That's exactly right," I interjected, trying to back Benno up. "Printing will require as much paper as we can get; there will never be a time when we don't want more."

Sylvester nodded while stroking his chin, then broke out into a mischievous smile. "Alright then. In that case, I will heed Rozemyne's request and order the construction of a workshop, an orphanage, and a monastery with a chapel."

"I am eternally grateful."

I really hadn't expected my request to be accepted so easily. Benno and I exchanged a nod, silently agreeing that we would immediately need to discuss which construction workshop we should hire and what orders we should make, but Sylvester interrupted us by suddenly pointing at Ferdinand.

"Ferdinand, you do it."

"That won't be a problem, but whose mana should we use for the protection magic?"

"Why not Rozemyne's? She can handle it."

They had suddenly started talking about something that I didn't understand in the slightest. A metaphorical question mark appeared over my head as Ferdinand gave Sylvester a nod, let out a short laugh, and then took out a pen and paper. He started writing something using one of those magic pens that didn't need any ink. I desperately wanted to peek at what he was scribbling down, but as it was bad manners to lean forward, I kept still.

"Rozemyne, will a workshop of the same size as the temple's suffice? How many rooms will the orphanage need?"

"A workshop of the same size will work just fine. As for the number of rooms, I believe that about half as many will do, even if more orphans enter the orphanage later."

"Agreed. Considering the city's population, that should be more than enough. The chapel needn't be particularly large, either. Should the orphanage be separated into male and female buildings as well?" Ferdinand asked, nodding at my replies as he continued to write on the paper.

I had no idea what he was noting down, or what he was thinking.

"There will need to be a basement storeroom for food and products that can be accessed by both the boys' and girls' buildings. I think the workshop should be in the basement of the boys' building, the kitchen in the basement of the girls' building, and the dining hall on the first floor of the girls' building."

"In that case, I will make the first floor of the boys' building the chapel, and place the hallways and staircases here. The dormitories will be on the second floor of each building. Your room, Rozemyne, will be registered with mana, and kept locked under most circumstances. I shall make it so that you can enter the room through the chapel, since you have both male and female attendants."

I could see Benno and Mark pale as the situation got more and more out of their control. In all honesty, I wasn't really sure what was happening either. But what I did know was that, rather than bringing this business to a construction workshop in the lower city, Ferdinand would be managing the construction himself.

"That should do it. How does this look?" Ferdinand asked, holding out the paper for Sylvester to see. He glanced over it, then gave a satisfied grin.

"Fast as ever, I see."

"Basing the architecture on the temple simplified matters greatly."

"Alright then, let's go. Eckhart, summon the guards."

Sylvester stood up smoothly, Ferdinand and Karstedt following his lead. Benno and Gustav also stood up, just as Eckhart opened the door and called in the guards. I slid off of my chair a full beat behind everyone else; I couldn't gracefully get down without the help of an attendant.

"Sylvester, where exactly are you planning to take us?" I asked.

"To Hasse so that Ferdinand can make the monastery. Where else?"

"W-Wait, right now?"

Sylvester nodded as the knights entered the room and formed a line. "Ferdinand, you take the lead. Karstedt, guard us all from the rear. I'll take Rozemyne; you four, get these three on highbeasts."

"Sir!" The guards nodded on reflex since it was an order from the archduke, but they all seemed confused.

Whew. I'm glad that I'm not the only one completely baffled by Sylvester doing this without warning.

"Eckhart, take Benno. Cornelius, take Gustav. Damuel, take their attendant. Brigitte, protect the aub's highbeast. Quickly!"

By the time Karstedt had given his speedy instructions, Sylvester was already striding toward the entrance hall. I hurried after him, worrying that he would forget I existed and leave without me otherwise.

"Stand down. Get out of my way," Sylvester declared in a powerful voice befitting an archduke. The eyes of every attendant and waiter who had been waiting in the hall shot open, and they immediately hurried over to the wall. I saw Freida look to me for an explanation, but I didn't really understand what was going on either.

"Go, Ferdinand."

"Understood. Open the door!"

No sooner had the attendants opened the double doors for him than Ferdinand summoned his white highbeast right in front of himself. He ignored the store employees clapping their hands over their mouths to contain their gasps, instead leaping onto his feathered white lion and soaring into the sky.

Sylvester followed his example by summoning a three-headed Cerberus-esque lion. He then hefted me up, climbed onto it, and flew out of the store. As the highbeasts burst out of the restaurant, those passing by yelped in surprise and dove to the ground. I tried to apologize to them, but the mana-driven highbeast I was on was moving at such a tremendous speed that it was hard to imagine they heard me.

"Sylvester, I think going to Hasse this soon is just plain reckless. It's too sudden."

I thought back to Gustav, who had been frozen in place with wide-open eyes, and Mark and Benno, whose faces had been twitching with terror. None of them were permitted to lose control of themselves in front of the archduke.

It kind of seemed like Gustav was confused throughout that entire meeting. That might be a problem... I just hope that the shock of riding on a highbeast doesn't give him a heart attack.

"Hmph," Sylvester huffed. "This is all according to our plan. Just as you all planned things out ahead of time, we three talked and made our own plans."

As we passed over the city's outer walls, the people down below pointed at us and yelled in surprise. We then soared past some farms and a small forest, taking us straight to Hasse. It was a pretty small city compared to Ehrenfest, not to mention it didn't even have a Noble's Quarter. The journey had taken half a day by carriage according to Lutz and Gil, but on highbeast, it took no time at all.

"Rozemyne, what type of land would be best suited for the workshop?" Ferdinand asked, scanning the area from above Hasse. I looked around as well, searching for a good place for a paper-making workshop.

"It would be nice to have both a forest and a river nearby."

"That seems like a good place, then," Sylvester said, looking down and pointing at a spot next to a water wheel. "Ferdinand, build it on the other side of that river—far away enough that it won't impact the water wheel."

Ferdinand looked around, gave an understanding nod, and then started to descend at Sylvester's instruction. Given that there were so many of us coming along, I had been sure that we were going to talk—or rather force—the city's authorities into letting us build here, but Ferdinand was the only one who flew down. He stopped his highbeast just a bit above the forest, at which point Sylvester started to soar up into the sky.

"Back off a little, everyone."

At Sylvester's order, everybody else followed suit and moved their highbeasts away. Sylvester only stopped flying up when Ferdinand looked about as small as my pinky finger.

Once Ferdinand had confirmed that we were all in place, he made his shining wand appear as per usual, then took some kind of shiny powder in his other hand. Ferdinand bobbed his wand like a conductor leading an orchestra, and the powder moved as though it had a mind of its own. We were far enough away that I couldn't actually hear him or tell what he was doing exactly, but I could see the shining powder float up into the air before forming a magic circle and starting to spin around.

"Sylvester, what is Ferdinand doing?" I asked.

"Making the monastery, of course. What else would he be doing?"

"Um... Come again?"

The large glowing circle floated higher into the air and shined dazzlingly bright. Then Ferdinand swung his wand down, and the circle began to slowly descend. It gradually vaporized the trees below as it touched them, turning their leaves, branches, and trunks into gleaming white powder, before doing the same to the flowers and even the grass on the forest floor. The huge storm of powder then started to spin inside the magic circle, everything else having been destroyed.

"Wh-What is that?"

"Not something you see too often. It's magic that only the archduke's family is permitted to use. Take a good look; you'll learn it at the Royal Academy one day, now that you're my adopted daughter."

As the magic circle came to rest on the ground, the earth it was covering quickly turned white. It started to twist, then drooped as though it was liquid.

Ferdinand took out the paper from before and threw it up into the air. It floated into the center of the magic circle as if carried by the wind, before burning up in golden flames. Then, the shining white earth started to change form entirely, as though it was concrete following Ferdinand's instructions. A big hole opened on one side, then rows of thick pillars shot up into the sky, white earth connecting the spaces between them like stage curtains.

Before I could even process what was happening, the white earth seemed to stop moving. It emitted a blinding light for a second, which then faded to reveal what looked like a tinier version of the temple. It had no noble section and was indeed of a smaller scale, but it was made of the same pure-white stone. Surrounding it was a circle of stone pavement just as big as the magic circle had been.

This was the monastery that Sylvester had mentioned. It was gleaming a radiant white, which made it look completely out of place beside the forest and river.

"See? Now you can get that workshop going in no time, huh?"

Sylvester was grinning with pride, but Benno and Mark were both as pale as ghosts; nobody had expected that the new workshop was going to be built in the blink of an eye.

Sylvester angled his highbeast down and started to descend. "We can take a look inside. C'mon, let's go."

"Are you sure it's okay for us to stand here?" I asked, lightly tapping my foot against the stone pavement once we had landed in front of the monastery. What I expected to be squishy white earth was instead the white stone that I had grown so used to seeing in the temple and the Noble's Quarter, and, to my surprise, it didn't react at all to me standing on it.

The monastery was a perfectly normal building, just as it appeared to be. It somehow had several glass windows and a door, but on the inside, it was empty. No furniture, no doors—the inside was pure white stone and nothing else.

"This will be the chapel. We'll need statues of the gods and a carpet. When can those be ready?" Sylvester asked.

Mark whispered something to Benno, who then replied. "I believe the statues will take about three months. The carpet will take some time as well." It seemed that he had already asked Mark to check how much it would cost and how long it would take for an art workshop to make the statues, since I had said that I wanted the workshop and chapel in the same building.

...That's Mark for you. He's a man who knows how to do his job. I love it.

"Speed it up and have them ready in two months. Make sure it's done in time for the Harvest Festival."

"Benno, I believe that the temple has a great deal of spare carpet," Ferdinand noted. "There should be more than enough for this chapel; I will give you what you need for this monastery."

Chapels needed a carpet for each season, and these took a long time to prepare.

"I thank you ever so much," I said. "That carpet will certainly be a big help."

"Rozemyne, there is no need to thank me. I will give you the carpet that you need now, and you shall donate the newly finished carpets to the temple when they are ready."

...Ferdinand, did you know that being nice can be its own reward sometimes?

That said, it was true that the new carpet we were going to have made wouldn't be ready in time for the Harvest Festival, so there was no need to look a gift horse in the mouth.

We walked into a hallway beside the chapel and climbed upstairs, leading us to the boys' dormitories. The doorways were completely empty.

"What will you do about the interior doors and furniture? If they aren't ready by winter, then the orphans will have a hard time living here," Sylvester murmured.

"Our top priority will be making sure that the chapel doors and the altar are completed prior to the Harvest Festival. As for furniture, we will need dinner tables, chairs, cabinets, and beds." Ferdinand listed off everything that we needed, while Benno noted it all down on his diptych.

"Benno, Gustav, and I can have the furniture finished quickly if we all use our respective wood workshops. Plus, if we pay a few of the wood workshops in this city to make some, then I'm sure that the people will view the monastery more positively."

Ingo's was the only carpentry workshop I could go to. He already had his hands full improving the printing press and making boards for the orphanage's winter handiwork, but I was hoping he could help us in finishing before the Harvest Festival.

"Seems like the workshop's gonna be up and running in no time, huh?"

"Sylvester, please don't ask us to do the unreasonable," I said. "This won't be like the temple's orphanage, where people's daily needs were already being met. This workshop won't be up and running anywhere near as fast."

The orphans in the temple were able to work hard, follow my orders, obey the older gray priests, and equally share the food and profit earned among themselves. But it was hard for me to say whether the workshop here would be ready to begin production anytime soon.

"They won't even be able to live here until the furniture and other living necessities have been prepared. Plus, the workshop won't start running the second we bring tools over."

"Fine. I'll wait a bit, but we made a whole miniature temple for you. Get it running fast."

"As you wish."

Once we had completed our tour, Benno, Mark, and Gustav gathered to talk about something. They were probably discussing who would take care of what, and when everything would be ready by.

Investment was necessary no matter the business you were starting. But as there weren't many orphans in Hasse, the initial investment would be especially high since we were quite literally starting from scratch. I looked over at Sylvester, who was with Ferdinand and Karstedt. I remembered Ferdinand saying that I would be given a budget for this since it was business for the duchy as a whole, so I was hoping to squeeze some money out of them.

"Sylvester, I think we might need some funding to cover the initial investment," I said.

"You spent all of your government funding on building this monastery. Get the rest yourself."

Not only had I failed to get any money, but he had rejected me without so much as a discussion. Apparently, that shining powder was fairly expensive. Of course it was. I had heard that something as simple as the parchment that merchants used for magic contracts was expensive; no way would a magic tool that could build an entire monastery be cheap. That said, it would still take a huge amount of money to get everything ready here. It seemed a bit unreasonable to expect me to earn it all myself.

"I can't cover that much all by myself."

"What do you think your status is for? Go and gather some donations."

Sylvester told me to exploit my position as the archduke's daughter to finagle donation money from other nobles. *Well, that definitely sounds like it could earn me a pretty penny.*

"Are you asking me to wander around the castle with a donation box?" I asked, thinking back to the fundraising people I had seen by grocery stores in my Urano days.

Sylvester rubbed his temples and shook his head. "Sheesh. Karstedt, let Elvira handle this."

"In that case, Rozemyne can stay home with us for now as Elvira shows her how to earn donations firsthand," Karstedt said, his eyes wrinkling in a gentle smile. It seemed that I would need to learn how noblewomen got donations, and having someone like Elvira teach me the ropes seemed like a great idea.

"Father, I thank you e—"

"Nope, that's not gonna happen," Sylvester interjected, interrupting my attempt to thank Karstedt and take him up on his kind offer. "I'll invite Elvira to the castle and she can work with Florencia on this. We're talking about the duchy's business here."

Now that he mentioned it, it made sense to handle the donations in the castle since this was duchy business. I nodded in agreement with Sylvester, but Karstedt smiled even wider and took a step forward, waving his hand in disagreement.

"Think about this carefully—who can say what villains might be lurking in the castle to eavesdrop on our plans? I think staying at my home will be safer and more secure."

"Nah, nah, nah. If you're talking about stopping information from being leaked, then Rozemyne needs to learn to be on guard about what she says at all times. Didn't you say that she has to get used to keeping her eyes and ears on her surroundings?"

They were towering over me on either side as they argued, each with peaceful yet sharp looks in their eyes. Having no idea what was going on, I took a step back toward Ferdinand, who was just quietly watching the proceedings, and tugged on his sleeve.

"I think they both have good points here. Why are they glaring at each other?"

Ferdinand looked at the two men with a hand on his chin, then laughed. "They are both correct because they are both attempting to argue their way into having your chef stay at their home."

They were fighting over something that hadn't even occurred to me. While they were discussing where I should do my donation work on the surface, they were actually fighting over where Ella would be staying. And honestly, that was something I couldn't have cared less about.

"...Wow, that sounds really tedious."

"Indeed. They both become quite aggravating when food is involved. How about you just travel to the castle from the temple, then? It won't take much time at all if you travel by highbeast with your knights rather than by carriage."

"Good point. They won't need to keep fighting if I decide not to live with either of them," I said with an impressed nod, just as Sylvester and Karstedt each plopped a hand on one of Ferdinand's shoulders.

"Now now, Ferdinand. Don't try to sneak her out from under our noses here."

...Seems like there's a third, slightly more subtle tedious person here.

Despite their peaceful expressions they all had scary looks in their eyes, so I scooted away and headed to where Benno was. It honestly didn't bother me where I ended up staying, so avoiding their dumb argument entirely seemed to be the best course of action.

"We need to have this all done before the Harvest Festival? We haven't got the time or money to do that," Benno said, his head in his hands.

"I wasn't expecting this either," Gustav sighed. "What's your plan, Benno?"

I stepped in between them and looked up. "I might be able to get the money by gathering donations from nobles, but there's no helping how little time we have."

My sudden appearance must have taken both them and Mark by surprise, as they all gasped and reflexively stepped back. They then scanned the area, taking care to see where Sylvester was and what the other nobles were doing. There were guards standing at the monastery's entrance and Sylvester's group was still preoccupied, but we were far away enough that we couldn't hear them, or vice versa.

Once Benno had confirmed that, he whispered to me, "Lady Rozemyne, are the nobles okay with your absence?"

"They're having a serious debate about where I'll be staying in the coming weeks. It's because I'll be bringing Ella with me wherever I go; she's the one they're interested in."

When I explained that they were arguing over my chef, Mark stroked his chin in thought. "Master Benno, let us assume that, rather than preparing everything the orphanage needs at once, we first deliver boxes of straw appropriate for sleeping on during the current weather. Then, we gradually replace these with beds as winter approaches. How long would it take to prepare the tools for the workshop, as well as the food and other daily necessities needed for the priests to live here?"

Benno scratched his head. "Even if the old geezer and I divide the work between us, we'll still need about a month."

"Yes, that sounds feasible. Though, in all honesty, I would like a bit more time than that," Gustav said with a frown.

It seemed they were both in agreement, so it was safe to say that it would take at least one month to prepare the skeleton of the orphanage, no matter what. Benno and Gustav glanced over at Sylvester while cradling their heads.

"You think he'll wait that long?" Benno asked. It was hard to imagine that someone who'd had an entire monastery built in a single day and then expected the workshop to be running a few days later would be very patient.

Mark smiled while writing something in his diptych. "You may count on me. I will ensure that we have both the funds and the time that we need, without any complaints."

"How will you do that?" I asked while looking up at Mark. He gave me a smile that seemed to say there was no problem at all.

"We will buy time by selling the recipes our customers want so much."

Mark's idea was to delay opening the Italian restaurant by one month (or potentially two) while we rushed to have the monastery prepared before fall. Meanwhile, we could lend our chefs to those who were interested for a fee and sell our recipes.

"The chefs will of course need payment even while the restaurant is closed, so all we need to do is have them work elsewhere."

...You're just going to refer to the Noble's Quarter and the castle as "elsewhere" like they're nowhere special, hm? But, that aside, it was a good idea—the chefs could earn money and would have something to do while we waited to open the restaurant. Meanwhile, Sylvester, Ferdinand, and Karstedt could each get one of my trained chefs to serve them.

When we returned from the monastery to the Italian restaurant, I called Hugo and Todd over to introduce them.

"These two are the chefs who cooked today's meal. They are two of the very few people who can make the recipes I invent," I said with a smile.

Sylvester, Ferdinand, and Karstedt looked at them with gleaming eyes. They honestly looked like carnivores about to pounce, and I noticed my two chefs recoil in fear of being targeted by the nobility.

"We were planning on sending out invitations to all sorts of major store owners after today's meal in order to lead into the opening of the Italian restaurant, but we need to prepare the monastery at once, don't we? To that end, we have decided to delay opening the restaurant a bit longer."

"...Doesn't that mean we won't be able to eat here again?" Sylvester asked, shooting me a dissatisfied glare. His hunger for my food was a good sign; the more he missed it while the restaurant was closed, the more he would be willing to do to get it.

"The waiters we borrowed from other stores will have places to work even if we keep the Italian restaurant closed, but the chefs have nowhere else to go. Therefore, I will lend you each a chef, for a fee, until the restaurant opens."

Sylvester twitched his finger, Ferdinand fixed me with a gaze, and Karstedt grinned in amusement. All three had taken the bait. I glanced at Mark, who nodded slightly while maintaining his peaceful smile.

"My recipes are somewhat unique, and so must be taught by a well-trained chef. For that reason, I will charge five large silvers per month for one chef. I will also charge one small gold for each recipe taught. I have currently taught my chefs thirty different recipes, including the ones served today."

"A small gold for each recipe? Isn't that a little expensive?" Karstedt asked, stroking his mustache with a surprised expression.

I widened my eyes as if shocked and offended. "Expensive? When I taught Freida the pound cake recipe, she paid me five small golds to monopolize the recipe for a single year. She agreed on the spot, saying that it was cheaper than she expected," I said, looking over to Freida and Gustav. "In my opinion, I'm giving you all an outrageous deal because of the consideration you've shown me, because we're family, and because we won't be signing monopolization contracts."

Freida put on a very merchant-esque smile. "Lady Rozemyne's recipes are simply that valuable. I believe that men of your stature are surrounded by high-quality food at all times and can thus understand how valuable today's food truly is. In fact, I would love to buy that bread recipe myself, and would be willing to pay as much as eight small golds for it."

I smiled at Freida's total lack of hesitation to announce what she wanted, at which point Benno began describing his own contracts with me to further support my position. "When my humble store, the Gilberta Company, bought exclusive rights to make and sell hairpins from Rozemyne, we paid one large gold and seven small golds. It was valuable information that only she knew."

But even though Benno and Freida were merchants, they were close associates of mine; it was hard to take their words at face value, and so Sylvester, Ferdinand, and Karstedt all wore dubious expressions as they searched for the truth.

"...I do not recall you charging for the sweets recipes you made for us at home."

"That is because you and Mother provided three rooms for me: one at home, one at the castle, and one at the temple. You also prepared my baptism clothes, hired tutors for me, and, above all else, welcomed me with all of your heart. I've already paid you back how I can, so now it makes sense that I would start charging."

I crossed my pointer fingers in an "X" to emphasize that I wasn't going to budge on the matter. Sylvester and Karstedt each knitted their brow in thought, while Ferdinand simply agreed to pay the price I had asked for with a composed expression.

"You ultimately intend to use this money for the orphanage, correct? I will have all thirty of those recipes you mentioned, and hire one chef for the one-month period. The money will be paid when the chef begins work. Which of your two will be coming to the temple?"

Mark once again whispered to Benno, who then gave Ferdinand an answer. "Todd. The chef standing on my left will join the temple's kitchen."

I glanced over at Todd. He had gone completely stone-faced, no doubt feeling the pressure as three nobles looked him over.

"We will need to spend tomorrow closing off the area and preparing the recipes, so I ask that we be allowed to send you the chefs the day after."

"Very well, then. Todd, come to the temple at second bell the day after tomorrow."

"Y-Yes, milord!" Todd squealed, kneeling on the spot.

At that sight, Ferdinand's lips slowly curled into a grin. "And now one chef remains..." he muttered.

There were three nobles who wanted a chef, but only two who were up for hire. Someone would be missing out.

"Alright, I'll pay. Send the other chef to our home, Rozemyne."

"Hold it, Karstedt. I'll—"

"Can you really move that much money without any scholars here? I think not," Ferdinand said, giving Sylvester an exasperated look. He apparently needed the permission of scholars before he could make a purchase like that. Doing things as the archduke wasn't quite as easy as it seemed.

"But you'll be paying when the chef arrives, yeah? They don't need the money to be paid right here, right now."

At that, Sylvester and Karstedt started to argue over who would get Hugo, causing every commoner present to tense up. It was clear by Benno's expression that he wanted me to do something about this. I nodded, and suggested that all of the commoners leave the room.

"I will inform you all when Hugo's workplace is decided. Would you all please clear the room for us?"

At my suggestion, every commoner gracefully—yet speedily— exited the room. Hugo, who was caught in the middle of a battle between nobles, had turned ghostly pale. He clutched his stomach and pulled Todd out of the room.

"Rozemyne, why don't you have three chefs?!"

Um... You can't really blame me for this. As I watched Sylvester continue to throw a tantrum, I fell into deep thought. "How about I lend him to whoever plans to buy the most recipes...?"

"Who wouldn't buy all of them?!" Sylvester shouted.

Well, well... Thank you for your business.

Sylvester had probably just blurted that out in the heat of the moment, but I didn't care as long as the recipes got sold.

"Very well, then. While I'm not sure whether you would actually be able to pay for them all due to that scholar business, I will keep your offer in mind, Sylvester. If you are permitted to spend the money, then I will send Hugo to the castle. Father can send his head chef there as well, so that Hugo can then teach both of your chefs. How does that sound?"

"...Acceptable. Be sure to send the chef over as soon as you can."

"Of course. I will bring him with me the day after tomorrow."

And so, Sylvester, Ferdinand, and Karstedt each settled on buying all of my recipes. We wrote out a contract and ironed out the rules of employment, which I took as an opportunity to mention that my chefs had each signed a magic contract that prevented the illicit spread of my recipes.

"If at any point you try to force any information out of my chef, I will take him home with me, and there will be no refunds," I said threateningly, trying to keep Hugo safe among the court chefs in the castle.

How to Gather Donations

Dazzling rays of sunlight poured in through the windows, illuminating a fancy tea party. Several musicians—including Rosina—were playing peaceful music in the room adorned by the season's flowers, as respectable ladies and their fine daughters conversed among themselves.

Today, I was the star. It was my first tea party as the archduke's adopted daughter, and this was an important place for me to earn donations.

"Hello, everyone. It is oh so nice to meet all of you," I said, repeating the line I had memorized while putting on the fake smile that had been drilled into me.

The ladies and girls introduced themselves to me one after another, all wearing similar smiles, but... honestly, there was no chance that I'd remember any of their names.

In order to attract more guests, we had framed the tea party as an opportunity to personally meet the archduke's adopted daughter. And not only were we serving the hippest tea party sweet of the season—pound cake—but also some Swiss rolls that Ella and Hugo had made. These were thin sponge cakes that were slathered with cream and in-season fruits before being rolled up, and had proven to be today's main attraction. Elvira and Florencia smiled brightly as they watched the fine ladies widen their eyes at the treats they had never seen before.

"Rozemyne's chefs made these," they said.

They were speaking the truth, but the gathered ladies all interpreted that as Elvira and Florencia accrediting their own chefs' work to me to establish my place as the archduke's adopted daughter. It was normal for a mother to care about her daughter's position in society, and I wasn't crass enough to correct the ladies' misunderstanding.

"I thank you all ever so much for coming," I said, speaking in what was honestly a pretty robotic voice as Elvira and Florencia addressed the attendees to ask for donations.

"Rozemyne has been starting an entire new industry. We would greatly appreciate your support."

"We are doing all we can to help her."

The fine ladies looked at me with widened eyes, hands placed daintily over their mouths as they gasped in surprise, before smiling and warmly saying that they were impressed to see me working so hard as the archduke's adopted daughter. Judging by the traces of amusement in their voices, I could guess that they assumed I wasn't actually doing anything, and that my parents were just attaching my name onto someone else's work.

"I could hardly refuse a request from Lady Florencia and Lady Elvira. I shall eagerly provide my support."

"I, too, owe much to the both of you."

Each woman who was approached readily made a donation, but not a single person asked me what kind of industry I was starting, nor did anyone ask how their money was going to be used. They were apparently just donating money because Elvira and Florencia had asked them to, and they owed the two women a lot. But even putting that aside, it would no doubt be hard for them to refuse since everyone here was a member of the same faction, and Florencia was the wife of the archduke.

Elvira and Florencia were casually going around and collecting money to show me how noble women earned donations, and I kept up my fake smile as I watched them. Before I knew it, our goal had been reached. That would be enough to complete the one orphanage, but if we were going to be spreading workshops throughout the entire duchy, a single round of donations wouldn't be enough.

But my honest opinion was that I just didn't have what it took to gather money at a noble tea party. I wasn't built to do that kind of work at all.

Brigitte came to my bedside with a troubled look on her face. "Lady Rozemyne, Lord Ferdinand is here," she reported.

I had been bedridden for two days since the tea party, so I was in no condition to accept visitors. In order to enter the northern building at all, one needed the permission of both the archduke and Rihyarda, the head attendant. The fact that Ferdinand was here must have meant that he already had their approval.

"Brigitte, where is Rihyarda?"

"Unfortunately, I could not find her."

Under normal circumstances, it was the duty of attendants to deal with visitors, not guards, but Rihyarda was nowhere to be found. And since it was Ferdinand, the brother of the archduke, that we were talking about, Brigitte had come to report the situation to me.

"Now now, Brigitte. Why did you leave your post?" Rihyarda said, arriving out of nowhere.

"Rihyarda, I..." Brigitte fell silent, too surprised by the sudden appearance to say anything.

Rihyarda moved her hands from the tea cart she had been pushing and placed them on her hips, a clear sign of an upcoming lecture. I hurriedly called out to stop her.

"Brigitte came to report a visitor to me since you were absent, Rihyarda. She said that Ferdinand is here. Did you prepare that tea for his visit?"

"Why, yes I did. I asked Lord Sylvester to summon him."

Rihyarda had apparently been so anxious about me being bedridden for two days that she had discussed the matter with Sylvester directly, who ended up directing Ferdinand to bring me a potion. I had asked her to wait another day, but she had apparently lost patience.

Two days of rest had already been enough to help me feel a lot better, so I was sure that another day would probably do the trick. But since the potion didn't taste as bad as it used to, I was more than happy to drink it and get my recovery over and done with.

Rihyarda stripped off my bed garments and dressed me in some casual indoor clothing. They were loose clothes that I could even sleep in if necessary.

"That should do it. Brigitte, let Ferdinand in."

Once Rihyarda had prepared the room for visitors and welcomed Ferdinand inside, we saw that he was accompanied by Elvira and Florencia for some reason.

"Oh my, Lady Elvira! And Lady Florencia! What brings you both here?" Rihyarda asked.

"I was planning on visiting Rozemyne after seeing Lady Florencia today, but we just happened to see you summon Lord Ferdinand," Elvira said. She had apparently wanted to check up on me since I had fallen ill right after the tea party, but I had no doubts that her actual goal here was to spend time with Ferdinand. "You truly are quite sickly, Rozemyne. I never would have thought that you would end up catching a fever after something as small as a tea party."

While her words were genuine enough, they were slightly undermined by the fact that her eyes were locked on Ferdinand and her voice was trembling a little with excitement. It was good to see her having fun, at least.

Rihyarda offered the guests seats, then pulled a chair over for me. The attendants must have been informed that Ferdinand would be arriving, and the young women who had been adjusting their makeup and clothes returned out of nowhere to make tea. It was funny, in a way, but I would have preferred them not all coming in at once and leaving the door unattended. If Ottilie hadn't been on break today, she definitely would have gotten angry with them.

"I heard you collapsed after the tea party," Ferdinand said, eyeing me carefully.

I nodded and took a sip of my tea, signifying that others could too.

While the tea party itself had been a pretty short event, it had taken several days of preparation to set up. Elvira and Florencia had only held it so that they could teach me how to gather donations, so I had spent most of my time just watching them, but that meant I also had to be present to witness everything that went into the preparations.

"I think I did a good job, all things considered. I made it through the entire tea party without collapsing. Why, is it just me, or have I gotten a lot stronger?"

"No, I do not believe the word 'strong' suits you in the least," Ferdinand disagreed. It seemed that I was the only one who felt that way, as nobody else praised my growth at all. Ferdinand was even giving me an exasperated look. "If you are so weak that a mere tea party is too much for you, how can you ever hope to socialize at all?"

"Now now, Lord Ferdinand—this is not a matter that is up for debate. As a noblewoman she must participate in social events, no matter what," Elvira said. Ferdinand had intended to just give me the potion and leave, but she was keeping him in place; he wasn't getting away any time soon.

"Lord Ferdinand, how do you suggest we enable Rozemyne to socialize despite her poor health? I think she will need to gather yet more donations in the future, if she is to help the archduke with this new, budding industry."

Our donation drive had been a success this time, but that was entirely thanks to Elvira and Florencia. The fact that she was indirectly suggesting I would be doing it on my own in the future was kind of a problem.

"I find it hard to rely on the goodwill of others. This donation drive went well since those ladies all trusted you and have known you both for a long time. I don't have anything like that."

"Relationships and trust are something you will have to build starting now."

Apparently, it was standard practice for noblewomen to donate money to each other. They would say things like, "I owe you for all you've done for me," or, "I owe you since you donated to me in the past." If that was how things worked here, then I had no choice but to adjust.

"Indeed. Of course, I would like to build trust with everyone, but considering how quickly the printing industry will be expanding, I would end up doing nothing but asking for money day in and day out. There is nothing that I can give them in return."

"Then what do you intend to do? You need this money, don't you?" Florencia asked with a surprised look.

Tea parties and the like were apparently the only means through which donations were gathered here. I suggested that I carry a donation box and wander around the castle, but my idea was immediately rejected; a request from me would essentially be an order given my status. Donations needed to be given based on goodwill, so those you asked needed to have the capacity to say no.

"I need something else... Some way to make people happily give me money. And I would like for that method to be related to the printing industry. I don't want people to give me money out of goodwill, I want them to give money to the printing industry itself."

The phrase "public company" flashed through my mind, but I wasn't familiar enough with economics to build one of those from the ground up. Besides, I didn't want people to invest in stocks; I just wanted a convenient way to get money out of them. After a moment of thought, I remembered the bazaar that my preschool had used to hold for fun.

"I have an idea. What about a (bazaar)? It's a place where you can bring things you don't need and sell them for cheap."

"But are there many things we own that we do not need? Anything that your family doesn't need is simply handed down to your servants, no?" Florencia asked, having no idea what I was talking about.

I put my head in my hands. Yet again, our upbringings had been way too different. I had been raised in the consumerist society of Japan, but the culture here was to keep using something until it broke for good. If there was something that you didn't need, then you just didn't buy it in the first place. Even nobles used hand-me-downs since children grew so fast—any ripped clothing would simply be repaired, or given to attendants or lesser families when they truly weren't needed anymore. Most households had very little that they didn't need.

"Mm... What about a (charity concert), then?"

"What might that be?" Florencia asked with a puzzled hand on her cheek. "I've never heard the phrase before."

"It's a public music performance, and the money earned is all donated. Ferdinand, would you be so kind as to play several harspiel songs for me?"

Judging by how fervently passionate the women had been during the baptism ceremony, it was a safe bet to say that the tickets would sell like hot cakes, not to mention that I could also sell printed goods to make some extra money. Merchandise would have to wait a bit, though, since photos weren't a thing in this world. We hadn't even finished multicolored printing yet.

"Why must I play the harspiel?" Ferdinand asked.

"Because you're the best harspiel player I know," I replied. I was trying to hide my true intentions, but could tell that he'd seen right through me. His brow furrowed in an utterly disinterested grimace.

"No. I have no reason to help you here; there is nothing that I gain from this."

"…Figures," I sighed. Ferdinand would never help me out of goodwill. Whenever he did something kind, it was probably part of some manipulative plot.

I was ready to give up then and there, but there was a sparkle in Elvira's eyes. She gave me a firm look, and ordered that I make the concert happen, no matter the cost.

Uh-oh. It looks like my small, seemingly harmless idea has created a monster.

As Elvira glared at me with a smile, I desperately racked my brain to come up with something. How could I make this work to Ferdinand's benefit? What was he interested in? Sadly, he was an expert of all trades who generally had everything he wanted, so nothing came to mind. Up until now, there had only been two things I owned that Ferdinand wanted.

"Ferdinand, I'll give you new songs if you promise to play them at the concert."

Ferdinand cocked an eyebrow. I had caught his interest, but it wasn't enough to get him involved in the concert… which meant I had to bait him with recipes, too.

"Erm, I will also provide you with recipes that I haven't even taught Ella."

He averted his eyes. It was a sign that he was tempted enough that he needed to look away to maintain his strength of will. One more push would probably make him fold, but, unfortunately, I couldn't think of anything else.

Still, I could feel immense pressure coming from Elvira as she silently signaled for me to finish Ferdinand off. But no matter how hard I thought, I couldn't think of anything else that would move him. He usually had me in the palm of his hand, but trying to manipulate him back was just beyond me. All I could do was shake my head.

"…I can't think of anything else."

"Then this discussion is over," Ferdinand said with some relief.

I could see Elvira trembling in shock. I hung my head, wanting nothing more than to apologize for failing so hard, when someone stepped forward from beside me.

"Listen here, boy! This discussion is *not* over!"

It was Rihyarda, standing with her hands on her hips and her head held high. Her lecture mode was fully engaged.

"Goodness, Ferdinand! Do you have no heart? Milady has only just recovered from days of illness, and you're turning down her one request?"

"But Rihyarda, I—"

"Milady did everything she could for you, did she not? She even offered you things that you want, my boy—not just any old rubbish. I can see right through you."

Rihyarda exploded in a lecture, giving Ferdinand no room to interject. He glanced around at everyone seated at the table, then shut his eyes tightly in despair. Elvira's eyes were gleaming with excitement; Florencia was observing the rare sight that was Ferdinand being scolded with great interest; and I was watching with my mouth wide open, overwhelmed by the sheer force of nature that was Rihyarda. Nobody could stop her.

"Don't be stingy, my boy. At least play a few harspiel songs for her."

"Rihyarda, I—"

"This is Rozemyne's own industry, backed by Lord Sylvester himself! What are you here for if not to support milady in her times of need?! Lord Sylvester won't hesitate to load even a young girl like her with work that she can't do on her own."

She knew him well, as expected of Sylvester's wet nurse. Ferdinand, unable to deny that, frowned and let out a deep sigh.

"Your answer, boy?!"

"...I shall play the songs."

"Good."

Thanks to Rihyarda's overwhelming victory, the charity concert had been set in motion.

"Do not expect me to do anything but play harspiel," Ferdinand said spitefully before leaving. Once he was gone, Elvira could finally drop her fine lady façade, and emotions exploded onto her face.

"Rozemyne, when will we be holding the concert?" she said, her dark-brown eyes shining as she leaned forward with an eager smile.

"You truly are fond of Ferdinand, aren't you?" Florencia asked.

"Oh, and are you not?"

"What I feel for him is largely companionship as someone who has also suffered the abuse of Veronica, but I must admit that he is quite the handsome man."

The two giggled while starting to formulate their plans, which reminded me that there was stuff in the temple that needed doing. "There will be the coming of age ceremony at the end of summer and the baptism ceremony at the beginning of autumn, and I will need to leave for the Harvest Festival. It's also possible that the Knight's Order will request aid around the end of autumn. So, while it will be rushing things a bit, I think we should hold the concert during the summer," I said, while mainly thinking that I wanted to save up money before winter preparations started.

And, most importantly of all, I could imagine Ferdinand coming up with all sorts of excuses to get out of playing when things got busy.

"In that case, we must hurry and prepare the invitations as soon as possible," Elvira said.

"Not invitations, Mother. Please prepare (tickets) and sell them for a proper price."

We were going out of our way to hold a concert, after all; it would be a waste not to sell tickets and make a profit off of them. It seemed that tickets weren't a thing here, though, as Elvira gave me a confused look.

"Rozemyne, what is a ticket?"

"It's similar to an invitation in that you need one to attend the concert, but it has a specific seat assigned to it, and one must pay to have one," I said, taking out a pen and ink from my desk to draw a map showing how the concert might look. "There were twenty-two women at the tea party, so I predict that we will have thirty participants. That means we'll need about five round tables. Ferdinand can play here. Where would you like to sit, Mother?"

"Where else but here?" Elvira tapped the center front-row seat; the expression on her face made it clear that she wouldn't give it up for anyone.

"A reasonable choice. And that is why the front-row seats will be expensive, while the ones further back will be less expensive."

"Oh? Visitors won't be seated based on their status?" Florencia asked, her indigo eyes blinking in surprise.

"Since this is a concert providing a chance to see Ferdinand play rather than a tea party, I do not think there is any need to uphold such strict social standards. Some will just want to enjoy the concert with others, listening to the harspiel, so those not interested in Ferdinand may want to buy a cheaper seat to save money."

"In that case, I will buy a cheaper ticket myself, and leave the more expensive seats to those who wish to see Ferdinand up close. That will make it easier for others to buy the cheap tickets as well, no?" Florencia asked with a refined giggle while looking at Elvira.

Normally, as the archduke's wife, Florencia would take the best seat. But if she showed through action that there was no pressure to buy the most expensive tickets, then others would gladly follow her example.

"Beyond that... what if you sell the tickets to people in order of status and ask where they want to sit? If you do that, I don't think there will be many complaints at all."

"Letting them decide on their own, Rozemyne? I fear that Sylvester has already corrupted you," Florencia said, peering at me with an incredibly worried look on her face.

...I'm sorry, Florencia. I've always been like this. You have a daughter who's lazy at heart now.

We moved on to pricing the tickets. The best seat—which had already been sold—would cost one small gold, while everything else would range from five to eight large silvers.

"I suggest the tea and sweets we serve be Lord Ferdinand's favorites," Elvira suggested, her voice bright from having secured the best seat. My idea of a concert differed from how nobles viewed music recitals here, so I decided it would be best to let Elvira handle these details. All I needed to do was inject a little business acumen into matters.

Merchandise would sell the best during the concert, and while I couldn't prepare any right away, I could have Ella and Hugo teach the court chefs how to make the cookies that Ferdinand liked the most, then have them mass produced.

"If we are going to be preparing sweets, I suggest we make extra and sell them after the concert as souvenirs to take home. I imagine those moved by Ferdinand's harspiel playing will be driven to buy them."

"Oh, I shall certainly buy one!" Elvira declared.

And so I already had one guaranteed customer. I had no doubts that there would be plenty more ready and waiting.

Once Florencia had decided on which room the concert would be held in, Elvira drew out the floor plan and made a chart detailing the seats.

"Please be sure to write who bought which ticket and where they will be sitting on the seating chart. That will minimize any chance of confusion on the day of the concert."

I explained that there were all sorts of problems that could occur, like tickets being lost or stolen, and Elvira nodded in understanding before firmly writing her name on the seating chart.

"Speaking of which, Rozemyne—you said that you wished to involve the printing industry in this concert. How do you intend to do that?" Florencia asked, having maintained a cool and observant head while we discussed the tickets, in sharp contrast to Elvira, who had completely given in to her excitement.

"You may leave that to me. I will work my absolute hardest to show everyone how wonderful printing can be."

...I'll have Wilma draw an illustration of Ferdinand and make it the front cover of the program. That way, I'll have the best marketing for printing that anyone could ask for. Eheheh.

My First Magic Training Regimen

"You may entrust the tickets to me," Elvira said, seemingly more invested in this than anyone. She seemed so motivated that I decided to let her and Florencia take care of the floor plan, invite the customers, prepare the sweets, and all other such matters by themselves.

"Elvira, please calm down. You won't be able to make the tickets unless we decide on a date first, no?"

"Yes, but, Lady Florencia, don't you want to hold this concert as soon as possible?" Elvira clasped her hands tightly, clearly wanting to hold the concert tomorrow if she could, while Florencia put a worried hand on her cheek and gave a small smile.

"I would like more time to prepare. This is not something we can allow to fail, is it?"

It seemed that Florencia wanted extra time to prepare since this was her first time holding a concert with tickets that cost money, and where things were being sold afterward. I was in full agreement with her. The more time to prepare, the better. Especially since I not only had to prepare the program, but also needed to provide Ferdinand new songs and recipes, with all the grueling work that entailed.

I would be safe while I was in the castle, but as soon as I returned to the temple, I had a feeling that Ferdinand would vent his frustration at being dominated by Rihyarda onto me. The more time we spent away from the temple preparing the concert, the more likely it was that his anger would fade.

...Hm? But wait... Since Ferdinand has such a good memory, is he the type of person who'd cling to ancient slights forever, holding grudges that only increase in wrathful intensity over time? Is going back now or later the better call here?

As I mulled things over, Florencia took her shining wand and chanted "*ordonnanz*," turning the feystone in her ring into a white communication bird. "We will hold the concert in one month's time. Please provide an alternate date if this inconveniences you," she said, before swiping her wand and sending the ordonnanz flying away. It went right through the wall and disappeared, just like I had seen it do many times by now.

It returned not long later, settling on a table and speaking in Ferdinand's voice. "One month from now will be fine. And my apologies, but please inform Rozemyne that her magic training will begin tomorrow. Her health should be fine if she drinks a potion beforehand," it said three times in a somewhat chilly voice before turning back into a feystone.

Was I the only one who felt a chill run down their spine and broke out in a cold sweat from that tone of voice?

"...Mothers, is it just me, or did Ferdinand seem exceptionally angry?"

"He certainly did not seem very pleased to me," Florencia said observantly.

"I-It was a very invigorating tone of voice," Elvira added. That was technically praise, but I could see her smile faltering a bit.

"I think it would be more accurate to say that it was a tone of voice chilling enough to freeze one's blood, Mother."

I drank the potion as instructed, and was fully recovered the next day. I was a bit worried about Ferdinand being so angry, but "magic training" had a nice ring to it. What was he going to teach me? Maybe he would let me read the magic books he had kept me away from all that time ago.

...There sure are a lot of books that I haven't read yet. I wonder if there's a magic textbook, like... "Fundamentals of Magic," or something...? Oh! Is this finally my opportunity to finish the Myne Decimal System?!

After remembering how I had struggled to categorize magic books in the past, I was more excited than ever for Ferdinand to arrive.

"Norbert has sent word that Ferdinand is here, milady," Rihyarda said. "Let's go to the waiting room."

At her guidance, my four guard knights and I traveled to a waiting room in the main building of the castle. It was a bit saddening that, when surrounded by four guards, I was completely buried in their midst.

"Good morning, Rozemyne." Ferdinand was sitting expressionlessly in the waiting room, his voice completely devoid of emotion. It was hard to tell whether he was mad or not, but the second I saw the stack of books in front of him, I ceased to care.

"Good morning, Ferdinand. Are those books for me?"

"Indeed they are."

...Yes, yes, yes! New books! All for me!

I cheered and did a small dance of glee on the inside, shaking pretend maracas with reckless abandon, but all I did in real life was look at the books with a smile. The fact that I hadn't just leapt at them goes to show how impressive noble training really was.

Cornelius and Angelica both let out groans behind me, the displeasure evident in their tones. It seemed that neither of them were avid readers.

What a waste.

"Rihyarda, bring these books to her room. We'll be off. Come, Rozemyne."

"As you wish, my boy."

I had been excitedly preparing to learn the fundamentals by reading books, only to have them so suddenly taken from me. I blinked in disbelief, and as Rihyarda left with the books, all I could do was sadly watch.

"...Where are we going?"

"Somewhere you can release your mana without issue."

Ferdinand made his highbeast appear on the balcony, and Brigitte did the same with hers. I would be riding with Brigitte since it was likely that Angelica wouldn't be able to support the weight of us both.

"Ow!"

As Brigitte picked me up to put me on her highbeast, my head bonked her metal breastplate. Knights didn't normally wear the full plate armor I had seen during the trombe extermination, instead opting for something more lightweight. They wore what was essentially a dress woven out of metal thread imbued with mana, with plate armor attached to the chest, hands, and from the knees down to the shins. Since Brigitte was a woman and her breastplate protruded more than Ferdinand's, it kept bumping against my head while I was sitting down.

"Forgive me, Lady Rozemyne," Brigitte said, before rubbing a hand over her breastplate. "It shouldn't hurt if I do this." The plate twisted and changed in an instant, no longer feeling hard and painful. Now it was nice and soft, like I was being enveloped in warmth. In fact, it was so nice and soft that I almost wanted to press my head into it to enjoy the feeling even more.

Brigitte had quite a confident and heroic look on her face when she had said she would fix it so, for her sake, I didn't point out that I could absolutely feel her boobs. I hadn't really noticed it before now due to her breastplate, but Brigitte actually had a pretty big chest.

...I see you there, Cornelius. I know you're of a spry young age, dear brother, but don't stare at us all slack-jawed. Learn from Damuel and politely avert your gaze.

Brigitte flew us to a tall, sizable building some distance away from the castle. Ferdinand had arrived first, and I could see that he was inside already. Brigitte set me down, but as she started to head inside as well, I hurriedly stopped her.

"Brigitte, you can return your breastplate to normal now."

"Oh yes, that's right." Having seemingly forgotten about it entirely, Brigitte touched her breastplate and reformed it to rigid metal again. I nodded in relief, then followed her inside, where we found a large white room that was completely empty.

"What kind of place is this?" I asked, the echo of my voice immediately making me jump.

"A building designed for knights to be able to practice fighting with large amounts of mana," Ferdinand responded. "It's built so that mana won't leak outside. I will teach Rozemyne how to wield her mana, so you all may train elsewhere. Especially you, Damuel. I hear that you are still in your growing period, and your amount of mana is increasing. Increase it as much as you can before it stops."

The knights gave sharp salutes, then moved to the other side of the building to begin training. I watched on with great interest to see what their training was like, but Ferdinand just poked my head.

"Ow!"

"Stay focused," he said. The look in his eyes was terrifying. Rihyarda wasn't here, and the knights were training elsewhere, meaning there was nobody here to take my side or protect me. I was alone with the enemy. The best thing I could do was try not to make him any angrier than he already was.

"Benno is busy with the monastery, no? I thought now would be a good opportunity to teach you magic. Children are normally not taught how to use magic prior to going to the Royal Academy, but you have already taught yourself how to direct the flow of your mana. I will be your teacher so that you might have some proper knowledge on the subject," he said. But despite how reasonable that sounded, the irritated look in his eyes all but confirmed that this was him getting back at me for the harspiel concert. "As you are not a student of the Royal Academy, you do not have a schtappe."

"Ferdinand, question—what's a schtappe?"

"This," Ferdinand said, whipping his arm and procuring a shining wand from seemingly nowhere.

I nodded, making a mental note that the shining wand that all students of the Royal Academy had was officially called a schtappe.

"Through possession of a schtappe, you will be able to control your mana more efficiently. But that isn't to say that you need one to control mana. I will first teach you to make a highbeast out of a feystone and ride it," Ferdinand said while putting on a thin leather glove. Then, he took out a clear, fist-sized feystone from the pouch on his belt. It was a feystone specifically made for turning into a highbeast, and was apparently the same kind of feystone as the ones that were in knights' gauntlets or kept on the belts of nobles.

"Give the feystone mana and morph it into the shape of an animal. You must then move it according to your will and fly through the air. There may be a trombe extermination in the autumn, and given that you cannot ride lower city carriages for extended periods of time, you would do well to learn this before we must leave for the Harvest Festival and Spring Prayer. Most importantly of all, you must learn the techniques necessary to harvest the ingredients you need. They will not be located in places that you can reach on your own without a highbeast," Ferdinand explained as he plopped the feystone into my hand.

I wrapped both of my hands around the feystone so as to not drop it, but instantly felt it start sucking out my mana. It was draining me so quickly that it was scary, so I hurriedly unlocked the box of mana I kept compressed inside of me.

"Ferdinand, it's stealing my mana at a really fast rate…"

"That is not a problem. You must first dye the feystone with your mana. This is necessary for it to move according to your will."

"What about the rings you've been lending me?! Those used my mana, but they didn't drain me like this!" I squeaked, still clasping the feystone with both hands, but Ferdinand just shook his head.

"Using feystones is not the same as using magic tools. I will explain the precise details later; the difference does not matter to you right now. And once again, I am reminded of just how much mana you truly have. The dyeing process is happening very quickly."

Ferdinand explained that a layknight with a low amount of mana had to pour so much into the feystone that it made them sick, and that it would sometimes take them days to fill the feystone completely. He also mentioned that dyeing a feystone with your own mana would make it so others couldn't use it—or rather, it would make it much harder for them. Those who had the same color of mana could use it, but the difference between using somebody else's feystone and using one dyed with your own mana was like the difference between mud and water.

As Ferdinand came to the end of his explanation, the feystone pulsed with light a single time, indicating that it had now been dyed with my mana.

"Now that the feystone has been dyed, you will begin training to change its shape. That should not take long, considering that you are already familiar with controlling mana. First, pour your mana into it, then imagine it swelling while using mana to change the stone's shape. You must eventually learn to change its shape at will, but for now, just changing the size will do."

I did as Ferdinand said, rubbing my fingers over the feystone and gradually pouring my mana into it. As I did so, I imagined the feystone swelling. I had assumed it would be tough to do, but the feystone easily swelled up just as I had imagined.

"Wow, it grew! It's like a (balloon)!" I exclaimed. The feystone had started at about the size of my fist, but was now as big as a softball.

"Continue pouring your mana into it as you set it on the ground, then try to maintain that flow even once you've removed your hand. Once you can do that, we will move on to morphing it into a particular shape."

"Okay."

I squatted down and set the feystone on the ground, removing my fingers one by one to slowly minimize the contact between us. I was worried that the flow of mana would cut off as soon as I stopped touching it, so I widened the metaphorical pipe to pour more mana in as I pulled my last finger away.

I couldn't see the mana flowing into the feystone, but I could feel it.

"Impressive," Ferdinand murmured as he looked down at the slowly growing feystone. It had gone from a softball, to a dodgeball, and then to a beach ball, which was making me increasingly nervous.

This won't burst, right? It's really going to be okay?

"Ferdinand, question—how long will this keep growing?"

"Until you cut off your mana or lock its shape. It needs to be large enough for you to ride on, so continue to make it bigger."

"Whew." I let out a sigh of relief and turned around to look up at Ferdinand. "So, unlike a (balloon), it won't suddenly burst—" But before I could finish my sentence, I heard the sound of cracking stone.

"You fool!" Ferdinand barked, before sweeping his cape around me. A second later, I heard a loud bang. It sounded exactly as I had imagined an exploding feystone balloon would. Small fragments clattered noisily against Ferdinand's cape, then made small clinking noises like pieces of glass as they fell to the ground.

"I believe I explained that the feystone would change according to your thoughts. Why in the world, then, would you imagine it bursting?! Of course the feystone would explode if you imagined that while you were changing its shape, you fool!"

"I'm sorry! I'm sorry!"

"Good grief. A valuable feystone, shattered into tiny pieces..." Ferdinand sighed, clearly exhausted.

I paled, only then remembering that feystones were valuable and expensive. This wasn't good. The feystone fragments were easy to find on the pure white ground, so I hurriedly started gathering them together. Once I had a few, I poured my mana into them and chanted, "Clay, clay, stick together. Be a sphere!" As commanded, the feystone softened like clay in my hands, allowing me to roll it all together in a ball.

"What are you doing? A shattered feystone will not come back together. We have no choice but to turn the fragments into powder and make a magic tool," Ferdinand said while looking down at me with exasperation, but I could feel the feystone fragments changing shape in my hands.

"It's fine. All I need to do is make the fragments like clay and they'll stick back together. See?"

I showed him the balled up feystone in my hand, and Ferdinand looked between it and me several times with an expression of complete and utter shock. He then took the feystone from me and examined it under the light for a moment, before eventually rubbing his temples.

"This simply does not make any sense…"

"What doesn't?"

"Never mind. Gather all of the fragments. Once you have done that, today's training will be over." Ferdinand waved a hand dismissively as if telling me to do whatever I wanted, then started massaging his temples again.

I gave an energetic nod, then started gathering the remaining fragments that were still scattered on the ground. I stuck each one into the increasingly large feystone ball while I worked, and, once I had enough, I poured more mana into it so that I could shape it all back into a smooth ball.

After a while of squatting and rolling around, I had picked up every fragment, but my legs were so numb that I couldn't even stand.

"It would be disastrous if you lost control of your mana without first understanding how to properly use it, so do not practice controlling mana on your own," Ferdinand told me the second we returned to my room.

Having just caused a feystone to burst, I hung my head and listened quietly. The very thought of making something explode here and hurting someone was so terrifying that I wasn't even considering practicing on my own.

"Good," Ferdinand replied, sensing my understanding. He then began stacking the magic-related books he had brought onto the table. "These are books from the castle's book room. They all concern the fundamentals of magic."

"Yaaay! I thank you ever so much," I said. But the moment I reached for the books, Ferdinand blocked my hand.

"Rihyarda, Rozemyne has a bad habit of completely losing sight of the world around her once she begins reading. She usually does not even respond when called. Observe her carefully and ensure that she maintains a proper lifestyle."

"Oh yes, oh yes. You may count on me, my boy. I am quite used to this."

"Furthermore, she is likely tired from her training today. There is a chance that she might fall ill again," Ferdinand said, glancing my way. The moment he said the words "fall ill again," I noticed Rihyarda's expression harden.

"Well then, milady—the reading can wait for tomorrow. As Ferdinand suggests, you must be tired from your first time practicing magic. You'll catch a fever if you don't get in bed early today."

"Um, wait... Rihyarda, I..."

The stack of books was being put away before my very eyes. I reached out to grab one, only for Rihyarda to slap away my hand and scold me.

"Oh yes, and I nearly forgot—Rozemyne, come to the temple tomorrow. I must receive those songs and recipes you promised me," Ferdinand said, grinning at the sight of me being scolded.

This is revenge! This is Ferdinand getting revenge for the harspiel concert! Seriously, how bad of a person do you have to be to put a stack of books I've never read before in front of me, then add more work to my schedule and order Rihyarda to carefully watch over me so I can't read them? Pretty bad, if you ask me.

"You're awful, Ferdinand!"

"Rihyarda and I are simply worried about your health. There is nothing awful about this at all," he said. Ferdinand was definitely just being spiteful; anyone could tell how smug he was. I glared at him, and he just sneered at me.

Okay, now I'm angry! If you're going to play dirty, Ferdinand, then so am I!

My plan had been for Wilma's illustration on the program to be a black-and-white cutout printing like the ones we had in our picture books, displaying an image of someone playing a harspiel. At most, someone might have been able to tell it was Ferdinand based on the hairstyle. I had wanted Elvira and the others to enjoy the idea more than anything else.

But I wasn't going to hold back anymore. The gloves were off. Copyrights for likenesses didn't exist in this world, and that meant there was nothing stopping me from going all out.

I'm gonna have the wax stencils finished this month, no matter what! I'll have Wilma draw a super detailed, super pretty picture of Ferdinand, then use mimeograph printing to stick it on every single program. And I'll make sure it's as detailed as possible!

Working Toward Wax Stencils

Despite living in the castle, the only time I saw my adoptive family (aside from when I was summoned by them) was during dinner. We ate breakfast in our own rooms, and during lunch Sylvester and Florencia would usually go to meetings that I wasn't allowed to attend. As a result, dinnertime was my one opportunity to talk to them.

"Sylvester, I will be returning to the temple tomorrow and shall remain there for about a month."

"...Why's that? Isn't the eatery done now?" Sylvester asked with a piercing gaze. It wasn't hard to tell that his deep-green eyes were searching for something fun to do.

"In order to improve printing technology, I will need to frequently meet and discuss matters with those building the tools. I will immediately return to report our findings whenever a new piece of technology is made."

Sylvester put on a regal expression and nodded, but I was sure that he'd make up some random excuse to come and "observe" me regardless.

"Sylvester, if you elect to come and observe the process, please do not fail to inform me ahead of time."

"I know, I know," Sylvester replied. I swallowed the urge to say that he definitely didn't know, and instead just finished eating.

Once we had said goodnight, we headed back to our rooms. For Wilfried and I, that meant heading to the northern building together.

"No fair, Rozemyne." Wilfried had looked sullen all through dinner, and was now glaring at me with his deep-green eyes that really resembled Sylvester's. But I wasn't sure what he was calling unfair.

"...What's not fair, might I ask?"

"I'm saying it's no fair, which means it's no fair!" he exclaimed. It was so far from an actual answer that I had no idea what he was trying to say.

I looked up at Lamprecht, confused, but he just gave me an uncomfortable frown. It seemed that now was a bad time for him to explain.

As soon as we arrived at the northern building, I started climbing the stairs to my room. "My sincerest apologies, Wilfried. I will be away for the following month, and I hope that you find peace in my absence. Good night."

Wilfried angrily shouted "You don't get it at all!" from the floor below, but I ignored him; I had things that needed doing.

Once in my room, I headed to my desk, grabbed a piece of paper, and started writing down everything I needed to finish while I was staying at the temple. Then, I listed everything that I needed to bring with me.

"Guuuh... I wish I had my diptych. This is such a waste of paper."

My own diptych had been returned to my family as part of Myne's belongings. Lutz mentioned that Tuuli was using it now. But even if I did have a diptych on me, it was hard to imagine that anyone here would let me use what was essentially an unadorned block of wood. Considering that it could have just been disposed of as something unfit for the archduke's adopted daughter, I was lucky that Tuuli had been given it at all... but I still wished that I had one myself.

...I know he's busy so this'll probably annoy him, but I'll ask Benno to order one for me.

With that decision made, my eyes fell on the cabinet that Rihyarda had put the books from Ferdinand in. It hurt so much knowing that I had new books so close to me but couldn't read them.

As I continued to stare at them regretfully, Rihyarda cleared her throat. "Please rest for today, milady."

Fine, fine. But I'm waking up early tomorrow so I can start reading.

The next day, I did indeed wake up early in the morning. But when I tried to get a book, I found that the cabinet wouldn't open. It was locked.

I ended up having to painfully wait for Rihyarda to come, and when she eventually did, she scolded me for not getting enough rest. And, to make matters worse, she sent me off to the temple as soon as I had finished breakfast. Her reasoning? "If you start reading, milady, you'll forget about your promises. Ferdinand told me that."

...Curse you, Ferdinand!

With pursed lips and dark feelings stirring in my heart, I got into my carriage and headed to the temple. Brigitte and Damuel were accompanying me, so even though we weren't in the same carriage, I was with my usual squad.

"Welcome back, Lady Rozemyne," Fran said on our arrival.

"It is good to see you, Fran," I replied as we made our way to the High Bishop's chambers.

"I was told that you would be staying in the castle for some time, so I was quite surprised yesterday when the High Priest informed me that you would be returning."

"I was surprised too when he instructed me to return," I said bitterly, my frustration at being summoned back without getting so much as a chance to read growing fiercer with each passing moment. The stack of books Ferdinand had given me belonged to the castle's book room, and as taking them outside the castle was forbidden, I would only get to read them when I returned. In other words, I was being denied books for an entire month.

"Lady Rozemyne, you appear to be quite upset. Has something happened?"

"Ferdinand is standing between me and my books; he forced me to come back before I even had a chance to start reading them. He must have a truly fierce need for those compositions and recipes," I said angrily, causing Fran to widen his eyes in surprise.

"...Is that so? He instructed me to contact the Gilberta Company since you had finished gathering donations. I believe they should be arriving soon," Fran said, throwing me off entirely. I had certainly been thinking I should give the money to Benno as quickly as possible since he would need it soon, but I hadn't expected Ferdinand to set up the meeting for us. "Shall we go to the orphanage director's chambers once you are finished changing? Nicola is waiting with sweets prepared."

"Oh, is she? I am quite looking forward to that," I said with a laugh, causing Fran to put a hand on his chest and let out a sigh of relief.

Monika changed my clothes while Fran counted the donation money we had gathered, and once we were done, I headed to the orphanage director's chambers. I inhaled deeply once I was there, feeling more relaxed in a room I was used to, then opened the door to my hidden room.

"Monika, please clean this room and bring in some writing utensils."

"As you wish."

Fran was maintaining a composed expression, but I had noticed him stiffening up a little whenever he was around the hidden room, so I was entrusting Monika with cleaning it and such.

"Fran, where are Gil and Wilma?"

"Gil is at the gate, waiting to welcome the Gilberta Company. Shall I go and summon Wilma so that you may speak to her?"

"I do want to ask Wilma to draw something for me, but it can wait until I've finished talking with Lutz and the others."

Fran began informing me what had happened while I was absent, and, soon enough, Benno and Lutz arrived. There was apparently so much work to do involving the monastery that Mark had decided to stay behind in the store.

"Lutz, Benno—thank you for coming. Follow me. I ask that Gil attend me and Damuel guard me."

We walked into my hidden room, and as soon as the door was closed, I leapt into Lutz's arms. I could guess that he had already seen it coming, as he accepted the hug without a trace of surprise.

"Lutz, Lutz, Lutz! You'll never believe it, but Ferdinand is a huge jerk!"

"...I'm really dang busy right now, y'know?"

"I'm busy, too! I had to hold a tea party to gather donations, and gave so many fake smiles that I ended up bedridden! Then Ferdinand forced me to start magic training because he's mad at me for something that's not my fault, and now he's being a huge bully out of spite! It's really hard for me right now."

Lutz narrowed his eyes. "The High Priest is bullying you? How? What's he doing?"

"He showed me a huge stack of books that I'd never seen before, then gave me so much to do that I didn't even get a chance to touch them. He even got someone to keep an eye on me to make sure I wasn't reading them! Isn't that just cruel?!"

"...Gotta say, I admire his courage. I'd be fearing for my life right now if I were him," Lutz said, shooting me a somewhat nervous glance. He had seen firsthand what kind of rampages I went on when books were taken from me. But his eyes only wavered for a second before he gave me a gentle pat on the head. "You've done a good job holding it in. Yep. I'm proud."

"Actually, I decided that I'm not going to hold it in. I'm so annoyed that I'm going to finish the wax stencils."

"How are those two things even connected?!" Lutz exclaimed. But that wasn't important. What mattered to me right now was finishing the wax stencils and making Ferdinand feel more awkward than he had ever felt in his entire life.

"That doesn't matter. Let's just make them together, okay?" I asked, clinging to Lutz.

That was when Benno's eyes shot open, and he unleashed his thunder on me. "You absolute *idiot!* Don't you know how busy the both of us already are?!"

"I need wax stencils for my scheme! Benno, don't you know how hard it is to gather money in noble society?!" I barked back.

Benno widened his eyes in surprise. His momentum had been completely blown away, and I didn't miss the opportunity to pile it on thick. Not even his thunder would shake my anger at being denied books.

"This is my only opportunity to make this kind of money. Wax stencils will bring in a stupid amount of profit if we can have them ready in time. So, basically, I'm borrowing Lutz for a month," I declared, wrapping my arms around him even tighter.

"Hey, don't decide something like that on your own," Lutz chided, before flicking my forehead. I put my hand over the spot where he'd flicked me and pursed my lips at him.

"You make the things I think up, don't you, Lutz? Are you really okay breaking that tradition?"

"Nah, but…"

"As much as I'd like to lend you Lutz, we've seriously got our hands full. We just don't have the stuff or the money we need," Benno said while scratching his head. The surplus from the Rozemyne Workshop apparently wasn't enough to keep them going anymore, and he had been talking to the guildmaster about how much of the load they would each be carrying.

"Don't worry about money, Benno. I gathered some donations which I'll be giving to you in a bit. It's enough to cover all of the initial costs."

"…Come again?"

Raising money was always the biggest problem for merchants, and that was especially true now given how much money we needed. As such, nobody could blame Benno for looking stunned when I mentioned that I had managed to solve the issue while he wasn't looking.

"Alright, I'll lend you Lutz. It'll be easier to make the orders with the money on hand, and fishing out the materials we need shouldn't be any trouble. If you need his help to raise more money, then have at it," Benno said with gleaming eyes. He had given me permission to use Lutz, and I would use that permission to its fullest.

"By the way—here. Consider this my thanks for connecting me with those nobles. You need one of these, don'tcha?" Benno jutted his chin out while Lutz gingerly took out something rectangular that was wrapped in cloth, which he then held out toward me with a mischievous smile.

"Please accept this gift, milady."

I took a surprised step back, before accepting the bundle from his hands. I then undid the cloth, wondering what the hard square thing inside it was.

"...Wow! A diptych!"

It was an extravagant diptych fit for a noble, ornately carved and polished to a shine with something like varnish. As I excitedly looked it over, Benno gave a laugh.

"I know that Tuuli's using your diptych now and figured you'd need a new one, so yeah, I had this made. We've put the crest of the Rozemyne Workshop on the front, the crest of Lord Karstedt's family on the back, and the crest of the archduke where your name would usually go," Benno explained while pointing at various spots on the diptych.

Lutz then pointed at the metal stylus that was attached to it. "We gave Johann an order to make the same one he made you before, so it should work just like you're used to."

"I really wanted a diptych. Thanks, Benno! And you too, Lutz!"

I giggled as I held the diptych, which was just big enough to fit perfectly into my hands. The joy of being gifted something right when I really needed it brought a natural smile to my face. It felt so nice to know that somebody was thinking about me, and that they knew me so well.

"So, where's that donation money of yours?"

"I entrusted it to Fran, so we'll have to leave the hidden room. I kind of want to recharge a bit more with Lutz, but since he'll be in the temple for a whole month, I guess we can continue this tomorrow. Eheheh."

Thanks to the diptych, my heart was soaring. I stepped out of my hidden room in a great mood, but since Brigitte was there, I still needed to act like a noble when I spoke to Fran.

"Fran, please give the donation money to Benno. Benno, I intend to let my mothers know how this donation money was used, so I ask that you give me a detailed report on how you spend it." The way I saw it, a detailed report that informed donors where their money went might make the next donation drive easier. "That is all the business I have with you, Benno. I imagine that preparing the monastery will be difficult, but I have complete faith in your abilities. Lutz and Gil, I would like to discuss matters of the workshop with you both, so stay here, if you please."

"I am honored," Benno said as he accepted the bag containing over three large golds, before putting it into his pocket and letting Monika escort him out of the temple.

I took a seat at the table. First, I wanted to hear how the wax stencils were progressing in the workshop. "Gil, how is the workshop? Are you making paper thin enough to be used for wax stencils?"

"We can make fairly thin paper using the wood from those growing trees. We tried using normal paper, but it just doesn't work. It will be a challenge unless we can find another kind of wood to use."

Gil mentioned that they could now make fairly thin paper out of trombe wood, but using that would make the stencils unreasonably expensive; the wood was rare and not something we could use so freely. The most ideal option would be to use a tree native to this region, like the volrin tree, but it seemed that volrin wasn't suited for making wax stencils.

In this one case, however, we could still make a profit while using trombe paper since the Ferdinand illustrations would no doubt fetch a high price. I also didn't really mind the increased production cost if it meant we'd be able to finish the wax stencils, so I decided to go ahead and make an experimental stencil using trombe wood.

"Have you had any luck using the iron that Johann made? I suppose that not even changing the type of wax helped to make the layer uniformly thin?"

"Not only does the wax not end up uniform, but when we tried cutting the stencil on top of the file Johann made, the wax cracked and became unusable."

Those cracks were forming either because the wax was too thick or too hard—in other words, I would need to add some kind of tree sap-like resin to soften it.

…What were the ratios for that again? I don't really remember… Either way, I guess it doesn't really matter since the wax and resin of this world will be made of slightly different stuff, especially due to all of the impurities.

"Lady Rozemyne, back when you put wax on the normal stencils to protect Wilma's illustrations, I remember you mentioning that it wouldn't be an issue if the thread from the cloth left an imprint on it. Is that true for wax stencils as well?"

"Absolutely not."

I had used baking paper back in my Urano days, but I couldn't make those here. I couldn't even think of something that could be used as a makeshift replacement. The only thing that came to mind was the wax coating machines that craftsmen used to make wax stencils on Earth: they pulled the paper between two rollers pushed against each other, which created a thin, even layer of wax.

"I think one of those wax coating machines will be necessary here, but… I wonder whether Johann would even be able to make one."

While I could roughly explain the concept, I didn't know enough to be able to draw a detailed blueprint or anything. We'd have to gradually make it through a process of trial and error, but I had no idea whether Johann could manage that given that he always needed detailed blueprints.

"Lutz, I would like to discuss this with Johann. Please call him over tomorrow. For now, I will head to the workshop to confirm whether the paper you have made is acceptably thin."

I stood up, and my two guard knights naturally stepped forward to follow me. But having Damuel and Brigitte come to the workshop with me would cause problems.

"...Could I ask you two to wait here, since there are business secrets at stake?"

"I am afraid not. You must have at least one guard with you at all times, Lady Rozemyne."

Unable to argue with Brigitte, I looked between her and Damuel. "In that case, I must ask that only Damuel accompany me. I have much to blackmail him with, and thus imagine that I would be able to silence him no matter what he sees."

"...Lady Rozemyne, do you not trust me?" Brigitte asked harshly, looking at me with a stiff frown.

I closed my eyes. "I appreciate that you are willing to accompany me, even to the lower city that all nobles consider unbearably foul, and so far you have served me well and true. But this is a separate issue."

Brigitte gave me a confused look; it seemed that she wasn't following me in the least. I knew how she felt about her family, and I did want to help her however I could, but this was a business matter. And considering how many obligations nobles had, I couldn't give them information this valuable for free.

"I do trust you, but you are directly connected with a landowning giebe. It is still beyond me to say whether you would be able to keep valuable information a secret from your family once it is in your possession. Damuel, on the other hand, is not from a family that owns land. And since his family lives in the Noble's Quarter, it will be much easier for me to control him if need be."

"...Understood." Brigitte looked at me with newfound fear in her eyes, then shot Damuel a sympathetic glance.

"Lady Rozemyne, when you say that you have much to blackmail me with, what might you be referring to?" Damuel asked.

"Ahaha. I shall keep that a secret for now."

With the now trembling Damuel as my guard, I headed to the workshop with Lutz and Gil, where the gray priests and children were making paper as usual.

"Continue your work, everyone. Pay me no mind," I said, before having Gil bring me the thinly made trombe paper so that I could examine it. As expected, trombe paper was a league above everything else; it felt so much better than volrin.

"There's such a huge difference in quality... Oh well. We might as well give it a try anyway."

As I looked over at the taue fruit stacked in one corner of the workshop, Lutz shot a glance at Damuel. "Are you sure this is a good idea?"

In all honesty, I wasn't. The fewer people who knew this secret, the better. But as I needed to have at least one guard with me at all times, Damuel was our safest bet through the process of elimination.

"Damuel, you must not speak of what you see here to anyone. Not a single person can know. Not my father, not Ferdinand, and certainly not Sylvester. Can you promise me that?"

Damuel's eyes wavered anxiously.

"If you speak a word of what you see, I might just let my tongue slip, and what a shame it would be if Sylvester learned of something that would make him tease you mercilessly."

"Wh-What? Erm, Aub Ehrenfest himself...?" Damuel asked, wearing a pitiful expression as he thought back to his time as a living sacrifice during Spring Prayer, when he had been teased nonstop by Sylvester.

"You'll keep this a secret, won't you, Damuel?" I asked with a smile.

Damuel gave a pained grimace, as if completely torn up inside. He then shut his eyes tight, knelt down, and crossed his arms over his chest. "I cannot make that promise. As a knight, I cannot keep my silence if ordered to speak by a superior. So... I ask that you allow me to keep my eyes closed." As Damuel couldn't report what he didn't know, he had concluded that the best course of action would be to remain completely ignorant.

I nodded. "In that case, do not leave the workshop under any circumstances. I pray that curiosity does not lead to your ruin."

"Thank you," Damuel replied.

And so, I went outside with Lutz and the others while Damuel and a few gray priests stayed behind inside the workshop.

An Illustration of Ferdinand

Lutz and Gil fetched baskets and blades to cut trombes, then took the children and gray priests to the girls' building as I followed behind.

"Would someone please summon Wilma, Delia, and Dirk from the girls' building?" I asked.

"Yes, yes! I can go!" several children cried out, before they all raced off. It wasn't long before Wilma and Delia, who had Dirk in her arms, came outside. Delia's expression was a little stiff.

"It's good to see you again, Delia. I'm glad you're doing well."

"I appreciate your concern. Dirk and I are doing just fine," Delia replied, offering me a small smile once I had spoken to her.

"Delia, Dirk has the Devouring. His mana was the reason that the toad—ahem—that the count and the High Bishop targeted him. As the count is still alive, Dirk continues to be bound to him in servitude."

The color drained from Delia's face. Count Bindewald was being kept alive so that his crimes could be properly investigated, and so that negotiations could be made with his home duchy of Ahrensbach. Sylvester's priority was making a politically beneficial deal, so it was hard to imagine that nullifying Dirk's contract was something he would even consider. It was safe to assume that Dirk's contract would remain in effect for as long as the count lived.

"Dirk has not been given a magic tool with which he can expel the mana building up inside his body. We must drain some so that it does not overwhelm him. Please have Dirk hold one of these red fruits."

I prompted Gil to give Delia a taue fruit, which she then gave to Dirk. His mana hadn't recovered much since he had been completely drained by the High Bishop back in spring, so the fruit barely grew large enough for the seeds to start bulging out a little.

"He should be fine for some time now. You may take Dirk back inside."

"Hear that? You're all okay now," Delia said to Dirk as she lovingly stroked his head.

Dirk had grown a lot over the past season, which meant that Kamil was probably bigger too. The nostalgia was so strong that I couldn't help but get a little teary-eyed, so I shook my head to drive away any sentimental thoughts.

…Nope, nope. I can't let myself start thinking like that or I'll want to go home again.

Instead, I focused my thoughts on printing. I needed Wilma to draw the program's cover art for me.

"Wilma, I have a request—could you draw an illustration of the High Priest for me?"

"I apologize, but that is beyond me. I have never seen the High Priest's face before," Wilma explained. Because she had a traumatic fear of blue priests, she had looked at Sylvester and Ferdinand as little as possible when they toured the orphanage. As a result, she hadn't gotten a good look at their faces.

I can't believe Wilma doesn't know what Ferdinand looks like! Though I suppose it does make sense, now that I think about it… I thought, paling in terror as my plot crumbled before my very eyes. "I-I shall invite him to my chambers, and you can—"

"I sincerely apologize, but I am still too terrified to even think about going to the noble section of the temple," Wilma said mournfully.

It certainly would be hard for her to go there, given that it was essentially a nest of blue priests, but still—it was hard to imagine that any blue priests would go after one of my attendants now that I was the High Bishop.

"Wilma, would you perhaps feel more comfortable if I stayed with you at all times? That way, nobody would even have a chance to approach you."

"I truly am sorry, Lady Rozemyne... But perhaps you could ask Rosina to sketch his face. I think that I would be able to draw an illustration based on her art," Wilma suggested with a regretful look on her face.

"I'll go and ask Rosina, then!" I exclaimed, now beaming with hope. Shrine maidens trained in art really were something else.

Wilma let out a small giggle, then returned to the orphanage with Delia and Dirk.

"Now then, is everyone ready?" I asked.

"Yes, milady!" Everyone responded in unison, holding their blades for chopping trombes.

I looked over them to confirm that everything was prepared, then Lutz gave a nod, signaling me to take the taue fruit from Gil. It was already half-grown from when Dirk had used it, and the moment I grasped the fruit, I could feel my mana being sucked into it. I watched carefully as the number of seeds increased, bubbling beneath the taue's surface as its skin hardened. Then, once the fruit was full of seeds, it began heating up.

"Here it comes!" I exclaimed, throwing it onto the dirt (without missing this time). Seeds shot in all directions, and I was instantly picked up by a gray priest who hurriedly escorted me behind the others. I observed their epic battle from the sidelines. It was more than apparent that they were more skilled than they had been last year—they were doing their job efficiently and without so much as a stumble.

We turned each of the four taue fruit we had gathered during the Star Festival and left on the workshop's dirt floor into trombes, and by the time we had cut them all down, the baskets we had brought with us were filled to the brim.

I looked over at the kids, who were flushed with satisfaction, and gave them a smile in return. "Now then, please use all of this to make paper. I expect another warm winter ahead of us."

The orphans all gave an enthusiastic "Yes, milady," at which point I decided to leave them to Gil and Lutz so that I could head back to the workshop to retrieve Damuel. When I arrived, I found him aimlessly walking around in circles like a lost puppy.

"Thank you for waiting, Damuel. We will be returning to my chambers now," I said, before heading to the High Bishop's chambers and immediately asking Rosina if she could draw an illustration of Ferdinand.

"Given her fear of men, it does not surprise me that Wilma would have avoided looking at him. But in any case, drawing the High Priest will be no problem at all. He has a very handsome face that is easy to draw," Rosina said with a giggle, elegantly sliding her pen across the paper as she started to draw Ferdinand.

Her art was beyond good. She drew Ferdinand's face from both the front and side, and all it took was a glance to recognize that it was him. Rosina's art was too impressive for someone who had only picked it up on the side.

"Th-This is incredible!" Monika exclaimed, her dark-brown eyes glimmering as she looked closely at Rosina's illustration.

"Monika, please deliver this to Wilma and ask her to draw an illustration of the High Priest."

"As you wish," Monika said, leaving the room with Rosina's sketch hugged close to her chest. A moment later, Fran returned from asking Ferdinand what his plans were.

"What did he say, Fran?"

"It seems he had a sudden visitor."

So you call me over to stop me from reading books, then have the gall to talk to another visitor first? Veeery interesting...

The dark feelings that had been partially dispelled by my meeting with Lutz and being given a diptych started swirling again.

"He said that you may peruse the books locked away in the temple's book room while you wait. Shall we go?" Fran continued.

The mention of locked-away books immediately blew away all of my dark feelings; my main priority here was reading new books. I stood up and gave Fran a smile. "At once! Fran, where might the key to these locked-away books be?"

"Right here."

Accompanied by Fran and my guards, I practically skipped to the book room. If you had asked me what the best part was about living in the High Bishop's chambers, I would answer that it was super close to the book room.

I opened the door to the book room with the key that had now been entrusted to me, then faced the locked bookshelf containing the temple's most valuable books. It was my first time even seeing them. Just what kind of books were stored behind that door, considered so valuable that they were kept separate from the others? Just thinking about it made my heart thump.

I slid the key into the lock, my heart pounding with excitement and nervousness, and the bookshelf door opened with a small click. Five large books were lined up inside, each with an ornately crafted cover.

"I will only need one book today, Fran. Please bring it to the reading table," I requested, eyes gleaming. It was hard for me to carry a big-print, sixty-centimeter-tall book on my own.

"...Lady Rozemyne, it appears that these are not books."

Indeed, the things lined up in the locked bookshelf weren't actually books—rather, they were boxes that had been carved to look like books, and inside of each one was a bunch of folded letters. I picked one up, and immediately noticed it was made of paper that was more like parchment than the plant paper I was making. When I opened it up, I saw that it didn't have the sender's name on it.

"Is this, by chance... a love letter?! Fran, should I really be allowed to read this?"

"Lady Rozemyne, as you are the High Bishop, I believe it is your duty to read the letters and report their contents to the High Priest."

Given where they were hidden, perhaps the letters were from the former High Bishop's lover. There were a lot here.

Oh no, what should I do? Now my heart's really beating fast...

"Well, no point wasting time, then." It seemed that the letters got older the further down into the box you went, so I turned the box over and started reading from the oldest one.

The High Bishop's anonymous girlfriend was apparently a noble girl who had been raised as the successor to her family for her entire life. But then her parents gave birth to a baby boy, and since he had more mana than her, he was selected as their next successor instead. The girl felt as though all of her pride and hard work up until that point had been for nothing, and so her heart was flooded with frustration. Her father predicted that this anger toward her little brother would lead to a civil war of sorts within the family, and so had her married off to a noble in another duchy. With both her mother and father completely absorbed in her little brother, the girl wrote to the High Bishop saying that, "You are the only one I can rely on."

Lady, I think you picked the wrong person to rely on...

It seemed that the girl continued to send letters here on a regular basis, even after she had been married away. Just what did she mean to the previous High Bishop? Given how carefully he was preserving her letters, it was clear she meant a lot to him. Priests couldn't marry, so perhaps he had a hidden crush on her.

I'd always thought he was just a greedy, lustful, perverted old man, but maybe he had an innocent side to him, too. Though that's really hard for me to imagine...

I read through letter after letter, until Monika eventually came to the book room in search of me. Only when Fran tapped me on the shoulder did I look up from reading.

"Lady Rozemyne, Wilma has a request for you," Monika said.

"And what might that be?"

"She would like to see the High Priest in person before drawing him."

Her attitude had done a complete one-eighty since I had last seen her, and while I was glad to hear that Wilma was increasingly working up the courage to come to my chambers, I didn't know how to feel knowing that it was a sketch of Ferdinand that had motivated her.

"...Well, that's fine. I shall go and get Wilma from the orphanage. Ferdinand should be visiting my chambers soon, anyway. Fran, I will be going to the orphanage with Monika, so please return to my chambers to prepare for Ferdinand's visit ahead of time."

When I went to the orphanage to fetch Wilma, she greeted me with an embarrassed smile. "My apologies, Lady Rozemyne. I just couldn't believe my eyes when I saw Rosina's sketch. Never in my life have I seen anyone with such perfect features."

"'Perfect... features'?"

"Yes. I could not imagine a face better suited for art. It is so beautifully composed. Were Sister Christine here, she would wish for him to exist by her side at all times, serving as a muse to observe and inspire her. Do you not feel the same way, Lady Rozemyne?"

Ferdinand apparently had such handsome facial features that Wilma wanted to use him as a model, and the art-loving shrine maiden of yesteryear, Sister Christine, would have wanted to have him with her as much as possible.

I honestly can't empathize at all.

"I do agree that Ferdinand has a handsome face, but he's generally expressionless, and gives off an overall cold impression. At times, I think of him as a moving statue. I much prefer a more living beauty—like what Fran has now that he has started showing a greater variety of expressions. There is much beauty in a peaceful, transparent, and caring expression," I expounded.

When Fran was little, he was probably a cute boy who looked very feminine. He was muscular enough that I didn't normally think about that, but whenever he looked surprised or laughed, he would look a lot younger than he actually was.

"Lady Rozemyne, I believe that is excessive praise for Fran."

"You think so? I won't deny that the High Priest is handsome, but I believe this is a matter of opinion, where different tastes lead to different conclusions. But even so, my attendants are far cooler than the High Priest's, and they are much cuter. That is simply a fact," I said firmly.

"Oh my…" Wilma and Monika said with a giggle, while Brigitte nodded in agreement.

Oh, looks like I have a silent ally. I get the feeling that Brigitte and I will be very good friends.

"Welcome back, Lady Rozemyne."

I returned to my chambers to find Rosina waiting with her harspiel, a trace of giddiness in her expression. Ferdinand was beside her, also holding a harspiel, while Fran was setting a pen and some paper on the table in front of them so that Ferdinand could write out the music I was about to teach him.

"Apologies for the wait, Rozemyne. I did not expect that visitor."

"Oh, it was no problem at all. I spent the time reading some very fascinating things. I don't mind lending them to you once I've finished reading them all," I said with a smile, while having Fran prepare a pen and some ink for Wilma as well. My words earned me a nod and a faint grin from Ferdinand.

"Now, then—you know what to do," Ferdinand said while readying his harspiel.

I thought about which song to give him, all the while watching Wilma's pen race across paper out of the corner of my eye. What would be a funny song for Ferdinand to unwittingly sing?

He lacks both kindness and compassion, so something about love, heroism, and friendship should be just perfect.

I selected a famous anime song and hummed it. After a bit, Ferdinand waved a hand, signaling me to stop. He then strummed his harspiel, fluidly arranging the notes into a song. Rosina watched excitedly, then shot a hand up.

"What is it, Rosina?" I asked.

"Um, High Priest! What do you think about arranging it like this?" Rosina asked, before strumming the tune in her own arrangement. Ferdinand stroked his chin, clearly impressed, then added something to the sheet music in front of him.

"That would do well for an orchestral arrangement," he said.

Rosina and Ferdinand proceeded to make the song together, regularly sharing their thoughts and opinions. Their discussions were so high-level that I couldn't even grasp a fraction of what they were saying, and the fact that my attendants and guard knights were watching them with impressed expressions led me to believe that none of them understood what was being said either.

Wilma, meanwhile, had a deadly serious look in her eyes as she continued to draw.

"Incidentally, Rozemyne… What kind of lyrics are attached to this song?" Ferdinand asked, causing my heart to skip a beat.

"U-Um, well… It goes like… 'I want to know what makes you happy. I don't want this to end before I know. We need love and courage'… Lines like that."

"I see. So it is a love song of yearning, then."

No! Not at all! I cackled on the inside, all the while maintaining a perfectly neutral expression. That, too, was thanks to my noble training. Who would have thought that an anime song adored by kids would end up as a melodramatic love song in another world?

Rosina and Ferdinand discussed what lyrics would match the song, deciding upon line after line in a speedy fashion. The lyrics ended up entirely different from what they originally were.

"This should suffice," Ferdinand said, before playing the new song from beginning to end. Bright, peaceful music flowed through the air as he sang in his deep, pleasantly reverberating voice, telling the tale of Ewigeliebe the God of Life offering up his love to Geduldh the Goddess of Earth. It was a song in which Ewigeliebe courted Geduldh by singing that he wished to know what made her happy, so while it was founded in religious legends, it was a love song.

Ferdinand's beautiful voice trickled into my ears, and despite knowing the original lyrics, I couldn't help but get goosebumps across my entire body. At some point in the past, I had thought that Ferdinand could get pretty much any girl he wanted by singing them a love song, and he had just given me even more reason to believe that.

Wilma had forgotten to draw at all, and was instead just staring at Ferdinand with widened eyes; Rosina had always liked Ferdinand as a fellow musician of culture, but now her pupils were basically hearts as she gazed upon him with a broad, dreamy smile; Monika and Nicola both had flushed cheeks; and Brigitte was looking at him in surprise.

It wasn't just the women looking at Ferdinand in awe; Fran and Damuel were both impressed by his playing as well.

...Is having Ferdinand play his harspiel at a concert going to be a lot more dangerous than I thought?

When I saw Wilma's excessively aesthetic illustration of Ferdinand, clearly drawn through rose-tinted glasses, I started to seriously rethink whether the concert was a good idea.

Johann and Zack

The next day, Lutz brought Johann and another boy to the orphanage director's chambers. It was probably more accurate to call him a man, given that he was the same age as Johann, but he was still young enough for me to instinctively use the term "boy." He had short crimson hair styled in what resembled a crew cut, and his gray eyes had an aggressive, competitive glint.

And, in sharp contrast to his enthusiasm, Johann was looking fairly stunned. I was wearing my High Bishop robes today. Up until now, he had thought that his patron was a rich commoner working with the Gilberta Company, and was now floored to learn that I was actually the tiny High Bishop who had apparently been the talk of the lower city ever since the Star Festival. I could hardly blame him for being shocked.

"Good morning, Lady Rozemyne," Lutz said politely, speaking in the formal tone he reserved for nobles.

Johann hurriedly dropped to his knees as well. "Good morning, erm… Lady Rozemyne?" He was looking at me with confusion, clearly not understanding my name change at all.

I launched into the small speech that I had discussed with Lutz and Benno ahead of time. "My apologies for summoning you so suddenly, Johann. As you can see, I have been given the duty of High Bishop, and thus can no longer visit you myself so easily. I would ask that you travel here yourself when necessary, if possible, but I understand if that isn't feasible."

"O-Oh, it is! I'll come! I'll walk here myself. I would never suggest you come all the way to my workshop!" Johann exclaimed. He was such an honest guy that he seemed to have concluded that I was an apprentice blue shrine maiden who had been sneaking out of the temple in disguise to walk around the lower city. Things went exactly as Lutz and Benno had said they would, which made me sigh in relief.

"That is much appreciated. Incidentally, Lutz... who is this with him?"

"Zack from the Verde Workshop. It seems he would like to receive your patronage as well," Lutz said.

I asked for more details, and learned that Johann's metal letter types had been presented to the Smithing Guild alongside the tasks of other new smiths to great praise. Zack's work had come behind Johann's in second place, and apparently the title of "Gutenberg" had played a significant part in that decision.

"It makes no sense that Johann would suddenly get so much praise after failing to get a patron—and leaving his customers dissatisfied—for so long," Zack said. "You just don't know the work other smiths can do, Lady Rozemyne. I believe I am more suitable for the title of 'Gutenberg' than he is. Please compare my work with his."

"...As you can see, Zack is quite eager to become a Gutenberg himself. I brought him here so that you may hear his case," Lutz said with a small smirk. The look in his eyes made it more than clear that he found Zack's eagerness to become a Gutenberg hilarious.

It turned out that Zack was very confident in his skills, and had some sort of one-way rivalry with Johann. I was more than happy to have such an enthusiastic craftsman join my legion of proud Gutenbergs—after all, the more skilled workers we had, the better.

"Before any decisions can be made, I must see how talented you truly are, Zack. Shall we go to the workshop?"

"Yes, milady!" Zack responded enthusiastically, before shooting Johann a victorious look.

I headed to the workshop with Lutz, Fran, and Damuel in tow. Gil was absent as he was taking the orphans to the forest; the gate guards recognized them now, which meant they could go on their own without Lutz or Tuuli accompanying them.

Once we had all gathered around a work table in one corner of the mostly empty workshop, in which only a few people were working, I took out some paper and ink to aid my explanation.

"I would like you to build a roller for making wax stencils."

"What are wax stencils?" Zack asked.

This was Zack's first time doing a job for my workshop, and Johann's first time entering the workshop, so Lutz explained the production process while showing them a thin wax stencil, a printing press, and a stylus that Johann had made.

"...So, for mimeograph printing, you need paper so thin you can see through it. You then need to coat it with a super thin layer of wax, but that layer has to be even. That's what we need a roller for."

"A roller? Like... the thing I made before?" Johann asked.

"No, not quite," I said with a shake of my head. I then looked over at Lutz, prompting him to read off of a cheat sheet I had prepared so that he could explain how it worked in my place.

"What Lady Rozemyne wants is a machine used to spread wax. It will be composed of two rollers, which are pressed against one another with a tray beneath them. You put the wax on the tray, then light a flame underneath to melt it. Like this." Lutz showed them the rough sketch I had drawn before continuing his explanation.

If you repeatedly turned the two rollers while the heated wax was below them, they would heat up too and get covered in melted wax. You could then slide a piece of paper between the two rollers, turning them just enough that the corners poked out the other end, before piercing these corners with thin bits of wood similar to toothpicks. One person would then turn the handle of the machine, while the other held onto the toothpicks and slowly pulled the paper out of the roller. The result would be a layer of wax so thin that it would dry while still suspended in the air, thus completing the wax paper.

"I apologize that I have nothing to offer but a rough explanation; I don't remember the details well enough to draw up any blueprints."

As Lutz gave his explanation, Johann looked over my sketches with a thoughtful frown. Meanwhile, Zack was listening with shining eyes as if completely fascinated, then started asking question upon question as he too started looking over the sketches.

"Lady Rozemyne—as long as the machine still accomplishes what you want, would you permit me to change its shape?"

"Of course. The important thing here is creating a machine that produces an evenly thin layer of wax. The appearance does not matter."

In the end, we decided that they would come back with rough blueprints in three days' time. It would then fall on me to decide which design we would use.

"I'm gonna become a Gutenberg, no matter what!" Zack declared, puffing out his chest. His gray eyes were burning so passionately bright that I could have sworn they had turned silver.

In response to the heated gaze from his so-called rival, Johann just shook his head with an exasperated expression. "I don't want to lose my patron, so I'm going to focus on doing work that Lady Rozemyne appreciates. But either way, I don't need the title. You can have it, Zack. Good luck out there."

The title of "Gutenberg" was purely symbolic, and Johann's dedication to results rather than appearances was exactly why it suited him perfectly. I could only hope that all of my workers would be so humble and dedicated to spreading printing.

But when I mentioned that, Lutz whispered something strange to me from behind. He said, "Johann's not being humble here, doofus."

In the three days during which Johann and Zack were making the blueprints, I decided to pick the songs that Ferdinand would be playing in the concert so that I could put together a schedule for the program. To that end, I burst into his room and requested his assistance.

"'Program'? Come again?"

"It's a printed document that lists the songs being played during the concert. Since we're holding this concert to gather money for the printing industry, I intend to sell printed goods once it's over. Each program is made using a single sheet of paper. The front will show a printed illustration, while the back will list each song and its lyrics."

The program would be like a movie pamphlet, and those who wanted to buy one could treasure it forever.

At my explanation, Ferdinand started to firmly massage his temples. His expression made it clear that, while he emotionally wanted to say that no program was needed, he had also rationally determined that it would be good to market the printing industry while we had an easy opportunity to do so.

"...Show me the finished program ahead of time."

"Consider it done."

I guess I'll go for a full black-and-white illustration for the program's cover. After all, I don't want to end up screwing myself if the wax stencils aren't ready in time.

"Shall we prioritize songs that the audience will be familiar with, adding only one or two new songs?" I asked.

"No, I would rather play new songs than ones I have played countless times before," Ferdinand replied.

With that in mind, I ultimately wrote up a schedule containing three songs based on classical music and two based on anime songs, with a break between the two genres. In total, five songs would be played.

"Good grief... Swear to me that you will never use Rihyarda against me again."

"I didn't ask Rihyarda to step in; she helped me out of sheer compassion. Personally, I had given up when I failed to convince you with what I had to offer," I explained. I hadn't expected Rihyarda to give him the final push, and I certainly hadn't expected Ferdinand to cave.

"If you don't stop Rihyarda as her master, then who will?"

"Considering that not even you could refuse her, Ferdinand, there is no chance whatsoever that I could on my own. Otherwise, I would have read all of those books you brought me before coming here. Why did you agree to do this concert in the first place?" I demanded with puffed-out cheeks.

Ferdinand averted his eyes. "...Although I was ultimately forced into this by Rihyarda, I am a man of my word. I will do whatever I have promised to do."

"Oh, I know you will. You have my full trust there."

When I returned to my chambers, I found Rosina playing the song she had arranged with Ferdinand. The fact that she had arranged it with him apparently made her love playing it. She was acting like a girl in love, and while that was cute, I was honestly pretty tired of the song by now. I almost wanted to ask her to stop playing it.

"I shall head to the orphanage to discuss the program," I said, needing Wilma to draw a full black-and-white stencil illustration of Ferdinand playing the harspiel both to draw his attention away from my true plot and so that I had a backup in case the wax stencils weren't ready in time.

...And when I informed her of that, Wilma's light-brown eyes shone with excitement.

"You may count on me. At the moment, I am overcome with such a powerful urge to draw that it feels as if Kunstzeal the Goddess of Art herself is granting me her divine protection. Lady Rozemyne, what manner of illustration do you need?" Wilma asked, before inviting me to her room in the orphanage where she had apparently drawn several pictures of Ferdinand already.

As Damuel and Fran were men, I left them in the dining hall and headed to Wilma's room with just Monika and Brigitte.

"Oh my! Wilma! These are spectacular!" Monika cried out as soon as we stepped inside.

"They certainly are impressive," Brigitte agreed.

My jaw dropped as I looked around the room; it was filled with so many stacks of Ferdinand drawings that I genuinely couldn't believe my eyes. Maybe she hadn't been joking when she mentioned that Kunstzeal had given her strength.

"I just kept thinking of more angles and styles to draw him in, and my hands simply couldn't stop."

Wilma's heart had been stolen by Ferdinand, and the resulting art fever was something to behold. Most of the paper I had given her for sketching had been used to draw him, and while I couldn't tell exactly how much, there was definitely some beautification going on. It was hard to deny that Wilma was looking at him through the rose-tinted glasses of a starstruck young girl. The real Ferdinand didn't shine anywhere near as much as he did in her illustrations, and he certainly didn't smile as much. Wilma and I were presumably looking at the same person, but we were seeing him in dramatically different ways.

…His expression does loosen up a bit when he's playing music, but he never smiles as gently as this. In fact, I reckon I'll die before I ever see him give a gentle smile at all.

Wilma had done a number of drawings showing Ferdinand playing the harspiel with Rosina, and while I was only going to sell illustrations of him by himself during the concert, they really were fantastic. Each one seemed to tell a romantic tale of a handsome man and a beautiful woman. She had also drawn him playing while I sang, and I immediately noticed that I looked about thirty percent shinier as well. It was as if the filter she was looking at Ferdinand through was so strong that it even affected how she saw me when I was beside him.

"So you would like a full-body illustration of Ferdinand playing the harspiel, cut into a stencil. I can finish that at once. Please come for it tomorrow afternoon."

I had never seen Wilma so full of life before. It was honestly kind of scary to think that Ferdinand had made her go from being afraid of men to… whatever this was. At this point, I had to accept that there would be women passing out or just completely losing their minds at the harspiel concert. In order to minimize any potential damages, it would probably be necessary to get the Knight's Order involved so that they could stop any rampaging fans and carry any collapsed women to the nearby medical room.

Wilma's prediction that she could have the illustration finished at once proved correct, as the stencil was ready the next day. It was a full-body picture just as I had ordered, and, in all honesty, it looked like she had put a lot more care and effort into it than she had the picture book illustrations.

"How is it, Lady Rozemyne?" Wilma asked, her eyes brimming with satisfaction despite it being clear from her face that she had barely slept last night.

"I think it's spectacular. Once I have Ferdinand's approval, I will send it to the workshop to be printed at once."

When I showed him, Ferdinand expressed his satisfaction through a contented "This will do." I had now managed to secure his permission to use the illustration for the programs, but I had a feeling that this was only because it wasn't a clear-cut picture of him. In fact, had it not been for the hairstyle and the general atmosphere surrounding the illustration, it might not have been recognizable as Ferdinand at all.

Before I knew it, it was time for Johann and Zack to submit their blueprints. They would be bringing them to the workshop, and so I was waiting there with Damuel and Fran. Behind me, gray priests were starting to print the programs. We would be using the same method to print the illustration as we had used previously, but this would be our first time printing using metal letter types. To that end, the priests were all tightly knitting their brows in concentration as they picked up the types and awkwardly lined them up on the stick.

"Lady Rozemyne, I have brought Lutz from the Gilberta Company and the smiths," Gil announced.

"Thank you, Gil. May I see your blueprints, then?"

With hunched shoulders and his head drooped a little, Johann took out a board. On it was a blueprint for a machine that looked and would supposedly work just as I had described, but it seemed that not even he was satisfied with it. The plans showed Johann's greatest weak point: while he could perfectly follow even the most detailed blueprints, he was bad at making his own plans based on customer needs.

Zack, in contrast, victoriously took out several boards, each with a blueprint on it. He had come up with various unique approaches to the wax coating machine, and each one appeared to have its own virtues. They were made well enough that I could understand why he was so confident and had so many patrons.

"These certainly are impressive," I said.

"Yeah. I could never think up anything like these," Johann added gloomily.

I couldn't blame him for hanging his head; following the blueprints that Zack had drawn up would make the machine I wanted a reality. Since he had based them on existing techniques, they would apparently be a lot easier to make than what Johann had drawn up based on my description alone.

"Zack, which of these would you most confidently suggest to me?"

"This one will probably work the best, but this one will be the most realistic to make," Zack replied.

I looked over the two blueprints he showed me and asked Johann what he thought. His expression turned serious as he began comparing the two. Then, once he had glared between them for a bit, he pointed at the one that Zack had said would work the best.

Zack narrowed his eyes and glared at Johann. "That one's not realistic! This part right here needs to be done so precisely that it'll be impossible to make!"

Johann slowly shook his head as he peered at the blueprint, the orange hair bundled in a ponytail behind his head shaking along with him. His face was full of confidence and his eyes shone with determination, and with a powerful nod, he declared that he could do it.

I clapped my hands once to stop Zack from leaping at Johann in anger; that kind of behavior would absolutely not be permitted in front of a patron. He stopped on a dime as he came back to his senses, then lowered his clenched fist.

"Now, I shall ask you each to make the machine you have picked. I intend to establish printing workshops in other cities as well, so having two functional waxing machines will be entirely acceptable. However, I will not pay for something that does not work."

Without any working examples to back up their arguments, any further debate was pointless; the competition could be settled once the products were completed.

Zack glared at Johann with the heated look of a rival, but Johann just glared at the blueprints.

"You may bring your machine and set it up here when you are finished, but ensure that you speak to Lutz and come here through him. Gil, will there be space for the machines?" I asked, and Gil pointed at a wide-open spot elsewhere with his chest proudly puffed out.

"We have plenty of space since we cleaned up."

"I see. Thank you. I have faith that you will both provide good work," I said.

I had assumed that would be the end of our conversation, but Lutz flashed a mischievous grin for just a second before taking out a letter. I looked up at him in surprise as he handed it to me.

"A hairpin craftswoman in our store has made a hair stick for you, Lady Rozemyne, and would like to show it to you as soon as possible. Would you be able to meet with her sometime soon?"

Tuuli. He was talking about Tuuli. I could see her again.

I gave a big, happy nod. "Please bring her to the orphanage director's chambers tomorrow afternoon!" I exclaimed, unable to hide the excitement in my voice.

Lutz nodded in response, a small grin creeping onto his face.

I did my best to keep my expression neutral as I exited the workshop with Fran and Damuel, but the moment I was outside, I heard Lutz burst into laughter behind me.

As soon as I was back in my room, I read the letter from my family.

Kamil was now able to roll over, and Mom was earning a stable income by making hairpins, which meant she could stay at home and look after Kamil until he was old enough to not need someone like Gerta around. I was glad beyond words that he wouldn't have to suffer being neglected by Gerta like I had.

Dad was busy working at the gate as commander, and he mentioned that Benno and the guildmaster were frequently passing in and out of the city. "Don't work them too hard, now," he wrote.

Tuuli said that she'd have the new hair stick ready when she saw me. I couldn't even begin to describe how excited I was to be able to see her soon.

I immediately got to work on my reply. I wrote that Ferdinand was bullying me by stopping me from reading books, that I was glad they had come to see me during the Star Festival, that I had successfully performed the Starbind Ceremony in the Noble's Quarter, and that I was working hard to develop the printing industry in the temple.

I folded the finished letter, and slid it between the pages of a finished picture book I intended to give to Tuuli. Then, I had Rosina bundle it together with something that I had asked her to prepare earlier.

"Lady Rozemyne, you are getting much too excited," Fran observed with a small grin as I squirmed in place. I knew in my head that I needed to act more like a proper noble girl, but I couldn't contain my excitement over seeing Tuuli again after so long.

"Lady Rozemyne, I have brought our store's hairpin craftswoman," Lutz said in a polite tone as he entered with Tuuli. I wanted to rush forward and leap into her arms like I always used to, and I wanted to cry tears of happiness at getting to see her again, but we were forbidden from addressing each other as family.

Tuuli was looking at me with the same tearful expression that I was no doubt wearing myself. Her lips trembled, but she swallowed the name "Myne" without ever saying it.

"Thank you for seeing me today, Lady Rozemyne. Here is the hair stick I made, using a new style of stitching…" Tuuli said, before taking out a hair stick bundled in cloth from the tote basket I used to carry. She had drawn inspiration from the method of using hide glue that I had taught Lutz and made a large flower with freely moving petals and a rigid stem.

"It's beautiful… I am always wearing the hair sticks that you make for me. As thanks for this new hair stick, I shall offer you this gift. I pray that it serves you well."

I gave her the second in my line of picture books, this one focusing on the subordinate gods beneath the Goddess of Water, as well as a collection of sketches detailing the clothes I had seen nobles wearing at the Starbind Ceremony, which I had asked Rosina to draw in return for teaching her the new songs I had taught Ferdinand. Hopefully they would help Tuuli in her design studies.

"I am honored," Tuuli said, probably having been taught how to speak to nobles by Mark and Benno. I had never heard her talk like that before, and it was clear as day how hard she was working to grow.

"...There is a baby in the temple's orphanage. He has started to crawl, and those taking care of him have noted how much of a handful he is. I would like to hear about any experience you might have with babies."

Tuuli paused for a moment in thought, then gave a small smile. "I hope that stories of my little brother Kamil will be to your liking. As of late, he has been spending much of his time looking at his black-and-white picture book. I am not exactly sure what he enjoys about it so much, but my mom usually keeps it spread out on the bed, leaning against the wall, and I always see him quietly looking at it on his own."

On top of that, Kamil had finally gotten big enough to hold onto the white rabbit rattle I had made for him. He could grab it, and track where the sound was coming from with his eyes.

"...May I bring you another hairpin when I finish one, Lady Rozemyne?"

"Yes, of course. I shall be waiting."

We shared gifts, pleasant words, and smiles, and while it pained me that I couldn't touch her, Tuuli's warm smile was enough to fill my heart with light.

Elvira and Lamprecht Attack

"Gil, Lutz—I would like you to print this on the program's back cover," I said, holding out the stencil that Wilma had made for me.

It was the day after I had met with Tuuli. Seeing her had warmed my heart but the loneliness had already set in again, so I was clinging to Lutz in the hidden room. Gil and Damuel were the only other people with us.

"How many do you need?"

"Mm… We'll be preparing thirty seats for attendees, so I guess we should make enough to accommodate people buying one to view, one to store, and one to share? That will be ninety in total."

"Say what?! That's way too many!" Lutz yelped in surprise before shooting me a confounded look. I personally thought that ninety wouldn't be enough, though that was just a gut feeling.

"If we don't finish the wax stencils in time then these programs will be the only printed merchandise we can sell at the concert, so I'm pretty confident that they'll sell well."

"Is that confidence founded in anything? If you're wrong then we're wasting a ton of resources here," Lutz responded, shooting me a glare very similar to Benno's that said he wouldn't permit any money to be wasted. He was becoming more like a merchant each day, and I couldn't help but feel proud.

"Wilma and the other girls' obsession should say it all. Those who didn't come to the concert will wish they had them. Even if we don't manage to sell them all, their reputation as the first printed product means it won't be long before their price shoots up crazy high—maybe in, like... a few decades? Possibly a century."

"'A few decades'?! That doesn't prove your point at all!" he barked back in disbelief. In my opinion, it was the most solid proof that one could ask for, but Lutz apparently just didn't get it. Either way, I was willing to compromise.

"We can print ninety, or we can round up to one hundred. Go with whichever your heart tells you."

"Why's the second number even bigger?!" Lutz exclaimed. Really though, I didn't think that one hundred would be enough either.

Gil, seeing that I wasn't about to budge on the issue, gave Lutz a slap on the back. "Lutz, I don't think you'll ever convince Lady Rozemyne to change her mind on this."

"I know that. I just needed to let it out to make myself feel better."

As today was Damuel's day off, I couldn't go to my hidden room or visit the workshop, so I went to the High Priest's chambers with Fran and Brigitte to help Ferdinand with his work. He had taken on most of my High Bishop work, so I pretty much just ended up helping him do a small portion of the stuff that was supposed to have been done by me in the first place.

"...It seems that our expenses for summer are much lower than they were for spring. Though our income has gone down a bit, too," I observed.

"What other reason could there be for that than the High Bishop being replaced?" Ferdinand replied without even lifting his head from his paperwork. But I couldn't understand how that alone would make such a dramatic difference.

"…Um, what exactly was the old High Bishop using all of this money on?"

"He could not distinguish the temple's money from his own. But if you wish to know everything that he secretly spent the money on, I am afraid that not even I know the full extent of his embezzling," Ferdinand said, briefly glancing my way before looking back at his work.

Ferdinand had only started managing the temple's finances about two years ago. He had inherited the position of High Priest after his predecessor left for the Sovereignty, and they had apparently been in a horrible enough state to make him feel dizzy. When it came to ability, the blue priests who had been raised in the temple and had lazily passed their days without putting much effort into anything were leagues below Ferdinand, who had been educated in the Royal Academy and trained to be the archduke's right-hand man.

"…It sounds like you had it rough, Ferdinand."

"I intend to make the temple budget clearer and properly managed while you are the High Bishop," Ferdinand said, just as an ordonnanz flew in through the window. It circled the room once, flapping its wings, then landed on Ferdinand's desk.

Nobles used ordonnanz—flying birds shaped from feystones—to communicate. They were apparently simple to use, and something that a student of the Royal Academy would master before the end of their first year. As such, children who were too young to attend the Royal Academy would have to communicate through their guardians. In my case, that was Rihyarda while I was in the castle, Ferdinand while I was in the temple, and Elvira whenever I was at home. If someone needed to send me a message, they would send an ordonnanz to one of these three depending on where I was.

"Lord Ferdinand, it's Lamprecht. My sincerest apologies, but I request a meeting with Rozemyne. There is a small matter regarding Lord Wilfried that I would like to briefly discuss with her," the ordonnanz said three times in Lamprecht's voice before returning to the shape of a feystone.

Oh yeah, Wilfried was calling me unfair or something before I returned to the temple; maybe it's about that. I can't think of anything else it could be...

"Rozemyne, when will you be available for a meeting?" Ferdinand asked.

I personally didn't mind when the meeting was held given that it was just supposed to be a brief conversation, but in the world of nobles, you couldn't just say that now was a good time. Ferdinand had always scheduled a date around three days in the future whenever I requested a meeting with him.

"...Well, I suppose three days from now will do."

"Agreed. Now then, face the bird and speak."

Ferdinand made his wand appear, then lightly tapped the feystone while saying "*ordonnanz*" to make it twist into the shape of a white bird. I faced it as instructed, and immediately felt a small wave of nervousness wash over me; it was like I was leaving someone a voicemail.

"Lamprecht, it's Rozemyne. I shall be awaiting your visit three days from now, in the afternoon."

Once that was done, the ordonnanz flew away. I had assumed that would be that, but then it returned in the blink of an eye. "Can the meeting be before noon? I don't get to see you very often, and I would like to share lunch with you afterward. It seems that Mother wants to join us, too."

It seemed that the whole thing about Wilfried was just a cover; his actual objective was meeting me for lunch.

"I imagine that Karstedt or Cornelius bragged to him about the Italian restaurant," Ferdinand said with an amused smirk, which reminded me—Elvira had only ever eaten Ella's sweets, not her actual cooking, while Lamprecht had eaten neither. But their head chef was still learning the recipes from Hugo in the castle; the only way for them to eat the food would be for them to come and visit me, since I had Ella with me.

"I'll prepare the same menu that Father, Eckhart, and Cornelius had," I replied to the ordonnanz, and a few moments later Lamprecht sent back his thanks in a tone that leaked both his relief at getting what he wanted, and his embarrassment that I had seen right through him.

And so came the day of the meeting. Since Elvira was going to be joining us, I had brought one of the freshly printed programs for her to check, as well as several illustrations that Wilma had drawn.

Ella and Nicola were working hard to prepare the food. They even had male helpers, since we had been training some priests so that we could send them to the new orphanage in the monastery, which was useful as we wouldn't need to worry about them getting exhausted when it came to the more physically taxing parts of cooking.

"Heya, Rozemyne. Good to see you're doing well. Sorry about coming down like this; I was worried you might be sick," Lamprecht said once Fran had guided him and Elvira into the room. They were both wearing bright smiles—Lamprecht because he was looking forward to the lunch, and Elvira because she knew that Ferdinand would be attending as my guardian.

"It is good to see you well, Rozemyne. I have no doubts that your good health is thanks to Lord Ferdinand's consideration. We truly are blessed to have him."

Once we had exchanged the lengthy greetings that all nobles gave, Lamprecht and Elvira were offered seats and a selection of tea. Nicola then carried in a plate of tea-flavored cookies, wearing an anxious expression as she set it on the table. Lamprecht eagerly leaned forward as I took the first sweet and bit into it; there was no escaping the noble tradition where hosts had to test their food for poison.

"These are (langues de chat). They're only light snacks, but as we are due to have lunch soon, please take care not to eat too many," I explained.

No sooner had the last word passed my lips than Lamprecht reached for a cookie. His expression looked so much like Cornelius's did whenever sweets were involved that I couldn't help but chuckle.

Lamprecht scarfed one down, then widened his eyes. "Has Cornelius tried these?"

"No, this is the first time that I am serving these to visitors, so Cornelius has not had one yet."

"I see…" Lamprecht replied, brimming with smugness.

Ferdinand took this opportunity to set down his tea and ask about the excuse that Lamprecht had made to visit. "Lamprecht, what is this business with Wilfried that you mentioned?"

Lamprecht gave a deliberate nod, then started to give a roundabout explanation full of vague noble euphemisms. Ferdinand was nodding as he listened, but I couldn't understand a word.

"Excuse me, dear brother, but your language is simply too complicated for me to understand."

"Huh? Erm…" Lamprecht furrowed his brow, not sure how else to explain, so I looked toward Ferdinand.

"Wilfried thinks it unfair that you are not being forced to study like he is," Ferdinand explained. Wilfried was apparently a ball of energy who spent his time running away from his tutors, and from his perspective, I was getting to walk around without tutors and even leave the castle whenever I wanted.

"Lamprecht, I advise that you inform Wilfried just how much of a fool he is being. Of course Rozemyne is being tutored. I have been instructing her personally while she is at the temple, and now that she is also being educated in Karstedt's estate, she is waiting for Wilfried to learn the alphabet."

Sylvester had seemingly decided that Wilfried would benefit from having a rival, given how much of a sore loser he was, so I was going to be learning history and geography with him once he had memorized the alphabet.

"I don't mind studying all day as it means I can read books. Please tell Wilfried that I am eager for him to learn his letters as soon as possible," I said, causing Lamprecht to cradle his head.

"You two are never going to get along…" he sighed.

I found it hard to disagree.

Wilfried wanted nothing more than to avoid studying, while I was willing to spend days—or perhaps even weeks—holed up in my room reading books. But considering that I was currently being denied access to a stack of exciting books, I was actually more envious of Wilfried's situation.

"Given that the archduke is pressing us for details about his son's studies, we can only hope that Lord Wilfried learns them soon. If possible, I would like Rozemyne to study with Lord Wilfried even just once in the meantime so that he can see just how enormous the gap between them is…"

"She does not have the time for that," Ferdinand replied as the manager of my schedule, immediately shutting down Lamprecht's request for my help. "There is much that Rozemyne must accomplish post haste. She has to practice magic in preparation for when she gathers the ingredients she needs, perform her duties as the High Bishop, and run the orphanage and its workshop—not to mention stay healthy in general. Wilfried's success ultimately comes down to him and those around him; it is not Rozemyne's job, but rather yours as his retainer."

Lamprecht was sitting with his mouth agape. "Lord Ferdinand, is that not too much work for her? She is but a child—one who has only just been baptized…"

"And that is why I refused your suggestion. Do not give her any more work than she already has."

Having Ferdinand list out everything that I needed to do made me feel even more busy than I actually was. I was pretty much just doing what he told me to, and since I was forbidden from working myself, I usually needed to leave the actual work to other people. When coupled with the fact that I never passed out in the temple because Fran was there to manage my health, I really didn't feel that busy at all.

"In Rozemyne's case, I know that she will consume and take in knowledge from whatever books are placed in front of her without needing to be prompted, so her studying can be done during her spare time."

"Bwuh?! No, please! Give me more time to read books! My spare time isn't enough!" I protested, only to have Ferdinand quickly shoot me down with a dismissive sneer. It seemed that I couldn't expect him to show me any consideration. ...*So mean.*

"Aside from the studying, it seems that Wilfried finds it unfair that only Rozemyne gets to talk with their father at the dinner table."

Dinner at the castle involved us discussing what we had done that day, and since Wilfried was always slipping out of class and running around the castle, most of his time at the dinner table was spent being scolded by his mother while Sylvester watched on without saying anything in particular. I had guessed that Sylvester couldn't scold his son in good conscience since he had done the same as a child, but neither could he support the bad behavior, so he had no choice but to remain silent.

"I suppose I do have conversations with him, but that's because I need to report on the printing business. Perhaps Wilfried should be given some work of his own to do?" I suggested.

Kids his age from the lower city would already be starting apprentice work. Maybe he would learn to be more responsible if he was given some simple jobs to do.

"Also, isn't Wilfried progressing quite slowly for someone his age? The child of a merchant would already know how to read and write before their baptism, and would be able to understand simple math. Even kids in the orphanage can do that. Do you not think it a mistake to spoil him and only start teaching him after his baptism just because he's the son of the archduke? I think it would have been better to start teaching him from a much younger age."

"Wilfried was taught from a young age and still learned nothing, which is precisely why Sylvester was so shocked when he toured your orphanage."

That reminded me—Sylvester had been pretty surprised when he saw the karuta and the picture books, but it seemed that his focus hadn't been on the products themselves, but rather on the kids who had learned to read them over a single winter. We had already proven that kids who studied using karuta and picture books learned incredibly quickly, but their progress depended on them having rivals to compete against, or at least friends to play with.

"It might increase the burden on Wilfried's attendants, but I will prepare a karuta deck for him."

"There is no need for you to take Wilfried's education upon yourself, Rozemyne. Good grief... Did I not just say that you are already overworked?" Ferdinand asked with a frown, but even he had to agree that Wilfried's inability to read or write was problematic for everyone. It was pure coincidence that I would benefit by getting to study (and thus read books) sooner.

Fourth bell rang to announce the beginning of lunch, at which point Ferdinand stated that it was best for a family to eat together and returned to his own chambers.

Lamprecht was chowing down faster than I had ever seen him eat before, and Elvira mentioned that she hoped our head chef would be coming home soon, so I could tell that they were both more than satisfied with the food.

After lunch, Elvira and I began discussing the concert. It seemed that they were experiencing a serious ticket shortage. Her intention had been to only invite women from her own faction, but ladies from other factions had expressed interest as well.

"Many of them had never shown any prior interest in Lord Ferdinand, but now it seems they have all changed their minds," Elvira ranted, but it was only natural that the ladies would have avoided Ferdinand for their own protection while Sylvester's mother was working against him. It seemed that those afraid of Veronica had kept a respectful distance from Ferdinand, rarely engaging with him in public. In other words, now that Veronica was gone, everyone who had been restraining their feelings was finally free to let them loose.

"…How many seats should we add?"

"Well, I imagine that just about every noblewoman in the city will be attending, so perhaps we should begin by rethinking where the concert is going to be held."

There were roughly three hundred nobles living in the Noble's Quarter of Ehrenfest, counting only those who had been baptized; if we estimated about half of them to be women, then we were looking at one hundred and fifty attendees. There would certainly be some among the crowd who weren't particularly interested in Ferdinand, but this was an event being attended by a throng of archnobles. It was the fate of a laynoble to follow after those superior to them, so I could imagine that many laynobles would be taking a hit from the ticket costs.

"Mother, I suggest that we add thirty more seats, and then prepare a standing gallery at a heavily discounted price for everybody else. Having to stand while watching will provide an excuse for those who don't wish to buy tickets, and a standing gallery should mean that fewer laynobles will need to break the bank to buy more expensive tickets."

Those in the standing gallery would be attending the concert all the same, so they wouldn't be put to shame by the archnobles who recommended they attend. The price would be comfortably affordable too, thanks to the programs being sold separately.

"Watching while standing? The thought never occurred to me," Elvira replied. "But the tickets certainly are expensive. It would be for the best to give those who can't afford them the opportunity to refuse."

With that done, I told Elvira which songs Ferdinand would be playing at the concert and showed her the finished program. It was using black-and-white art from a cut-out stencil, but since that was still new technology here, she was head over heels for the illustration. I jotted down on my diptych that we would be needing a *lot* more copies printed—one hundred more, to be precise—as I continued my report.

"The programs will be sold separately from the tickets, and the money we make from them will be added to our donations."

"Then I shall buy one at once. Buying this program is a form of donating—it is a moral, highly commendable act, is it not?" Elvira asked, her dark-brown eyes gleaming with excitement. I could already imagine her going out of her way to buy every single illustration of Ferdinand ever released under the guise of donating to a good cause.

Forgive me, Father. Forgive me...

"You sure come up with good ideas at the drop of a hat, huh, Rozemyne?" Lamprecht said in an impressed tone as he continued to shovel langues de chat into his mouth despite having only just eaten lunch.

I looked at him, then remembered the security problem that we were bound to have. "Excuse me, dear brother. I would like for the Knight's Order to station guards in the concert hall, but who should I ask to make that happen? Father? Or perhaps Sylvester?" We would be hosting even more people than expected, which meant that our need for guards was more urgent than I had thought.

"Knights in the concert hall? Oh my. For what purpose?" Elvira asked.

"I believe that more than a few ladies will pass out from the excitement, or alternatively just completely lose control of themselves. I think we should even prepare a medical room to take them to."

"Hold on a second, Rozemyne—this is just a harspiel concert, isn't it?" Lamprecht asked dubiously.

I gave a nod. "It is. I wouldn't have been worried either had I not seen how women reacted to Ferdinand playing the harspiel; Wilma and Rosina were both drooling over him less than a verse into his first song."

It wasn't hard to imagine someone like Elvira who was already obsessed with Ferdinand just absolutely losing her mind.

"I think it would be easier for me to just demonstrate," I said, before standing up from my chair, unfurling one of Wilma's illustrations and spreading it out so they could see.

"My my myyy! What do we have here? Allow me to take a closer look!" Elvira abruptly stood up from her chair with a clatter, and briskly walked to my side of the table. She still moved with grace and elegance, but her sheer speed was nothing short of intimidating.

I looked at Lamprecht as I held out the illustration to Elvira. "Imagine one hundred ladies in a state like this, and think of the chaos that would ensue without the Knight's Order."

"...I'll try asking Father. The resting room close to the large hall should be suitable for medical situations. Anything else you need?"

"I would like you to prepare a stage similar to the one used in the Starbind Ceremony, to prevent the audience from getting too close to Ferdinand while he plays."

I thought back to the idol concerts on Earth and listed off whatever safety precautions and other bits of advice I could think of. Meanwhile, Elvira was sighing and gasping in awe as she pored over the illustration.

"Rozemyne, may I have this?"

"I intend to use that illustration as a base for printing once I complete the wax stencils, so I'll have to ask you to buy a printed version on the day of the concert. If I am unable to finish the stencils in time, then you may have it."

"Very well, then," Elvira said as she reluctantly handed back the illustration. She was staring at it so intently that I decided to give her a copy of the program, just to keep her mind occupied.

"The printing business is all about reproducing exact copies of things en masse. We already have one hundred copies of this program, for example, and I intend to make even more, so I ask that you encourage everyone to bring their money pouches and spend freely."

...Please do your best to make this concert a success, dear mother.

I was listening to a report on Johann and Zack's progress in my hidden room; they were gradually bringing new parts to the workshop, and the waxing machines were slowly coming together. While we were waiting for the machines to be finished, I asked Lutz and Gil to begin making wax that had just a bit of pine resin mixed into it to increase its pliability.

"How much is 'just a bit'?" Gil asked, but Lutz immediately put a hand on his shoulder.

"That means we need to experiment using different amounts of resin while also changing the type of wax to make a bunch of products so that we can pick the best one. That's what Myne did for ages to get the paper-making ratios right."

"For real...?" Gil asked in disbelief. Up until now, he had only ever had to follow instructions to the letter, and he started to head back to the workshop to research with an exhausted look on his face.

Once I had seen them off, I got to work reading through the remaining letters that the High Bishop had hidden in the book room. It turned out that they weren't all innocent love letters—in fact, quite a few looked pretty suspicious. Some concerned bribes, others involved under-the-table deals with nobles, and a bunch were requests for flower offerings.

"So Viscount Gerlach *was* connected to the High Bishop. I knew it."

Ferdinand had made me put a veil on before I could greet certain people during Spring Prayer, and I could see now that most of them had connections to the High Bishop. I wrote up a list of people to be wary of as I continued reading the oh-so suspicious-looking letters.

"I should probably show these to Ferdinand. Fran, please send word to him."

"As you wish."

The letters could potentially prove useful in Sylvester's or Ferdinand's future political endeavors. I wanted to keep the love letters hidden, though, so I put them back on the bookshelf.

"Ferdinand, I have something for you."

I entered Ferdinand's room with Fran, who was carrying the box shaped to look like four books. He immediately gave it a dubious look.

"What in the world are these? They must not be normal books if you are bringing them here."

"They were books stored on the bookshelf that only the High Bishop can open... or so they appear. In reality, this is just a box that has been shaped to look like four books. Inside are a bunch of letters that serve as evidence of his crimes. Will they be of use to your plots with Sylvester?"

Ferdinand opened the book-shaped box and furrowed his brow. He took out a few letters, checked who they were from, and then gave an evil smirk. "There certainly are a good number of these, hm?"

"You can have them all. All I ask for is the box; I love things like this," I said while pointing at the book-shaped box decorated with leather and gemstones.

Ferdinand dismissively waved his hand, an exasperated look on his face. "All I desire are the contents. You may use the box as you wish. Just give me a moment to remove the letters."

"I thank you ever so much."

At that, one of Ferdinand's attendants started packing the letters into a regular wooden box. Ferdinand stopped writing and set his pen aside, having apparently reached a stopping point in his work.

"Rozemyne, is your schedule free for the rest of today?"

"Yes. I've received today's report from Gil and Lutz, and I have given them instructions. It seems that Hasse's orphanage has started to show signs of progress. But in any case... do you need my help with something?" I asked.

Ferdinand shook his head and began to clean off his desk. "No, I merely wish to continue your magic training as soon as possible. If you do not learn to create a highbeast soon, then it won't be ready in time for the Harvest Festival. Follow me to the castle."

"Allow me to get changed, then."

I returned to my chambers and was changed from my High Bishop robes to my noble clothes, wrapping a belt over the top that Ferdinand had given to me. Nobles apparently needed belts to hang magic tools off of. The balled-up feystone I had dyed with my mana had been embedded in a gold bird cage ornament similar to the ones worn by Ferdinand and other nobles, and was hanging from my belt.

"Shall we go, Lady Rozemyne?"

Once Brigitte had set me on her highbeast, we flew off toward the castle's magic training area. I would have to make my own highbeast this time for sure.

Finishing My Highbeast and the Wax Stencils

When we arrived, Damuel and Brigitte were instructed to train on the opposite side of the arena to us. I turned to face Ferdinand as soon as they were gone; it was time to begin.

"Now then, start by changing the size of your feystone to practice what you learned last time. And take care not to imagine it exploding this time," he said, reminding me of my past failure as a warning.

I took out my feystone and tightly gripped it so as to not drop it. This time, as I changed its size, I imagined it as a sturdy bowling ball instead of something flimsy like a balloon. It wasn't long before I heard Ferdinand's voice again.

"Very good. Next, practice locking its shape. Pour mana into it until it is the size you have imagined, then stop. It should be quite easy for you to consciously halt the flow of your mana."

Since I regularly stopped and started my mana flow during my offerings to the divine instruments, this step was just as easy for me as Ferdinand had predicted. Once I was able to easily change the ball from the size of a ping-pong ball, to a basketball, to a massive inflatable beach ball, Ferdinand told me that was enough.

"Now you will practice changing its shape."

I turned the round feystone into a pyramid, then a cube, then a spiked pufferfish-looking thing, then a book, and then a pen. It took me a while to form the shapes at first, but as I got used to the process, I became able to instantly turn the feystone into whatever I envisioned in my head.

"You truly are a fast learner," Ferdinand said, complimenting me in a tone that suggested a mix of both respect and exasperation. That was rare for him. "Rozemyne, this is your final task: remove all unnecessary thoughts from your mind and imagine an animal that you can ride."

When I tried to picture a rideable animal, the first things that came to mind were the bouncy spring rides that could be found all over amusement parks—the kind where you would slide a coin in and then ride for three minutes.

"Once you have decided on a form, cut off your mana to lock it… What in the world is that?"

"Um… A (panda) ride."

It had a single seat and was pretty small—in fact, it was less like an amusement park ride and more like a toy that a toddler would sit on and move about with its feet. In other words, it was absolutely pathetic.

While I sadly shook my head at my failed attempt, Ferdinand looked down at it with thoroughly dubious eyes. "Can this thing fly?"

"…I imagine that would be a little difficult."

"It seems to me that 'a little' is a vast understatement," Ferdinand said while rubbing his temples. "You are a fast learner, but your lack of common sense may never be improved."

I personally had no idea where his criticisms were coming from; he had asked me to make an animal ride, and I did.

"Okay. I'll make it a little bigger so you can tell it's rideable."

"No, focus on the shape before the size. Can you make a lion like this?" Ferdinand asked, brushing a hand against his feystone and forming his highbeast in the blink of an eye. Just seeing that made it clear how trained his movements were. I could only imagine how much practice it would take before I could do that myself.

"Ehrenfest's insignia is a lion, and the archduke rides one that has three heads. Children of the archduke tend to use lions as well. It is not mandatory, of course, but it is a long-standing tradition."

I had assumed that Sylvester rode a Cerberus-esque lion because he had the mind of a little boy who would like that kind of thing, but as it turned out, there was actually a lot more meaning behind it. And as his adopted daughter, I would be permitted to use a lion myself.

"Okay. I'll do my best."

Ferdinand's highbeast was so realistic that I found it kind of scary, so I wanted my own highbeast to be a cute lion. I nodded, trying to picture a lion that I wouldn't mind riding on, then poured mana into my feystone. It swelled in size and actually took the shape of a lion this time, but despite it growing as big as an amusement park ride would be, Ferdinand grimaced even harder than before.

"Your aesthetic sense is catastrophically poor. What foul manner of beast have you summoned in place of a lion?"

"Wait, 'foul'? This is pretty cute, in my opinion." I had made a lion to ride on, as requested, but my cartoony take was apparently no good in Ferdinand's eyes.

"Can you even ride that thing?"

"I can try. Oomph."

I climbed onto its back and successfully grabbed the handles I had made in place of reins, but it didn't move like I had thought it would. Well, that wasn't quite true—it *only* moved like I thought it would, since it moved based on my thoughts. I had envisioned it as an amusement park ride, and with that in mind, I couldn't get it up into the air at all; my best efforts to move its feet just caused it to shuffle very slowly.

That was a big problem. No matter how hard I thought, I just couldn't work out the motions to make an animal fly. It didn't feel like it would be leaving the ground any time soon.

"A lion I can ride, but one that can also fly through the sky..." I murmured to myself, deep in thought. Lions were a bit different from cats, but I had a feeling that I could make a flying highbeast by copying what I had seen in that one famous movie with the cat bus running along power lines. It was one fast bus—definitely one that could run through the sky.

The highbeast that I actually ended up making was pretty heavily influenced by thoughts of cats, so the Lionbus ended up looking less like a lion and more like a cat with a shower hat for a mane, but, oh well.

"What in the world is that?"

"As you can see, it's a (Lionbus)."

I stood in front of the Lionbus and a window dropped down to form an entrance for me. I climbed inside, joy welling in my heart because it had moved exactly as I had imagined, and saw that there was a steering wheel and driver's seat right by the entrance. These parts had probably been made based on my subconscious knowledge of cars, and perhaps due to me having owned a driver's license back in my Urano days, the area around the driver's seat was more detailed than the outside of the bus. Incidentally, I only knew how to drive automatic cars. The Lionbus also had a seatbelt so that I wouldn't have to worry about falling out, and I had a feeling that it would probably be pretty warm in here even during the winter.

"That is a waste of mana. Make it smaller," Ferdinand said from outside the bus.

I tried shrinking it a little, and the minibus-sized highbeast became as small as a one-person car. It had a lion head and legs, just like before.

"Rozemyne, the form of your highbeast is highly irregular. Will it truly be able to fly?"

"I'll give it a try."

I sat down in the driver's seat and fastened my seat belt, then gripped the steering wheel and poured a bit of mana into it as I pressed the accelerator. The lion's feet started to move.

"Wow! It moved!"

I drove laps around the practice area, then thought *"fly"* while pulling the top of the steering wheel toward me. The lion's head pointed upward as the whole thing lifted off of the ground like a plane, and my body was pushed against the seat as it steadily gained height.

"Wooow! It's flying!"

It seemed that I could fly around by changing the angle of the steering wheel, and I made it all the way up to the ceiling of the training building.

"How was that, Ferdinand? I think it's pretty good," I said, proudly puffing out my chest once I had gotten out of my Lionbus. But Ferdinand just looked perturbed.

"...Do you truly intend to ride that?"

"Absolutely!"

I could make it smaller when I was alone, or bigger when I needed more people. It would be perfect for any situation, not to mention much safer than most highbeasts as there was no risk of anybody falling off. And, of course, it was infinitely cuter and more functional than Ferdinand's scary, realistic lion.

"If you insist on riding that, then I ask that you change the animal you are basing it on. I would rather that bizarre creature not be associated with Ehrenfest's lion."

"Aw, what? But it's so cute," I said, looking at my Lionbus. But Ferdinand simply furrowed his brow as he followed my gaze, before marking it off as, quote, unquote, "not beautiful."

"Well, whatever you say. I guess I'll take this opportunity to make it even cuter."

"I will repeat that your aesthetic sense is unnatural and will never produce anything even remotely close to cute."

He sure was being mean over our tastes being just a little different. In fact, he was being so mean that I wanted to make it even cuter than I was planning to out of spite.

"...What is this? A feybeast? It looks entirely like a large grun. If this really is the route you wish to take, then at least model it after a shumil; that will make it easier for other nobles to accept."

"What's a shumil? I've never seen one, so that's out of the question. And no, it's not a grun or whatever. It's a (red panda). Don't you think his lovable face and bushy tail are just adorable?"

"Not in the least."

There apparently existed a feybeast here that resembled a red panda—also known as a "lesser panda" back in Japan—but given that feybeasts sounded scary, I would rather red pandas not be associated with them. Ferdinand ignored my protests and continued to glare at my highbeast, then pointed sharply at its tail.

"That tail will do nothing but get in the way. At least make it half as long."

"No way! Don't ask me to cut off Lessy's tail! That's too cruel!"

"You've named it now? ...But regardless, the tail is a waste of mana. What purpose does it serve?"

We stared each other down for a bit. I ultimately did cut the tail down to be half as long, but I had managed to secure the bus shape for my highbeast. Thus, the Pandabus was born.

"Now then, let us return to the temple at once. You will be riding your own highbeast."

After a bit more practice in the room, we went back to the temple on our highbeasts. We stayed pretty low as we flew over the Noble's Quarter just in case I did fall.

"Rozemyne, you are going too slowly."

"Okay! Mm... BWAH?!" I stepped on the accelerator to go faster, and the Pandabus shot up to an incredible speed. I reflexively pulled my foot away, which cut off my mana like an emergency brake.

"Eep!"

Driving a mana-powered highbeast was nothing like driving a normal car, and it was surprisingly tough to keep the flow of my mana consistent. We ended up arriving at the temple before I had mastered the art of slowly putting my mana into the highbeast so that I could maintain a steady speed while flying.

My guard knights had followed behind us, their schtappes at the ready just in case my Pandabus were to fall. Only once they confirmed that I had landed safely did they make their schtappes and highbeasts disappear.

"Your struggles are due to your sizable amount of mana. It will no doubt be hard for you to fly while you are still figuring out how to execute minor mana adjustments, but only through struggling will you learn. Practice to the best of your ability such that you will be able to fly comfortably before the Harvest Festival."

"...Okay," I said, my shoulders slumped in sorrow over my failure.

Ferdinand cleared his throat. "Ahem! You mastered this faster than I had expected. I imagine that you will have at least a little time to read over the coming few days."

"Really?!"

From there, I spent my days practicing to fly my highbeast, organizing the book room, learning the harspiel under Rosina, practicing the prayers for the summer coming of age ceremony and autumn baptism ceremony, and doing other such matters.

At times, an ordonnanz would fly in to announce a lunch meeting regarding the concert. These were attended by Elvira, who was acting as the lead director; Eckhart, who was the head of security; and Cornelius, who had wormed his way in under the justification that he was my guard. Karstedt was able to enjoy Hugo's cooking since he ate in the castle with Sylvester, but meals in the knights' barracks were made by another chef, so Lamprecht had started coming to the temple on his days off for lunch and sweets.

In short, my attendants would be given no time to rest until our head chef had finished his training, and when I saw how nervous Nicola got whenever she was serving nobles, I couldn't help but feel a little bad.

It was the evening five days before Ferdinand's concert. While I was cataloging the books in the book room, Gil came rushing in, his eyes shining.

"Lady Rozemyne, Zack finished his wax coating machine. I thought you would like to see it."

I speedily put away my half-completed catalog, then went to the workshop with Gil and Damuel at once. I instructed the gray priests to continue their work as usual then called out to Lutz and Zack, who were talking about something as they looked over the machine.

"Good day, Zack. I was informed that you had finished the wax coating machine."

"It's right here, milady."

Sitting on the work table was a machine just small enough for an adult to carry with both hands. Lutz was already preparing to melt some wax on it, and there was trombe paper ready nearby. Impressed by how effectively Mark had educated Lutz, I peered at the machine myself.

"Please take care not to touch the machine, Lady Rozemyne. The flame has been lit so it is already quite hot. We will be melting the wax here, and shall then move this part here like this to wax the paper," Lutz said in a ridiculously polite tone of voice as he raised his head. There was a neutral expression plastered over his face, but he was no doubt cackling on the inside.

"In that case, please cut the paper to be as large as my diptych, then run it through the machine."

Lutz and Gil split the trombe paper between themselves and began cutting it into A6-sized sheets. While they were doing that, I moved over to Johann, who was working silently some distance away. His machine looked a lot bigger and more complicated than Zack's, but I could tell that it perfectly matched the plans Zack had made. His ability to make things exactly as they were on a blueprint reminded me that, indeed, Johann's skills were top-class.

"How is your machine coming along, Johann?"

"Ah, Lady Rozemyne. It's still a work in progress... It should take a couple more days, but I think it'll be exactly what you want. Zack's blueprints really are impressive," he said with a fervent look in his eyes as he took out a few parts and started fitting them together. It was clear that he was focused on his work, so I moved away at once so as to not get in his way.

"We're ready, Lady Rozemyne."

Lutz slotted the paper between the rollers, which he then rotated by hand rather than using a crank. The core of each roller was made of wood, so while the metal parts heated up and got wax on them, the parts he was touching stayed reasonably cool.

"I think this should be appropriate for the size of paper that this workshop deals with," Zack said as he glanced over at the wax coating machine that Johann was making. Given that Zack's machine required the rollers to be moved by hand, it needed to stay small enough that anyone could use it. But he was right—our workshop only dealt with A4-sized paper for picture books, so the wax stencils didn't need to be that big. Plus, a small machine meant small rollers, and small rollers needed less melted wax to get the job done.

"Now then, let's experiment using the wax that Lutz and Gil made to see what works best."

Lutz and Gil had numbered and organized the various combinations of wax and resin that they had made prior to today. There were three types of wax, and each one had been mixed with one of three set amounts of pine resin, making for nine combinations in total.

"Hmmmph!"

I could guess that Lutz and Zack had tried out several kinds already, as they were working the machine and spreading the wax with experienced hands. Once they had coated two sheets with the first kind of wax, they cleaned the machine and got to work preparing the next kind.

Once they were all done, the pieces of wax paper were presented to me. My job was to check the finished products and determine whether they were good enough to be used or not. Gil speedily handed me a file and a stylus, and I started cutting into the paper.

"This one seems usable enough. This one... not so much. It's too hard to cut. This one isn't any good, either. It's a bit cracked. Oh, but this one is good."

As expected, the wax had been evenly distributed thanks to the rollers, and it looked beautiful. It was pliable too thanks to the resin, meaning it didn't crack when cut into. In the end, I was able to pick the type of wax that seemed the easiest to use out of all the kinds presented to me.

"Now then, Lutz—please make the wax copying the ratios that you used for this kind. I will need about twenty sheets of wax paper the size of picture book pages. Call Wilma tomorrow to begin cutting them into stencils. We will be using mimeograph printing for the art."

"As you wish."

Leaving the rest to Lutz and Gil, I looked up at Zack with a bright smile. "Zack, thanks to you, I now have a finished wax coating machine. Your accomplishments are fit for me to award you the title of 'Gutenberg.' I ask that you work to spread printing alongside the others."

"Y-Yes, milady! Thank you!" Zack immediately knelt down, beaming with pride, but then quickly looked up with a confused expression. "Erm, what do you mean by 'the others'?"

"I refer to your fellow Gutenbergs, of course: Johann and Zack the smiths, Heidi and Josef the ink makers, Ingo the carpenter, and Benno and Lutz the merchants. Mark as well, now that I think about it. Plus all those who work in the Rozemyne Workshop. They are all your Gutenberg allies."

Zack looked over at Johann in search of an explanation, only to see his coworker hanging his head in abject desolation for some reason. He then rapidly looked between me and Johann. "H-Hold on a second... What? 'Gutenberg' isn't a title reserved for the best craftsman?!"

"It is a title awarded to all those involved in printing. From this day onward, you may proudly refer to yourself as a Gutenberg," I said, not about to let someone as skilled as Zack escape my grasp.

Zack simply blinked in confusion as I left the workshop. Behind me, I could hear Lutz say "I told you it wasn't anything special" between bursts of laughter, while Gil excitedly exclaimed "I'm a Gutenberg too!"

Uh huh. Uh huh. Keep up the good work, everyone.

Upon returning to my chambers, I had Monika go and tell Wilma our plans for tomorrow. It was finally time to begin mimeograph printing, and I started writing down the steps and important notes about the process onto a board in preparation.

"Good morning, Lady Rozemyne," Wilma said. Lutz and Gil had brought the file and stylus to the orphanage's dining hall since she said the tables there were easier to work on than the ones in the workshop.

As Lutz waited for her to get ready, he read aloud the list of instructions that I had prepared explaining how the wax stencil cutting process went. "Place the wax paper over the illustration, then lightly trace the stylus across it. A thin white line should appear where the stylus touched."

Once the illustration had been traced onto the wax paper, the next step was to cut the paper on top of the file to form the stencil. The file would be fitted into a wooden frame, then the wax paper was placed over it and pinned to the frame using thin needles. In my Urano days we had held it down with scotch tape, but that didn't exist here and thin needles were the next best thing.

"I will now begin," Wilma said nervously, taking the stylus and beginning to trace the illustration. That seemed easy enough for her, and she quickly finished without any problems. Next, she pinned the wax paper over the file and began cutting it with the stylus.

"These white parts will turn black when printed. There are styluses of many different thicknesses, so please use the one best suited to the situation."

"Understood."

Wilma was cutting in the illustration of Ferdinand sitting and playing the harspiel. It went down to his knees so that the entire instrument could be seen, and unlike the full-body illustration we had used for the cut-out stencil, this one showed his face in such great detail that you could immediately tell that it was him in the picture. He would no doubt be furious if he saw it.

The light sound of scraping could be heard all around the hall. The gray priests watched on with interest at first, but once they realized that it would take a while they returned to their workshop duties. Some children did the same, while others continued watching Wilma work.

"Lutz, please go and check to see whether the printers are ready," I said once the wax stencil was almost finished, and Lutz nodded before leaving the dining hall.

"How is this, Lady Rozemyne?" Wilma asked, looking up from the stencil with a satisfied expression. In her hands was a beautiful illustration, complete with shading that had been done using lines of various widths and intensities. It would probably look different once it was printed, but I could tell at a glance that it was well made.

"I think the illustration will look just wonderful. Let us go, Wilma."

"As you wish, Lady Rozemyne."

The printing tools were ready in the workshop, and everyone was waiting for Wilma's wax stencil. Lutz placed it on top of a sheet of normal paper and, with experienced movements, began rolling ink over it.

"Lutz, take care to be gentle when putting the ink on. Some of the lines are very thin."

"Understood, milady."

The ink-covered roller smoothly moved across the netting. When he pulled off the wooden frame, there was a beautifully printed illustration; the thin lines from Wilma's original picture were all clearly there, as was the shading. The printing had been a success, meaning that we'd now be able to produce a wider variety of art than we could using just the original cut-out stencils.

"It's a success, Lady Rozemyne."

I felt my heart leap with joy at the finished mimeograph print. We now had one more means of expression available to us. Illustrations weren't the only thing this would let us print—sheet music had been hard to slice out with cutters, but now it would be beyond simple to print.

"Now then, Lady Rozemyne—we finished the wax coating machine and have used a lot of expensive paper to complete the wax stencils. Do you think we'll make a return on our investment?" Lutz asked, holding up the art with a grin.

The illustration was so stunning that there was no doubt in the world that we'd be making back more than we had invested. I looked at Lutz, Wilma, and everybody else in the workshop before giving a confident smile of my own.

"We surely will. Your expectations shall be met without fail."

The Harspiel Concert

I returned to the castle the day before the concert. I needed to iron out the final details with Elvira and the others, plus Ella needed to go to the castle's kitchen so that she could mass-produce cookies as an experienced sweets chef.

While Fran and Gil were carrying my things, Monika and I headed to Ferdinand's room to inform him of our departure. As soon as we stepped inside, he met me with a thoroughly displeased expression.

"I am not accompanying you, and I will not help to prepare the concert. Did I not say that already?"

"You did, and that is quite alright. All I need you to do is play the harspiel tomorrow."

Given that Wilma was currently in the process of stacking illustrations of him into a carriage, I was honestly grateful that Ferdinand wasn't coming with us. I said my farewells, then left the room with a smile.

Leading up to today, I had printed as many illustrations of Ferdinand as I could. There were three different versions, and we had a hundred of each; keeping them limited in quantity was the best way to encourage people to buy them.

...Okay, that wasn't entirely true. I had wanted to make as many as possible since I knew that they would sell like hotcakes, but I simply didn't have the time. If I'd been able to, I would have printed a greater variety of illustrations, too!

We made our way to the castle. Ella and Rosina were in the carriage for attendants, while my two guard knights and I got into the carriage for nobles.

"Come now, Rozemyne. We are simply out of time!"

Elvira and Florencia were already waiting for me in the castle. They brought me to the concert hall before I could even go to my room, and we started checking over everything there.

The seats for tomorrow were already prepared. I walked over to the stage where Ferdinand would be playing, checked to make sure that there was enough space around, and then took a look at the standing gallery. Despite the name "standing gallery," the reality was that we were dealing with a group of elegant noblewomen and daughters here. For this reason, the standing gallery was made up of a number of seats placed in close proximity to one another, separated only at certain points to allow those of different factions to sit apart.

Once I had finished looking over the concert hall, I checked the sound-amplifying magic tools, ensured that the sweets were being prepared, and then discussed the matter of security. There were several doors for entering and exiting the hall—one for Ferdinand, one for the waiters, and one for attendees. I also checked the empty rooms that would serve as medical rooms, if necessary.

"I see that everything has been prepared exactly as discussed," I said.

Once I had double-checked everything to do with the concert, I ended up being given the role of concert host. There were three reasons for this: nobody had ever hosted a concert before so we were all equally fit for the position, I was young enough that the ladies wouldn't envy me for getting to stand on stage with Ferdinand, and I was the one who was gathering donations in the first place.

"Incidentally, Rozemyne, how did the illustration come out?" Elvira asked, leaning forward in anticipation after we had finished ironing out the details.

"Perfectly," I responded while puffing out my chest. She would love them for sure.

"Allow me to look," Elvira instantly replied.

"I would like to see as well," Florencia said.

Since they both wanted to see the illustrations, we moved things to my room, where the boxes of pictures had already been carried. Elvira was able to enter the northern building with Florencia's permission, so there was no problem with us talking there.

Rihyarda sent off an ordonnanz telling my attendants to prepare for our arrival, so tea had already been prepared by the time we reached my room.

I lined up three letter-sized boxes on the table that Lutz had prepared for the illustrations to be carried in. They were reasonably thin which made them pretty easy to carry, and were apparently used in the Gilberta Company for storing documents. I opened each one with a delicate yet deliberate movement to add to the excitement.

"My my myyy!" Elvira exclaimed, her eyes glimmering as she examined the illustrations.

Florencia seemed shocked at how many copies of the same illustration we had, and started flipping through them to make sure that they really were all the same. "I had heard about your printing before, but now that I see the results, I find myself at a complete loss for words. Is this what printing can do?"

"Yes, Florencia. I would like to build orphanages and workshops in other cities to spread printing further, and it is to that end that I am seeking donations."

"One look at these illustrations is all I need to understand the value in what you are doing. It truly is wonderful."

With that done, I started training both my attendants and Florencia's attendants how to sell things during the concert. First would be the programs, and then once the concert was over we would bring in the sweets and illustrations on carts and sell those.

"Oh? But would things not be more orderly if we sold the illustrations before the concert?"

"No, I think it would be best to wait for Ferdinand to finish playing and leave. It is safe to assume that he will confiscate them all the moment he sees them, and that is what we need to avoid above all else."

"That certainly would be problematic... I say we do as Rozemyne says and ensure that Lord Ferdinand does not catch sight of them," Elvira said with a serious look on her face, before starting to iron out where the attendants would wait and where the carts would be pushed to.

I took this opportunity to ask Florencia about something exceedingly important. "Erm, Florencia... Does my dear adoptive father Sylvester know about this concert?"

"He has heard that we will be holding a large-scale tea party, but that is all. It would be best if he does not learn the details, as I am sure that he wouldn't be able to resist coming and making a mess of things for his own amusement. That is precisely why I have had magic tools prepared to keep sounds from leaking out of the room. Take care not to mention a word of this at dinner tonight, Rozemyne."

Florencia offered me a graceful smile, her hands firmly gripping Sylvester's reins. I was in full agreement; it was a safe bet that Sylvester would come to crash the party as soon as he found out, so keeping quiet was the best option for all of us.

With that fear settled, I got to work writing a script that I could read as the host. I naturally included a bit about the virtues of printing, and I could imagine that a passage about Ferdinand taking part out of the goodness of his heart would likely be necessary as well. I didn't have the time to do much else, though.

And so came the day of the concert. I looked around the room while waiting for the attendees to arrive. The sound-related magic tools were functioning without issue; the waiters had tea and sweets at the ready; Ferdinand had arrived and was waiting in a back room; and there were twenty members of the Knight's Order, including Eckhart, stationed throughout the room at regular intervals. Most of them had apparently heard Ferdinand play the harspiel before, and were just using guard duty as an excuse to listen to him again.

"My my... Will we be able to hear the harspiel in such a sizable room?" one attendee asked.

"Look at the stage; they seem to have prepared a number of magic tools to that very end."

"I wonder why there are knights posted around us. They aren't just standing attendees, are they?"

Chatter filled the room as I nervously climbed the stage. I inhaled deeply, then held the voice-amplifying magic tool that Florencia had given me up to my mouth like a microphone.

"I thank you all for attending this harspiel concert starring Lord Ferdinand himself. This is a charity concert to raise donations to provide food, work, and housing to orphans in Hasse. The sales from the tickets you have purchased will all go toward the construction of an orphanage, and if you look to your side you will see that we are selling programs for today's event. The money from these sales will be added to our donations, so I would be very grateful to all those who perform the generous and moral act of purchasing one."

I held up a stencil illustration, and Elvira and Florencia stood up to be the first customers. They were essentially leading the way for everybody else, which seemed to have worked as the women belonging to Florencia's faction also got up.

"My, have a look. They're all the same illustration."

"This artist is exceedingly talented. What a beautiful illustration this is."

I could see Elvira sitting closer to the stage than anyone else, showing off her program to the noblewomen sitting beside her. We were charging three large silvers per copy.

"Technology that produces identical copies of text and illustrations is known as printing. I intend to give orphans work in the printing industry, which will be to both their benefit and ours. All I humbly ask for is your monetary support."

With Rihyarda and Ottilie handling sales, the noblewomen steadily bought more and more programs.

"Goodness, she certainly is kind to go so far for the sake of orphans. If only she would direct that kindness to those who deserve it more…"

"I thought this was excessively expensive for a single piece of paper, but this illustration truly is amazing. I cannot say that I've ever seen this style of art before."

"This is the first time I have ever seen an illustration copied so perfectly and so many times before."

The standing gallery was mostly filled with laynobles, as expected, so very few of them moved to buy the programs. But they did seem interested in them; when one person bought one, the others all swarmed around her.

"We have also prepared tea and sweets that Lord Ferdinand is known to have a taste for. We have more in the kitchen so, if you like them, I would be very grateful if you bought some once the concert is over."

With waiters serving tea and sweets to the tables, it did feel very much like a tea party. The sight of so many high-class ladies discussing the songs they weren't familiar with while poring over the artistry of the illustrations made it unlike any concert that I was familiar with. But as they only ever listened to music during tea parties, a whole concert centered around music was a new experience for them.

"Now then—Lord Ferdinand shall begin," I said, before leaving the stage and speed-walking to Ferdinand's waiting room.

"Ferdinand, are you ready to play?" I asked, and Ferdinand, wearing the long-sleeved robes of a noble, stood up with his harspiel.

The moment we stepped into the concert hall, I noticed Ferdinand freeze in place. He resumed walking a split second later, but I heard him quietly murmur "Why are there so many...?"

"Everybody here has donated money to me," I said. That wasn't a lie, since just buying a ticket counted as donating money.

"Still, there are too many. This is simply a ridiculous number of people."

"I merely waited in the temple while Mother and Florencia prepared the concert, so I assumed this was a normal turnout for a noble event. Is that not the case?" I asked, playing dumb as I guided Ferdinand to his seat in the middle of the stage.

Once there, I again colorfully expressed my gratitude to him to the audience, talking about how he pitied the suffering orphans and was helping spread printing for their sake. Ferdinand's face twisted into a momentary grimace, but he was a skilled noble (unlike me) and was thus able to quickly read the room. Wearing a plastered-on smile, he looked over the audience.

"I shall now play the harspiel as an expression of my gratitude to all of you who have donated in support of our efforts," Ferdinand said, before sitting down in his seat and readying his harspiel. The anger in his eyes screamed "I will remember this," but I didn't let that bother me.

Light streamed in through the windows, beaming down onto Ferdinand from his right and making his harspiel gleam. He lowered his head a little, causing his light-blue hair to fall and cast a shadow across his face, and as his fingers touched the strings, a few notes poured forth. A deep *bwong* came from his left hand, a sharp *ting* from his right; it seemed that he was checking the sounds.

Ferdinand raised his head and looked at me. He was ready.

I looked around the audience and saw that the archnoble ladies and daughters who had paid top dollar to sit in the front row were already giving Ferdinand heated, sensual looks.

"Ferdinand has prepared new songs to play for you all. This first is one dedicated to Leidenschaft the God of Fire."

Ferdinand looked down at his harspiel, then began to smoothly strum it. He supported the neck of the instrument with his left hand while playing with his middle finger. His left hand made low sounds reverberate through the air, while his right produced sharper, clearer sounds.

A moment later, Ferdinand's usually expressionless face softened. The furrows that were always present between his brows disappeared, and the sharp edges in his golden eyes smoothed over. It was hard to tell from a distance, but his lips were also curved ever so slightly into a natural smile.

That alone was enough to dramatically change how the audience saw him, and the customers in the front row were all trembling with their hands over their mouths.

I'm glad to see Elvira's having a good time.

Ferdinand's long fingers with visible knuckles practically caressed the harspiel as he strummed its strings. He played note after note, masterfully melding them together to form music so gentle that it almost seemed to melt into the air; it was as beautiful as ever. The man himself was always being mean or giving dark, evil smiles, but when the songs he played were so sweet and tender, it was like he was someone else entirely.

I had assumed that there would be a big fuss, with Elvira's throbbing heart taking over as soon as Ferdinand started playing. But perhaps due to their good upbringings, everybody was just quietly listening to the music, looking flushed and spellbound.

When Ferdinand started to sing in his low, beautiful, reverberating voice, I felt a shiver run down my spine. The sound-amplifying magic tools were no doubt playing a part in this, but it felt as though I were wearing headphones and he was whispering right into my ears.

"Haaah…"

"Ohoooh…"

And then came the heavy, sensual sighs. Elvira was normally full of bubbly excitement when it came to Ferdinand, but all things considered, she knew him pretty well. She was listening with glittering eyes and a hand on her cheek, but the younger daughters who had never had a chance to see Ferdinand before were blushing bright red with tear-filled eyes, their hands either pressing against their hearts or covering their faces. Some were resting their heads against the table to try and hide their expressions, while others struggled to remain calm so as to not attract any unnecessary attention. But one thing was for sure: a storm was raging in all of their hearts.

Aah… If I strain my ears just a little, I can hear their inner voices wailing and writhing.

The noble daughters were having a huge moment, but since they weren't causing any problems, the knights stayed at their posts and kept their eyes on Ferdinand. For a moment, I thought that we wouldn't be needing their help after all, but that was when it happened… He started playing the love song where the God of Life doted on the Goddess of Earth, and a woman fainted.

Things were bad enough already given that we were using a magic tool to amplify his voice so that those sitting near the back could hear. What would happen when they heard Ferdinand sweetly pleading for their love in his beautiful voice? It was a song that managed to take even my breath away, and I already knew what the lyrics were. From what I could see, it was enough to make the noble daughters' hearts throb, pounding so hard that they couldn't even control themselves.

…This is a popular anime song aimed at kids, you know!

It was a lengthy song that had proven powerful enough to make Wilma's fear of men temporarily melt away, and naturally, it was having a huge effect on these noblewomen. One let out a sweet, heavy sigh before collapsing onto the table in front of her.

"Angelica, please direct the knights to take that woman to the infirmary," I instructed in a quiet voice, and Angelica vanished from behind me without making a sound. It was only a matter of moments before several other women started to collapse, and the knights had to start hurriedly carrying them out of the hall.

Meanwhile, Elvira was trembling in place. She was no doubt fighting as hard as she could to stop herself from passing out, given that she had previously said she would never be so foolish as to fall unconscious and miss the rare opportunity to hear Ferdinand playing the harspiel.

Good luck, Mother.

Angelica slid back into place behind me while the Knight's Order continued working wonders, and informed me that Eckhart wanted to see me. I exited the concert hall midway through Ferdinand's performance, where I found that Eckhart wasn't the only one waiting for me.

"Looks like you've been having a lotta fun without me, huh, Rozemyne?"

"Sylvester..."

He was standing in the hallway beaming a crude grin, while Karstedt was standing beside him cradling his head. According to Eckhart, Sylvester had passed by the concert hall just as some of the noble ladies were being carried out.

Sylvester's dark-green eyes gleamed. "I don't think you informed me of this, Rozemyne."

"Goodness. I thought for sure that Florencia would have said something..."

"Don't think you can fool me."

I glanced at the door to the concert hall with cold sweat running down my back. It was all going so well. I had to avoid him messing it up, no matter the cost.

"I did not believe you had any interest in gathering donations, Sylvester. But if you wish to assist as Aub Ehrenfest, I would find nothing more encouraging," I said.

Sylvester simply raised a dubious eyebrow in response, so I racked my brain as hard as I could to find a peaceful solution to all of this.

"I would like to entrust you with the valuable position of concluding the concert with one final song. If you go and retrieve your harspiel now, then I am sure you can still make it in time. The true protagonist of a story is always late, after all!"

"Y'know, I like the way you put that. Karstedt, fetch my harspiel!" he ordered.

Karstedt shot me an extremely worried look. "Are you sure about this, Rozemyne?"

"It is better than him ruining everything," I replied.

Once Karstedt had gone to get the harspiel, I asked Sylvester for a song that he could play without needing to discuss things with Ferdinand first, then noted it down on my diptych. Karstedt came back with the harspiel in no time at all.

"Lady Rozemyne, the concert has concluded," Brigitte said quietly after exiting the concert hall. I hurriedly went back inside and climbed onto the stage.

"I shall now introduce a special visitor. Aub Ehrenfest, please come in."

The door was opened by the knights stationed by it, and in came Sylvester carrying his harspiel. Damuel followed behind carrying a chair, which he set on the stage beside Ferdinand.

Sylvester's sudden appearance was a surprise even to me, which of course meant a stir ran through the audience. Nobody had expected a standard tea party to be extended without warning by a visit from the archduke. The attendees started to flounder, and I had to hold back the urge to yell that I was feeling the exact same way.

Ferdinand glared at me and murmured "I was not informed of this," to which I whispered back "He found us just a second ago." Meanwhile, I could see Florencia shrugging her shoulders a bit, worried but no doubt unsurprised to have been found out.

The noblewomen and daughters who had been quietly listening to the music before were now chattering about Sylvester's appearance, so I held up the voice-amplifying magic tool to my mouth and started making excuses.

"Aub Ehrenfest has said that he would like to put his full weight behind the printing industry, and thus is taking it upon himself to show his gratitude to all of you who have donated to help our cause. To that end, he has taken time out of his busy schedule to rush over and assist our humble concert," I said, knowing that anyone would believe Sylvester's appearance had been planned from the start when they saw how confidently he was holding his harspiel. "The song that Lord Ferdinand and Aub Ehrenfest are going to play for you today is one that you are all very familiar with."

I announced the song—namely the one that Sylvester had played during Spring Prayer—and signaled Ferdinand with my eyes. He let out a small sigh and played a few test notes on his harspiel once again.

Perhaps due to it being a song that everyone here was familiar with, or perhaps due to Sylvester loudly declaring that everyone was to sing along with him, this performance had become the most exciting one of all. It truly was a spectacular finale to the concert, with everyone singing along and feeling like a part of something greater than themselves.

When the song was over, the hall broke out in a spontaneous round of applause. The attendees made their shining wands appear and raised them high into the air in a show of respect and praise while Ferdinand and Sylvester exited the room.

"I believe we can all agree that this has been a spectacular concert. Now, might I suggest buying some of our products as a way of remembering this day? The profits made from them will also go toward our donations. For the sake of a good cause—for the sake of donating—please strongly consider purchasing them."

Now that Ferdinand and Sylvester were gone, it was time for business. Attendants entered the room with carts and traveled from the most expensive seats to the least, selling illustrations and cookies. Of course, the carts also carried the leftover programs.

Cookies were being sold at a price of one small silver for ten, but the illustrations were five large silvers each. The programs were still a more comfortable three large silvers each, so I had assumed the extra-fancy illustrations would only be bought by the more affluent nobles like Elvira. In reality, however, everyone was clawing to buy a ton of them.

Seeing other people spend money must have been a surefire way to loosen one's purse strings, as I saw more than a few ladies reach for cookies after much deep thought, and others glaring at their purses for a while before picking up an illustration and gazing at the art. Even those in the standing gallery looked eager to spend.

Ferdinand's love song had been enough to make them pass out, and their hearts seemed to have no way of resisting Wilma's beautiful illustrations. The noble daughters who purchased them gazed at them longingly, then rolled them up to keep them from creasing and hugged them to their chests. Apparently, the illustrations were a literal treasure to them.

...And so the illustrations have sold out. Thank you all very much for your patronage.

"Thank you ever so much for attending today. I shall report the total amount of money that we have gathered today and where it was spent later in the winter. Everyone, please watch your step and carefully exit the concert hall."

I saw the noblewomen off as they stumbled out of the room, their legs wavering like they were in the middle of a dream. It was safe to say that Ferdinand's charity concert had been an overwhelming success. I let out a sigh of relief, and saw Elvira joyously smiling over the full set of illustrations she had purchased.

"I shall hear your excuses."

It was several days after the concert, and Ferdinand had summoned me to his lecture room just like in the old days. His light-golden eyes were filled with wrath, and his voice was chilly to the point where I was sure it was freezing the air.

Three illustrations were laid out before him. I had thought that I had managed to sell them without him finding out, but seeing him in possession of all three made me want to pass out where I stood.

"Sylvester showed these to me while guffawing about how he saw a knight with them. Given that the name of the author was so kindly written on the back, I discovered the culprit with little issue."

NOOOOOO! I know it's a printing tradition and all, but I can't believe I included publishing information! What was I thinking?!

Ferdinand gave me a harsh scolding and made me swear that I'd never sell them again.

Epilogue

"Lutz, the customers have all left," Mark said. "You have a report to give Master Benno, no?"

At that, Lutz headed to Benno's office in the back of the store; he needed to inform him how much they had made from the harspiel concert.

"The money brought in from the concert totaled twelve large golds, eight small golds, and six large silvers. The overall profit exceeded ten large golds after subtracting various expenses."

Lutz went through the totals that he and Rozemyne had calculated, and Benno's eye twitched at the shockingly high numbers. Not even Lutz had expected her to earn so much. Rozemyne had asked him to print more before the concert, but he had been so certain they already had enough that he had deliberately slowed down production.

...I really didn't expect all the stuff to sell out. Sometimes it's good to be wrong, I guess.

"Sounds like we've gotta plan a second concert," Benno said, wearing the confident grin of someone who was planning to make tons of money.

"There likely won't be a second one; the High Priest found out about the illustrations being sold and got really mad at her," Lutz explained. Benno's subsequent agonized groan made him hesitant to explain that Rozemyne had only been found out because she printed the name of her workshop on the back. "I believe she was told to never sell merchandise like that ever again. Lady Rozemyne begged him to reconsider, even offering him a portion of the profits, but he said that he didn't need the money and firmly refused."

Ferdinand already had a stable source of income as a priest in the temple, he was compensated each time he helped the archduke or the Knight's Order carry out their duties, and he was given money whenever he designed or sold a new magic tool. This was all in addition to the wealth that he had inherited from his deceased father. To Ferdinand, a portion of the illustrations' profits was nothing; he had absolutely no need whatsoever to suffer for loose change.

"Nobles sure are something, huh? You can show them over ten large golds of profit and they'll still call it loose change," Benno said, clearly impressed. But Rozemyne was also a noble, and she had cursed all of the rich people in the world after hearing Ferdinand declare that.

Lutz wasn't sure how to respond. "...But in any case, Master Benno—with this much money, we shouldn't have any problems in Hasse, right? That's what Lady Rozemyne was most concerned about."

Ingo and his wife—the owners of the carpentry workshop that Rozemyne exclusively gave business to—were currently living in the monastery in Hasse, working day in and day out to ensure it was ready for the orphans. Lutz's own father, Deid, would also be heading there soon, having been contacted by the Gilberta Company. Even with the craftsmen from Hasse helping them, Rozemyne, Benno, and Gustav didn't have enough people in their respective workshops, so they were in the process of gathering as many external carpenters and builders as they could.

"It's more than enough. With this money, we can get things ready a lot faster," Benno said with a firm nod. "We just finished bringing daily necessities over to Hasse, so the craftsmen can live there while they work. There's food, firewood, and the materials needed to make paper. Won't be long before we can take some gray priests and shrine maidens there to make the place more livable. How are things on the temple's end?"

Lutz took out and looked over his diptych, into which he had written the words "workers selected," "training started," "request," "winter preparations," "hide glue," and "hair sticks."

"The temple has finished selecting the gray priests and shrine maidens to go to Hasse, and is currently training them as chefs and workshop workers. They want us to let them know once we've settled on a date to take them. I also have a request from Lady Rozemyne—she would like to use a portion of the donations gathered from the concert for winter preparations, with the Gilberta Company helping to butcher meat and such like we did last year. Nobody lives near the monastery in Hasse, so she is considering making hide glue there."

Having been given a request from a noble, Benno nodded with a grimace. "Well, our high and mighty noble friend has given us a huge load of money; might as well help the temple out with their winter prep."

With the winter preparations matter sorted, Lutz somewhat hesitantly moved on to the next topic. "...Furthermore, Lady Rozemyne has said she would like to order more hair sticks, and she has requested that we keep bringing Tuuli to her chambers. Tuuli has not been fully educated in noble manners, but what do you think, Master Benno?"

It was Benno's job to decide whether they could keep sending Tuuli to the archduke's adopted daughter as a craftswoman of the Gilberta Company. Meeting a single time for a reunion was one thing, but regular visits would require much better behavior.

Benno frowned and didn't answer, so Lutz pushed a little harder. "Lady Rozemyne has said that she strongly, *strongly* suggests we continue sending Tuuli there."

"'Strongly'? Is she saying that knowing a commoner can't refuse a noble?" Benno asked with a grimace. But Lutz could empathize with how Rozemyne felt, so she had his full support this time.

"I believe that Lady Rozemyne doesn't want to miss any opportunity that she might have to see her. The only time she gets to see her right now is when she's receiving her hair sticks, and that only happens once a season at most. Hair stick orders made from her home in the castle or the Noble's Quarter don't count either, as Tuuli cannot go to these places for obvious reasons. Lady Rozemyne is aware of all of this." She knew that her request was only feasible when she was in her orphanage director chambers. "Plus, Tuuli needs a place to practice her manners like how I do in the Rozemyne Workshop. She can't practice at home, just like I can't."

Benno fell into thought for a bit, then looked up. "...Alright, we can take her with us. She definitely does need a place to practice. Tell Tuuli to consider this an opportunity for her to improve her manners, and that she shouldn't open her mouth outside of the hidden room."

Two days later, Lutz, Benno, and Tuuli went to the orphanage director's chambers. Once Benno had given the standard noble greetings, Rozemyne ordered the three to step into her hidden room alongside Gil and Damuel. Her aura drastically softened the moment they were inside, and while she looked at Tuuli with eyes full of nostalgia, she didn't call out her name. Tuuli remained silent as well; the magic contract forbade them from addressing each other as family, and Benno hadn't told Tuuli that she could speak yet.

As the two looked at each other, Benno gave Tuuli the hard gaze of an instructor. "Tuuli, nobody's gonna criticize you for loosening up a bit in this room, but you need to stay polite. You've gotta learn how to interact with nobles somewhere, so consider this a place where you can mess up a little without consequence."

Tuuli nodded, a serious expression on her face. She had learned a lot about manners and speech over the past season in her fervent attempt to become a craftswoman skilled enough to meet Rozemyne, but she wasn't quite good enough to safely interact with most nobles. Not even Lutz was, which was why he couldn't go to the Noble's Quarter.

"Rozemyne, if you want to keep having Tuuli deliver your hair stick orders, then help her learn while she's here. She's not presentable to the public at all yet."

Rozemyne's expression tightened. She gave a big nod, then turned to face Tuuli on the other side of the table from her. At that, Tuuli nervously took out a bundle of cloth from a wooden box, opened it, then lined the hair sticks up on the table.

Rozemyne held up a hand to stop her. "You mustn't rush, Tuuli. Relax and take all the time you need. In fact, allow me to demonstrate how it should be done. Watch carefully, for I have been taught by experienced archnoble wives," Rozemyne said, returning the hair sticks to their box before pulling it over to her. She then took a deep breath, and, once again, her entire aura seemed to change in an instant.

She touched the box's lid with a warm, peaceful smile. Each movement she made was careful and precise, yet her pale fingers moved with incredible grace. She slowly opened the box, following a practiced rhythm that drew everyone's eyes and focus to her hands, then took out the contents with both hands and undid the cloth as smoothly as a stream of moving water.

...*What in the heck?* Never before had Lutz seen such elegant movements. All she was doing was opening a box and removing its contents, but she was doing it so gently that he hadn't even heard a noise when she set the lid down. The cloth had almost seemed to unfold on its own, and the hair sticks now resting on Rozemyne's small white fingertips seemed all the more fancy just from being in contact with her. Lutz had just witnessed how much of an impact the way something was treated could have on how high-class it seemed, and it was such a shock to him that he felt as though he had been hit over the head.

"What do you think?" Rozemyne asked.

Lutz had no doubt that she was on an entirely different level from him. They had started at the same point, to be sure, and Lutz had even been working hard to improve his manners, but he was still nowhere even close to her. It seemed impossible that she could have grown so much over a single season.

Benno looked impressed, too. "You sure do look like an archnoble when you do that. Gotta say, I'm amazed you've learned that much in such a short space of time. Even if you have good teachers, you don't get that skilled without a lot of hard work. I figure you two can already guess this on your own, but fixing your movements up like that after you've grown up doing something else isn't easy."

"I was quite desperate to learn since the High Priest had offered me the keys to the book room as a reward," Rozemyne said with a smile.

Everyone laughed a little, but she had put a great deal of effort into her studies and the results made that apparent. Lutz would need to train just as hard if he wanted to become a merchant capable of doing business with her.

"Tuuli, try copying what Lady Rozemyne just did," Benno instructed.

Tuuli started taking out the flowery hair sticks while doing her best to copy what Rozemyne had done, and while her movements were a bit stiff, they were still a great deal better than what she had done just moments prior. Having an example to try and replicate in her head made a huge difference.

Meanwhile, Lutz closed his eyes and tried remembering how Rozemyne's fingers had moved. He replayed what he had seen again and again, trying to burn the image of her graceful white fingers into his brain. ...*How much am I going to need to practice before I can move like that?* he thought to himself.

Before he knew it, Tuuli had lined up all of the colorful flowers on the table.

"Lady Rozemyne, if you desire a ceremonial hair stick, then I would suggest one that uses larger and more extravagant flowers," Benno said, getting Tuuli to repeat his words. "What do you think of these? If we make them the divine color of autumn, I believe it would suit the flowing night sky that is your hair quite well."

Lutz had never had Benno as a long-term teacher, nor had he ever gotten to see Benno do business with customers in the Noble's Quarter. For this reason, he was fully focused on watching Benno do business with Rozemyne, his noble customer. Gil was doing the same.

"A valid perspective. I prefer flowers that are closer to this size, but I certainly would like their petals to move like they did on the last hair stick."

"I am glad to hear that you liked it. In that case, we shall make flowers of this size in the divine color of autumn."

Through further conversation, they settled on the center of the flower being dark yellow and the petals being light yellow, but the way that they spoke to one another wasn't anything like when Myne and Benno had used to discuss things; this was a noble and a humble merchant talking, and they were both making faces that Lutz didn't recognize at all.

It was only then that Lutz realized that Rozemyne had been relaxed and casual even outside of the hidden room. He had been sure that he could catch up to her one day, but now he knew that he was wrong. After just a single season, Rozemyne was wearing the face of the archduke's adopted daughter; it wouldn't be easy to reach her level at all.

"And what about the other flowers, Lady Rozemyne? What color would you like for those?" Benno asked, referring to the smaller flowers on the hair stick.

Rozemyne tilted her head and placed a hand on her cheek, then looked at Tuuli with a smile. "Given that this is an autumn hair stick, I believe it would be cute for there to be fruit decorations alongside the flowers. Please design an ornament that is reminiscent of a bountiful autumn forest."

It seemed that this was something they had already discussed when they were sisters, as Tuuli simply nodded in understanding and wrote down "autumn fruits" in her diptych. Her handwriting was still much too crude for anyone except her to be able to read, but given how she hadn't even known how to read last year, that was still impressive progress.

Am I making progress too? Lutz asked himself. He thought he had been. Everybody said that he was. But a feeling of unease spread through his chest nonetheless.

"Not even vast stores of wealth can guarantee one the opportunity to learn how to behave like a noble. The experience that these young ones have gained today is priceless; I am sure this will help them enormously in their growth. Lady Rozemyne, I offer you my thanks from the bottom of my heart," Benno said, before kneeling despite the fact that they were in the hidden room. Seeing that, Lutz and Tuuli copied him, kneeling in the same way.

Rozemyne had previously said that people didn't change that easily, and even Benno had asserted that she was still the same person on the inside. But even if that was true—even if people stayed the same on the inside—Lutz could feel a larger gap than he had ever expected forming between him and Rozemyne. He had slacked in his training, assuming that she wouldn't change that much, but during that time she had steadily gotten even further out of his reach.

Lutz could feel the cold sweat running down his back. *The amount I've been working isn't gonna cut it anymore... I've gotta push myself even harder.*

Being My Little Sister's Knight

Mother had said that she had important news and gathered Eckhart and I at the dinner table to discuss it over tea. The news was important enough to warrant using sound-blocking magic tools, and when she told us what it was, I couldn't believe my ears.

"You truly intend to take in a girl raised in the temple?!" I exclaimed, reflexively standing up from my chair, but Mother simply motioned for me to sit back down without criticizing me for my rude outburst. Once I was seated again, she nodded with a serious expression.

"Yes, Cornelius. She will be baptized as the daughter of Karstedt and I. Then, she will be adopted by Aub Ehrenfest."

"Aub Ehrenfest is adopting a girl raised in the temple?!"

It wasn't easy for me to believe that a girl due to be adopted by the archduke would have been raised in the temple, nor was it easy for me to accept that she would soon become my little sister. Everything was happening too suddenly. I looked over at Eckhart in confusion, hoping that he would share my reluctance and express his own disapproval, but it appeared that he had already accepted her. His blue eyes crinkled in a smile as he started telling me about our future little sister.

"Rozemyne had much to do with Lady Veronica's fall from grace. She is Father's daughter whom he placed in the temple under Lord Ferdinand's protection. She has dark-blue hair that looks to be blessed by the God of Darkness, complementing her golden eyes that look to be blessed by the Goddess of Light. The archduke decided to adopt her upon hearing about her enormous quantity of mana."

"What are you talking about, Eckhart? Father never had a daugh—" I began, but Mother cut me off.

"She is Rozemary's daughter."

Rozemary? As in... Father's third wife?!

I couldn't believe it. The air had turned to poison whenever Father's second and third wife met, and they would bitterly engage in a verbal sparring contest that always hurt to listen to. Their families were involved in the feud as well, and Mother always struggled to act as an arbitrator between them.

"Does Father intend to bring discord into our family again?"

"We shall claim that she is my daughter instead to avoid that."

"Hold on a second. You remember how awful things were here before Rozemary climbed the towering stairway, right? Things are finally peaceful, and now you want to bring Rozemary's daughter into the main estate—as your own daughter, no less? This is like a nightmare."

Father's second and third wives lived in buildings that were separate from the main estate, so I rarely ever saw them. That was the only reason I had managed to endure their feud. But if this new girl was going to be treated as Mother's daughter, then she would be living in the main building prior to moving to the castle.

"You don't need to worry that much, Cornelius," Eckhart said.

"...And why is that, Eckhart? You and Father might be okay with this since you're adults and have rooms elsewhere, but I'm going to be stuck here living with her."

As guards of the archduke's family, Lamprecht and Father had rooms in the knights' barracks, while Eckhart had flown the nest and now owned his own home. I, on the other hand, had nowhere to run. I glared at Eckhart, and he glared right back.

"You're not appreciating the significance of her having been trained under Lord Ferdinand himself," Eckhart said. "He would never send her here if she wasn't already a model archnoble daughter. Lamprecht and I saw her perform the Healing Ritual during the last trombe extermination mission, and it was quite an impressive sight."

Well, I think you view Lord Ferdinand too highly, brother...

I knew that I would have been scolded for saying that out loud, so I kept my complaints to myself. Eckhart thought the world of Ferdinand, and I had been told many times over how fine of a man he was. But, due in part to my age, I had never met Ferdinand myself, so this boundless praise didn't really mean much to me. Besides, if he really was so amazing, then he should have just gotten rid of Veronica before she forced him into the temple.

"I must say, dear Eckhart—your confidence in this matter brings much peace to my heart. Oh, and by the way... Cornelius, you will serve as Rozemyne's guard."

"Mother, please don't decide such things on your own. I don't want to be a retainer to anyone in the archduke's family. You should know that."

Father served an Aub who had essentially been a puppet of his mother, Eckhart's life was being swung all over the place by his lord's ups and downs, and Lamprecht spent every day suffering under his selfish master. I didn't want to endure a fate like that, and I had said this to Mother over and over again. Why would she tell me to guard an adopted member of the archduke's family who I hadn't even met before?

"Neither of us have any choice in the matter; there are very few knights who would be willing to guard Rozemyne."

Nobody knew what kind of girl Rozemyne was yet, or how Veronica's fall would impact Florencia and the Leisegang family. For that reason, they apparently needed a knight who was of a high enough status to serve the archduke, but who also wasn't too involved in either faction. There was also the fact that, since Rozemyne was set to become the High Bishop, the knight would need to be someone who was willing to enter the temple. Once these criteria were all taken into account, there really weren't many options.

...Yeah, no way are there any female knights who'd be willing to go to the temple.

"Of course, there is also the fact that I would like at least one member of our family to stay with her while she is in the castle. You may leave her side when she becomes old enough to select her own retainers, but I will ask you to guard her for two or three years."

Veronica's fall had sent tremors throughout the entire Noble's Quarter. It was obvious that we'd want as much information as we could get on matters surrounding the archduke's family, and if she would be joining their home as Mother's daughter then we would want someone trusted nearby so that we could stay informed of her situation in the castle. And then there was the fact that I was the only one in the family who didn't yet have a master. As a proper archnoble, it wasn't my place to refuse. I gave a silent nod, keeping my dissatisfaction in my chest as I was unable to complain any further.

It was with that dissatisfaction still stirring inside of me that I met my new little sister Rozemyne for the first time. Eckhart had been right when he said that she had been raised well despite being brought up in the temple. In fact, she seemed about as well behaved as I would have expected for the daughter of Rozemary, a mednoble. Despite not having been baptized yet, she had for some reason been given a ring that could expel mana, and she was able to give a proper noble greeting.

"Elvira, regarding Rozemyne's future education..." Once they had finished exchanging greetings, Ferdinand got straight to the point. Rozemyne was the topic of conversation, but she couldn't make any contributions herself as she was just a kid. She shrunk into her chair, stuck with nowhere else to go, and I could see her hands trembling a little in her lap.

...My sympathies.

A girl raised in the temple had been brought to an archnoble estate out of nowhere to be adopted by the archduke. Anyone would be nervous. The stiff smile that she was forcing onto her young face no doubt belied the immense pressure she was feeling beneath the surface, but the adults were so absorbed in their conversation that they paid no mind to her and how anxious she was bound to be in a strange new place.

Might as well help her out a bit... I thought before calling out to her. "Rozemyne, sounds like you're gonna have a lot of work dropped on you after this. Think you'll be able to handle it?"

"I shall do my best to become a little sister who you can be proud of, Cornelius. I have already made a promise to Lord Ferdinand and Lord Sylvester, so failure is not an option for me," she responded.

While her voice made it clear that Rozemyne was still quite young, there was a fierce resolve in her golden eyes unlike anything I ever would have expected from a little girl. I had no idea what promise she had made to Ferdinand and the archduke, but I could tell that it was something significant. Something that she had to follow through on. Something that demanded she charge forward without ever looking back. Her golden eyes looked like those of a knight who had sworn to protect their liege, which made me like her at least a tiny bit more.

I like seeing eyes like that.

"Y'know, I don't think you have much to worry about. I know I'll be proud to have you as my little sister."

Rozemyne's eyes widened, then a happy smile spread across her face. "I thank you ever so much, Cornelius."

She looked a lot cuter when she was happy than she did when nervous. I let out a sigh of relief upon seeing her relax, at which point I felt someone's gaze on me. I turned and made eye contact with a grinning Ferdinand.

"It is good to see you two getting along," he said, no doubt having planned for this to happen. His smug look kind of annoyed me, but like a proper noble, I just smiled and paid it no mind.

Rozemyne's archnoble education started the next morning. Her schedule was packed with studying for the entire day, and while it might have been necessary, it was a brutal amount for a young girl like her. I would have just thrown up my hands and given up in her situation, but Rozemyne didn't say a word of complaint, instead tearing through her assignments one by one.

Her talent both for learning and for playing the harspiel was shocking, and the tutors who told Mother about her results absolutely lathered her with praise. Rozemyne herself complained that she was having a hard time remembering the names of nobles, but she was learning them so quickly that it hardly seemed like she was struggling at all. I could tell that she was really smart.

Ferdinand had been most worried about her language and how she carried herself, but with Mother training her, she was acting more like an archnoble each day. Even when we were eating meals, I could see her focusing on her hands as she attempted to master proper eating etiquette.

"Mother, is Rozemyne still studying?" I asked, picking up the cup of tea that my attendant had brewed for me when Mother invited me to the table. I had just gotten home from my apprentice knight training, but Rozemyne was still in her room.

Mother nodded. "She is indeed. I believe that Rozemyne is putting her all into her studies so that she may acquire the keys to the book room. It is very easy to see how dedicated she is; every day she shows clear signs of improvement, and her talents make it more than clear why she caught Lord Ferdinand's attention. You will need to work extra hard to stay ahead of her, Cornelius. Otherwise you will be very embarrassed when you return to the Royal Academy with her," Mother said with a pleased smile as she sipped her tea.

Ferdinand was visiting every other day or so to check up on Rozemyne, which did wonders for Mother's mood and in turn led to Father coming home more regularly. Mother and Father generally treated each other coldly because of the drama between wives, but now they were talking normally. Everything they spoke about was in relation to Rozemyne's baptism or her education, but still, it was a relief just to see them not at each other's throats.

There was also the fact that, once Lamprecht had become Wilfried's retainer, Mother had no one at home to speak to except me. But now she was talking to Rozemyne about beauty and fashion trends. As expected, she was finding it a lot more entertaining talking to another girl, and I often found them both eagerly discussing Ferdinand. I had been wary about another girl joining the family since I had only ever had brothers and Father's second and third wives had been nothing but trouble for me, but I couldn't deny that her presence here was having a real positive impact.

"So, Cornelius—what do you think of these sweets? Rozemyne's personal chef knows many unusual recipes, and she has just started trading recipes with our own head chef."

The strange-looking sweets were apparently known as "cookies." I was a bit hungry after training so, out of curiosity, I bit into one. It was crunchy and had a comfortable amount of sweetness, which made it very easy to eat—so easy, in fact, that I found myself eating more and more while I was listening to Mother talk.

"I'm currently prioritizing recipes that I can serve at tea parties, but at some point I would like to exchange for main courses as well."

...I've always been a fan of tasty sweets and delicious food. Honestly, it feels pretty good to have a little sister who's so talented.

I didn't really have the highest opinion of the temple-bred nobles who had returned to society en masse after the Sovereignty's purge, but maybe Rozemyne was entirely unlike them given that she had been put under Ferdinand's custody. The way she spoke about the temple was also a lot different from how the others had; apparently it was a really formal place with a lot of restrictions.

"I ate breakfast at second bell, then went over my schedule for the day with my attendants when I was done. After that, I practiced harspiel until third bell, at which point I headed to the High Priest's chambers to help Ferdinand with his work. Math is my specialty."

"Oh yeah, your math tutor did have a lot of praise for your ability."

"Lunch was at fourth bell, after which I would memorize religious verses for rituals, visit the orphanage as the orphanage director, or summon merchants to my chambers. After that, I would go to the temple's book room, assuming I had any time to spare."

As far as I could tell from what Rozemyne had said, she couldn't leave the temple freely to, say, visit a friend's house with her parents, and she was too weak to run around outside.

...A girl this young having nothing to do in her free time but read quietly in a book room? Sheesh, now that's torture. As someone who liked gathering in the nobles' forest and the exercise I got from my apprentice knight training, I couldn't help but want to show her more of the outside world.

"Rozemyne, is there anything you want to do? Once you've finished all of the stuff you need to do before your baptism, I'll take you anywhere you want to go," I said, and Rozemyne beamed a smile.

"Really?! I want to go to the book room and read some books, then."

"No, no! Not the book room! Anywhere else?!" I said, hurriedly turning her down. She immediately gave me a troubled frown, let her eyes wander around the room for a moment, and then looked at me tearfully.

"I'm sorry, Cornelius... but that's all I can think of."

...Of course. The only real respite they ever gave her was the book room, so of course she doesn't know where else she would go. That's no good at all. I can't leave her with Ferdinand if he's never going to take her outside the temple for anything but work! I've gotta help her myself!

"Give up. Some plans are doomed to fail." Ferdinand shot me down the second I suggested taking Rozemyne outside to play, and, perhaps due to her weakness, he even went as far as to tell me not to take her outside unless I could cast healing magic and mix healing potions for her.

"I understand, but she has finished all of the work that she had to do before her baptism; I think she needs some time to rest and enjoy herself. She needs to see the world outside the temple."

"A place where Rozemyne can enjoy herself without putting her at risk, hm? Your only option would be your estate's book room, then. You will still need to keep a close eye on her, but this will be a perfect opportunity for you to get used to serving as her knight."

I wasn't sure what he expected me to do if she was just going to be reading books, but Ferdinand claimed it would be good training. He started teaching me to keep an eye on her walking pace on the way to the library, as well as how long the books I gave her should be and how I could confiscate them from her.

I know she's weak and all, but do we really need to be this cautious when she's just reading books inside?

"If all else fails and the situation gets out of hand, summon me with an ordonnanz."

The next day, I guided Rozemyne to our estate's book room, though I was still confused by how neurotic Ferdinand's instructions had seemed. If you asked me, there was nothing fun in that stuffy book room packed with nothing but hard books and boring documents; I would have much rather been taking Rozemyne outside, but making her happy was the most important thing here.

When I told Rozemyne that Ferdinand had permitted her to visit our book room as a reward for finishing her work, she looked up at me with the happiest smile I had ever seen in my life.

"I can't believe this estate has a book room... From the very bottom of my heart, I am glad to have joined your family. I am glad to have finished my work so quickly. Praise be to the gods!" she declared, suddenly assuming the praying posture.

She really was raised in the temple, I thought to myself in bemusement before holding out a hand. I couldn't properly escort her due to me being so much taller than her, but we could at least hold hands while slowly walking together.

"You sure like to exaggerate, huh? There's a lot out there that's more fun than a book room."

"There is nothing I will ever find more fun than books, Cornelius." Rozemyne's golden eyes were twinkling with pure joy, and as she spoke, she sped up to walk faster than normal. She must have been really eager to visit the book room.

"You like books that much, Rozemyne?"

"Yes. I love them. What kind of books are in this book room? They must be different from the ones in the temple. I positively can't wait," Rozemyne said, looking more energetic than usual.

Then, when we got to the book room, she suddenly passed out right in front of me. She had been smiling and talking like normal, but out of nowhere her knees collapsed and she fell onto the ground, where she stopped moving entirely.

"Wh-What?! WHAT?!"

My hand was still grasping hers and, as pathetic as it was, all I could do was panic. I was stuck there floundering for a moment until I remembered that Ferdinand had given me permission to summon him. I hurriedly took out my schtappe and sent an ordonnanz to him, believing that he was in the temple.

"Lord Ferdinand, Rozemyne lost consciousness and collapsed out of nowhere!"

"Unsurprising. It is possible that she hit her head, so take care not to abruptly move her."

Ferdinand flew over on his highbeast right after sending his response. He checked Rozemyne, told an attendant to carry her off to bed, and then silently looked down at me. "I repeatedly warned you to be very careful as Rozemyne is weak and sickly, but I imagine you did not take me seriously. You thought I was being neurotic and overprotective, so you did not stop her when she sped up in excitement on the way to the book room, did you?"

"...You're exactly right," I said sadly. I didn't have any room to protest whatsoever; never in my wildest dreams had I thought that she would pass out just from walking down the hall.

"This is how poorly she fares inside. Going outside is, indeed, out of the question. Do you understand that now?"

"Absolutely. I now also understand why I must become Rozemyne's knight." There needed to be someone there to teach her retainers that Ferdinand's warnings were true and beyond necessary. Otherwise, if she were to collapse in the castle, her attendants would be punished for failing to keep her healthy while her knights would be punished for failing to keep her safe.

"Your understanding in the matter is appreciated," Ferdinand said, slightly raising an eyebrow as he continued to look down on me. "Damuel has served her for half a year in the temple, but he is a laynoble; he does not have the status to advise her retainers. You will be playing an essential role here as both her family and an archnoble.

"When it comes to protecting Rozemyne, what you must be wary of above all else are her reckless family members: Sylvester, who is always barreling ahead and doing things his own way; Wilfried, who is well known for being a self-centered hooligan; and finally, your own grandfather, who seems to be putting his all into his granddaughter's baptism ceremony. You will need to pay them all great heed. If you carelessly take your eyes off of Rozemyne, she will no doubt die in the most ridiculous of ways while you are not looking."

I instinctively knew that he wasn't just making an empty threat; he was stating a simple, immovable fact. My duty was to keep Rozemyne alive until she had chosen her retainers, at which point I could retire as her knight.

"Lord Ferdinand, would it be possible to make Lord Wilfried and my grandfather understand how weak Rozemyne is before she acquires her retainers, so that no disaster strikes in the castle? If possible, I would like this to be done under your observation."

She was so weak that it would be impossible to protect her if others didn't understand the extent of her weakness. For this reason, it was important for them to learn before she moved to the castle.

"Hm. I will see whether I can think of an effective plan," Ferdinand replied, tapping a finger against his temple.

One Stressed-Out Chef

"Hugo, a cart from the Othmar Company with the desserts for tomorrow is here! I dunno why, but Leise is with them!"

I reflexively clicked my tongue; tomorrow was the day that the archduke's party would be arriving at the Italian restaurant.

As it turned out, the apprentice blue shrine maiden whom I had been training under had been an archnoble girl all along. Her devoted efforts in the workshop and the orphanage had been praised widely enough for her to be recognized and adopted by the archduke, which also involved her name being changed from "Myne" to "Rozemyne" for some reason. I didn't know much about noble affairs so that wasn't a big deal to me, and as a commoner chef, there wasn't much of a difference between serving a laynoble or an archnoble or whatever.

To be honest, I knew that being the archduke's adopted daughter was a big deal, but it was so far beyond my realm of understanding that it didn't really click. Looking back, I was blown away by how crazy of a place I had been training in.

So yeah, I was pretty uninvolved when it came to the whole noble business, but the archduke getting interested in the eatery that his adopted daughter had been funding and wanting to go was another matter entirely. That involved me directly. I would have to serve food to the archduke.

Under normal circumstances, it would be unthinkable for the archduke to travel to the lower city just to visit an eatery, even if it had been funded by his daughter. That was why Benno from the Gilberta Company and his new funding partner from the Othmar Company were doing everything they could to ensure that there were no mishaps whatsoever—they were selecting the highest quality meat and vegetables, carrying them in, double checking things with the waiters, and keeping in regular contact with the temple.

We were better at making Lady Rozemyne's food since she had been available to give us indirect instructions, but frustratingly enough, Leise was better when it came to baking sweets. That was why the guildmaster's granddaughter, Freida, had decided to put her in charge of making the desserts tomorrow—namely the pound cake, sponge cake, and mille crepes. We were still responsible for any final touch-ups, but that didn't change the fact that she was stealing our work, which really didn't feel great. I wanted to bake some desserts of my own to upstage her, but I was too busy making the consommé.

"Sixth bell rang just a second ago. What's Leise doing here when we're so busy?!" I fumed. It wasn't that I was annoyed to see Leise, I had just been planning to clean up a little before she arrived. Honest. But unfortunately, it seemed that she had heard me loud and clear; she barged into the kitchen, carrying a big plate topped with a dome-shaped metal cover, and glared at me.

"I came to deliver some desserts and taste-test your stuff. What else? Are you making somethin' you don't want me seeing? Don't tell me you messed up on the consommé, of all things," she said with a snort.

"Like heck we did! We're friggin' busy making dinner! What are you doing here?!"

I had been at the guildmaster's place learning noble recipes until just recently, so I knew when Leise was going to be at her busiest—that is, right now. It didn't make any sense for her to come here; anybody else could have brought the desserts.

"I finished dinner prep a long time ago and decided to leave the rest to my assistants," Leise said dismissively before putting her plate down and extending a hand toward me. "So, Hugo—did you manage to make some consommé that won't embarrass you and everyone else?"

Consommé was an essential part of Lady Rozemyne's menu, but it was by far the most exhausting and time-consuming of all of the recipes. To make matters worse, it was the dish that was most unlike anything nobles usually ate, so failing here would cause everything else to fail, too.

That was why I had spent my afternoon focusing on the consommé, refusing to leave the pot for even a moment and instead just shouting my instructions to Todd and my assistants. Consommé was the result of very, very carefully cooking the top-class ingredients that the Othmar Company had provided, and the aroma wafting through the kitchen alone was enough to make it clear how well made it was.

...And it's even better knowing that Leise still can't make double consommé.

I returned Leise's smug look and poured some still-steaming consommé into a small taste-testing bowl, similar to the ones we had used back in Lady Rozemyne's kitchen. "Have a taste and see for yourself."

Leise took the bowl of consommé and swished it around a bit, looking for any cloudiness among the pure liquid. She then gave it a sniff, before slowly easing the bowl's contents into her mouth.

...Gaaah! My stomach's killing me!

Not only was Leise both Todd's and my teacher in regard to noble food, she was my ultimate rival when it came to seeing who could make Lady Rozemyne's recipes better. I was confident in this dish, but it was still nerve-wracking having to wait for her judgment. I knew that I'd die inside if she scrunched up her face while tasting it, but all I could do was wait nervously.

Leise frowned, unamused. "Looks like I really don't need to butt in," she said, thrusting the bowl back at me before shouting to the people outside the kitchen. "C'mon, bring it all in!"

Heck yeah! I won!

Basking in a sense of victory, I set the carried-in desserts into the winter prep room of the kitchen where it was coldest and moved the pot of consommé to the storage room. At times like this, I wished that I had the big ice room that we had in the temple on hand, but as it ran on mana—something that only nobles had—neither the guildmaster's place nor the Italian restaurant had one. It was a real shame, since it was beyond convenient.

Todd and I thoroughly checked that everything was ready for tomorrow, then I finished cleaning up and locked the doors to go home. *Ended up leaving kinda late...* I thought to myself as I power-walked through the fancy northern part of the city. The Italian restaurant was located in a nice spot in town, just northeast of the city center, so heading straight down would take me to the main street connecting the east and west gates.

I glanced at the bustling east gate as the sky darkened and then entered a narrow side alley, turning away the women looking for customers. When I reached the well closest to my place, I stopped for a moment and looked up, hoping to see my very-recent girlfriend Kirke. Luckily, there was a shadow in the window to her room.

"Welcome home, Hugo!" she called down. "Tomorrow's the big day, isn't it? Good luck!"

"Yep, it's gonna be great!" I called back. I knew that everyone would be able to hear me since it was summer and their windows were open, but I didn't care; it had taken training under an apprentice blue shrine maiden and being selected as the head chef of the Gilberta Company's high-class eatery for fate to finally bless me with a girl.

Listen up, everyone. Hear how happy I am. At next year's summer festival, I'm gonna be the star of the show!

After years of throwing taues during the Star Festival, it was finally my time to be the star. I hadn't made it in time for this year's festival, but next year would be my year; I was going to dodge taues from lonely, jealous losers and run home with my new wife. To that end, I needed to make sure that tomorrow's lunch succeeded no matter what—both for my future as a chef, and for my marriage.

I'm gonna do it!

And so, the day of my most important challenge finally came. I desperately cooked with Todd and my assistants, feeling such a tight knot in my stomach that I was close to throwing up. The whole time, Todd and I kept reminding ourselves that we were fine. Lady Rozemyne herself had assured us that we were good enough. Everything would be okay.

"The archduke and all of the nobles said that they had never tasted anything like this cooking before, and each person was beyond satisfied," Mark said as he pushed a cart back into the kitchen, having finished serving dessert.

Only once hearing that the customers were satisfied—that I had succeeded—did the tension drain from my body, and a smile spread across Mark's face as he saw Todd and me fall to our knees on the spot.

"Excellent work, everyone," he continued. "I know that you all wish to rest, but remember that it is now time for the waiters and attendants to eat. Give it one last push."

At Mark's instructions, we prepared meals for everyone else. The attendants from the temple and the musicians ate in the side room, while waiters searched for places to sit at empty tables around the kitchen or by the doors in some halls. Todd and I hadn't been raised to be as proper as the attendants or employees of major stores, so we were fine eating while standing. The food tasted so good that it almost moved me to tears, maybe due to the immense relief of having succeeded.

But the story didn't end there. For some reason, the nobles then flew out of the restaurant on strange flying animals, bringing Benno, Mark, and the guildmaster along with them. We saw them off in a daze, but the passersby in the street were throwing a huge, panicked fuss. Screams and yells could be heard coming from outside, and then we had people rush into the eatery to ask what was going on.

With all those in charge having been taken away, the only two who could deal with the crowd were Freida and Fran, the latter being one of Lady Rozemyne's attendants. They politely apologized and explained that nobles did as nobles would, offering to pass on complaints if anybody had any. But few seemed interested in complaining directly to nobles, and so the crowd naturally dispersed.

Once everything calmed down and we had finished cleaning up the kitchen, the nobles came back. Mark slid away from the group, entering the dining hall and summoning Todd and me.

"Hugo, Todd—I have important news. Due to very profound circumstances involving the archduke, the opening of the Italian restaurant will be delayed by a month or possibly two. You will, of course, still be paid during this time, but we would ask you to continue working for that pay. Is that acceptable?"

I didn't mind as long as we weren't getting fired out of nowhere; doing work for pay was just the way of the world.

Todd and I nodded together, and Mark gave a smile. "Thank you very much. I appreciate your understanding in this matter. Now, would you rather work in the Noble's Quarter or the temple for the next month?"

"What?!"

"The plan today was to sell Lady Rozemyne's recipes to the three important visitors who came to eat today, but Lady Rozemyne's recipes are a bit unusual, are they not? There needs to be someone who can teach the others directly, and to that end we would like you two to teach their chefs."

Lady Rozemyne's recipes certainly were strange; a lot of prep work went into maximizing the flavor, and some of the cooking methods were hard to believe at first. Someone looking at them on paper would almost certainly expect the food to taste bad. From my experience, I had found that the more experience a person had, the harder it would be for them to believe and understand the recipes. Ella was younger than me and she had gotten used to them pretty quickly, while Todd still ended up getting confused while we were cooking. In fact, there wasn't even any guarantee that noble chefs would take us seriously even when we were teaching them directly.

"I've gotta go to the temple," Todd said, the blood draining from his face as he clutched my arm. "Please, Hugo. I'll die before I go to the Noble's Quarter."

He was useless whenever he got too nervous, and he feared nobles so much that he even tried his best to avoid Lady Rozemyne whenever he was in the temple. That said, he was at least familiar with the temple, and it would no doubt be better to have him go there than brave the Noble's Quarter.

"Yeah, I don't think you'd survive there either. You can take the temple."

"Thanks, Hugo. I owe you one!"

Not that I'm gonna have a good time in the Noble's Quarter, either. Pretty sure I'm gonna be throwing up every day from the stress!

"I see it's settled, then. Please come with me to the dining hall."

Mark brought Todd and me to the dining hall, where we were introduced as today's chefs by Lady Rozemyne. After fussy negotiations that seemed to be centered around money, we were rented to the nobles as teachers for one month.

On my way home, I saw Kirke among the women preparing dinner by the well. I said hello, grinning at the thought that, by this time next year, we'd be married and she'd be making that food for me. It kind of felt like we were already newlyweds.

"Hi, Hugo. How'd it go? Did everything turn out okay?"

"Yeah. In fact, it went so well that I'm gonna be going to the Noble's Quarter for a whole month. I'll be teaching noble chefs how to cook these new recipes."

"Really?! Wow! Teaching in the Noble's Quarter! That's amazing!" Kirke exclaimed, her eyes glittering. I held my head up with pride, only for my mom to emerge from the crowd of women and scold me for not telling her first.

Sorry, Mom. Kirke's a lot more important to me right now.

Kirke saw me off on the day I was leaving for the Noble's Quarter. "Good luck! It'll be lonely, but I'll be here waiting for you," she said.

Once I had said my goodbyes, I headed to the central plaza where I met with Todd, and together we went to the temple. When second bell rang, we identified ourselves to the gray priest standing guard, who took us not to the familiar orphanage director's chambers but to the High Bishop's chambers deep, deep within the temple.

"Good morning, Lady Rozemyne."

"Good morning, Hugo. Good morning, Todd. I imagine it will be a great struggle to work in the kitchen of a noble who isn't me, but I trust that you will both do well," Lady Rozemyne said in the expensive-looking clothes of a proper noble girl. "Zahm, Todd is here."

At that, a gray priest apparently called Zahm began lining up large golds and silvers on the table.

...That's my first time seeing a large gold! Woah, and there are so many!

"This seems to be the correct amount. Zahm, please guide Todd to Ferdinand's kitchen. Fran, please gather the money and contact Ferdinand."

"As you wish." Zahm took away the uneasy-looking Todd while Fran put the money into a bag and exited the room. In their place came Nicola, who had sometimes helped out in the kitchen, and Ella, who had become Lady Rozemyne's personal chef.

"Lady Rozemyne, I have brought Ella."

"Thank you, Nicola. I now ask that you take Hugo and Ella to the carriage for attendants."

"As you wish. Ella, Hugo—please follow me."

We followed Nicola to the temple's gate, where we found unbelievably beautiful carriages for noble use. Lady Rozemyne would be living in the castle from today onward, so carriages had been sent for her as well.

"Please wait here until Lady Rozemyne and the High Priest are ready," Nicola said. Commoners couldn't enter the Noble's Quarter without noble approval.

"Thanks, Nicola," Ella replied. "I know it'll be hard without me for a bit, but I'm sure you'll be fine."

"I will be, now that a lot of gray priests and shrine maidens are learning. I can't wait for you to learn a lot of new recipes and come back to teach me more," Nicola said, before turning on her heel and heading off.

Ella waved Nicola goodbye as she left. I could guess that a lot had happened with Ella over the winter while Todd and I were gone, as she looked a lot more mature than she used to.

"Wait. Did you come of age?"

It was only once we had stepped into the carriage and were out of sight that I could finally relax, at which point I noticed something that I hadn't before. Of course Ella looked more mature; she had her hair tied up.

"Uh huh. Back in spring. Though I missed the coming of age ceremony since I was in the Noble's Quarter."

"That's a shame."

"Mm? I don't really think so. Lady Rozemyne gave me new recipes to celebrate, and a small meat grinder to use in the kitchen since we girls lack arm strength. Eheheh… It really is something else. I'll show it to you later; I have it packed."

Meat grinders were machines that minced meat. The ones in the city were pretty large and owned by butchers who used them to crush a lot of meat for turning into sausage, and those definitely weren't small enough for an individual to own. I had never thought there existed small meat grinders.

"That sounds like it'd make it a lot easier to make ground beef. No fair."

"She said she'd ask a smith she knows to make other cooking tools for me, too. Us women have it rough in the Noble's Quarter, so she wants it to be as easy as possible for me to cook…"

It sounded like Lady Rozemyne had really taken a shine to Ella; she had never given me any tools to make cooking easier. Again—no fair.

"Hey, Ella. That reminds me. Where in the Noble's Quarter are we going?"

"Hm? Where else but the archduke's castle? Kinda slow on the uptake there, Hugo."

"The castle?! I mean, I'd heard that we were going to the Noble's Quarter, but nothing else!"

I had assumed that Lady Rozemyne would be going to the castle while I would be sent to the knight commander's home, but according to Ella, she and I were both going to the castle's kitchen. Ella was a woman who had just come of age, and people would no doubt be judging her by her looks more than her talents. That was why she would be teaming up with me until she was a regular member of the castle's kitchen.

On top of that, the knight commander would be sending his estate's head chef to the castle to learn recipes. Ella knew that chef, and had taught him some recipes before. He apparently still looked down on her, but was sucking it up because he wanted to know Lady Rozemyne's recipes that badly.

"I thought I was going to be thrown into a kitchen even bigger than the one in Lord Karstedt's estate all alone, so I'm glad you're here with me, Hugo. It feels like such a long time ago that we were first going to the temple's kitchen together... That time, it was Benno taking us to the temple. Now it's Lady Rozemyne taking us to the archduke's castle. It's only for a bit, but we're court chefs now, huh?"

"Just the thought is making my stomach hurt..."

The very idea of a commoner chef suddenly shooting up to be a court chef of the archduke was staggering, especially after hearing Ella talk about how prideful and arrogant noble chefs were.

"Hugo, you're actually more of a scaredy-shumil than Todd, aren't you? It's not every day you get a whole new workplace like this. Let's do our best to sniff out new recipes. It's good to have a goal to work toward."

"Alright! Y'know, you're right. I'm even gonna go and talk to Kirke's dad when I get back from the Noble's Quarter."

"Wha...? 'Kirke'? Hugo, did you get a girlfriend?" Ella asked, her mouth agape. It was written all over her face that she couldn't believe it.

...*Believe it or not, I don't care! Facts are facts!*

"Yep, not too long ago. Working for a noble in the temple got my name out there, and before I knew it, we were dating. I can't imagine it'd be too hard for you to get a boyfriend, and I very much recommend it. It's a lot easier to work hard when you've got a special someone to impress."

"Wow, very cool. I'll definitely keep that in mind," Ella replied, clearly not interested at all. She was so obsessed with cooking that, despite coming of age, she still seemed to be a little kid who had no interest in romance.

"We're not working here forever, but you can't get much more prestigious than a court chef. You think Kirke's dad will let me marry her on that alone?"

"Assuming she doesn't break up with you while you're away at the castle."

"Ella, don't say that!"

I've been stuck throwing taues at the Star Festival over the last couple of years, but next year will be different. I'll do it. Once I get back from training in the castle, I'll go straight to Kirke's dad and ask for his permission!

Afterword

Hello again. It's me, Miya Kazuki. Thank you very much for reading *Ascendance of a Bookworm: Part 3 Volume 1*. Part 3 begins with this volume.

Rozemyne was baptized as Karstedt's daughter before immediately being adopted by the archduke, thereby becoming a member of the archduke's family. The number of people involved with her has blown up immensely, including a ton of new family members and retainers. It's hard even for Rozemyne to keep all their names and faces in order. Dear readers, please feel absolutely free to learn them at your own pace as the story progresses. (Hahaha.)

The overarching goal of Part 3 is for Rozemyne to adjust to noble society and make the potion that'll heal her body. In this volume, she did the exact opposite: extorting money from her guardians through recipes, gathering money from a unique charity concert, selling merchandise at said concert, and so on. But I ask that you read on warmly as she continues to fail at fitting in.

The potion she needs to make requires her to gather a variety of materials, and to this end she made her own highbeast for transportation. She yet again approached this in an inventive way, and while the Pandabus may have earned her firm disapproval from Ferdinand, it is ideal for transporting luggage and lets her travel without needing to worry about being blown around by the wind.

Rozemyne is busy as the archduke's adopted daughter, a higher-up in the printing industry, the High Bishop, and the orphanage director, but she still finds herself constantly thinking about her family in the lower city. She interacts with them in small ways as best she can, while also making sure that she doesn't break the magic contract.

And finally, thanks to all the power and authority vested in her now, Rozemyne has been steadily moving the printing industry along. Both Johann and Zack were tasked with making machines to manufacture wax paper, with the latter being the first person to actually want to be a Gutenberg. As you might remember, Zack appeared in Part 2 Volume 3's short story: "The Title of 'Gutenberg.'" They're all working hard for the sake of printing.

Not only were lots of new characters introduced in this volume, but there's the four-panel comic at the end as well. Shiina-sama definitely has her hands full with work. I feel guilty, but at the same time I'm happy to have so many cute illustrations. Thank you very much, Shiina You-sama.

And finally, I offer up my highest thanks to everyone who read this book. May we meet again in Part 3 Volume 2.

July 2016, Miya Kazuki

COMING OUT OF NOWHERE... AGAIN, IT'S THE...
END OF VOLUME BONUSES!

A COMFY LIFE WITH MY FAMILY

Art by You Shiina

Adoptive Brother

A LOT HAS HAPPENED, AND NOW I HAVE MORE FAMILY MEMBERS.

It's complicated.

Older Brother 2

D...S!

SIGH

I REALLY WANT A BEEF AND EGG BOWL...

LEARNING

I'VE BEEN ABLE TO EAT A LOT OF TASTY FOOD LATELY.

THANKS TO ALL MY CHEFS,

EEP!

LEMME EAT ONE! LEMME EAT ONE NOW!

THE HECK'S THAT?! SOUNDS LIKE SOMETHING TASTY!

IT WAS THEN THAT I LEARNED TO BE CAREFUL ABOUT WHAT I MUMBLE TO MYSELF.

N-No, wait!

Oden

Cooked Fish

Miso

BUT SOMETIMES I WISH I COULD EAT MORE JAPANESE THINGS, LIKE SOY SAUCE AND STUFF.

AESTHETIC SENSE

THE KIND OF GUY WHO WOULD POP UP IN A SHOUJO MANGA.

IT SEEMS THAT ALL THE GIRLS THINK FERDINAND IS LIKE...

SCRITCH SCRITCH

IF HE WAS, MAYBE HE'D BE DRAWN LIKE THIS?

MENACING

SHUDDER

!!

TICKING TIME BOMB

STEP STEP STEP STE

STEP STEP STE STEP

AH.

BLINK

FLINCH!

CALM DOWN, CORNELIUS.

I just remembered something, that's all.

YOU ALRIGHT?! ARE YOU GONNA COLLAPSE?! DOES IT HURT ANYWHERE?!

The 1st ASCENDANCE OF A BOOKWORM Character Poll!

To celebrate starting part 3 we will announce the top 20 characters as decided by you, the readers! Take a look at these poll results that far exceeded our expectations!

This poll was held from June 10th to July 10th of 2016.

Total number of votes

12,118!

HMPH. AS EX-PECTED.

1st

Ferdinand the High Priest

3,295 votes

THANK YOU, EVERY-ONE.

W-WAIT, REALLY?!

2nd

Myne

2,991 votes

3rd

Damuel

1,353 votes

4th Lutz
1,305 votes

Benno **5th**
878 votes

HEY, NOT BAD.

I'M SUR-PRISED.

8th Sylvester 147 votes

7th Fran 358 votes

6th Tuuli 590 votes

10th Mark 115 votes

9th Gunther 133 votes

11th	Freida	96 votes
12th	Wilma	74 votes
13th	Johann	69 votes
14th	Heidi	62 votes
15th	Gil	58 votes
16th	Delia	57 votes
17th	Effa	56 votes
18th	Karstedt	40 votes
19th	Bezewanst the High Bishop	38 votes
20th	Otto	37 votes

✲ Comment from Miya Kazuki ✲

What do you think about these rankings, everyone? I was worried we wouldn't get too many votes when we started this online poll, but we got more than I ever would have thought. Thank you.

Myne and Ferdinand ended up about where I expected, but I thought Lutz and Benno would be competing for third place, so Damuel getting it caught me by surprise. Still, Lutz might have won if only he had a few more votes thrown his way. I have to say, Sylvester rushing in to narrowly make the top 10 is very much like him.

✲ Comment from You Shiina ✲

I was totally on board with the first and second place results, but when I saw Damuel come in third I was like... wait, whaaat?! Damuel's that popular?! He doesn't seem to have done much up to the point I'm at so far... (Sorry).

Either way, now I'm excited to see what he gets up to in future volumes.

Thank you all for reading!

ASCENDANCE OF A BOOKWORM

I'll do anything to become a librarian!

Part 3 Adopted Daughter of an Archduke Vol. 2

Author: **Miya Kazuki**
Illustrator: **You Shiina**

NOVEL:
PART 3 VOL. 2
ON SALE NOW!

MANGA:
PART 1 VOL. 7
ON SALE NOW!

J-Novel Club Lineup

Ebook Releases Series List

* Novel and Manga Editions
** Manga Only

Keep an eye out at j-novel.club for further new title announcements!